C-2088　　CAREER EXAMINATION SERIES

This is your
PASSBOOK for...

School Lunch Director

Test Preparation Study Guide
Questions & Answers

COPYRIGHT NOTICE

This book is SOLELY intended for, is sold ONLY to, and its use is RESTRICTED to individual, bona fide applicants or candidates who qualify by virtue of having seriously filed applications for appropriate license, certificate, professional and/or promotional advancement, higher school matriculation, scholarship, or other legitimate requirements of education and/or governmental authorities.

This book is NOT intended for use, class instruction, tutoring, training, duplication, copying, reprinting, excerption, or adaptation, etc., by:

1) Other publishers
2) Proprietors and/or Instructors of "Coaching" and/or Preparatory Courses
3) Personnel and/or Training Divisions of commercial, industrial, and governmental organizations
4) Schools, colleges, or universities and/or their departments and staffs, including teachers and other personnel
5) Testing Agencies or Bureaus
6) Study groups which seek by the purchase of a single volume to copy and/or duplicate and/or adapt this material for use by the group as a whole without having purchased individual volumes for each of the members of the group
7) Et al.

Such persons would be in violation of appropriate Federal and State statutes.

PROVISION OF LICENSING AGREEMENTS – Recognized educational, commercial, industrial, and governmental institutions and organizations, and others legitimately engaged in educational pursuits, including training, testing, and measurement activities, may address request for a licensing agreement to the copyright owners, who will determine whether, and under what conditions, including fees and charges, the materials in this book may be used them. In other words, a licensing facility exists for the legitimate use of the material in this book on other than an individual basis. However, it is asseverated and affirmed here that the material in this book CANNOT be used without the receipt of the express permission of such a licensing agreement from the Publishers. Inquiries re licensing should be addressed to the company, attention rights and permissions department.

All rights reserved, including the right of reproduction in whole or in part, in any form or by any means, electronic or mechanical, including photocopying, recording, or by any information storage and retrieval system, without permission in writing from the Publisher.

Copyright © 2024 by
National Learning Corporation

212 Michael Drive, Syosset, NY 11791
(516) 921-8888 • www.passbooks.com
E-mail: info@passbooks.com

PUBLISHED IN THE UNITED STATES OF AMERICA

PASSBOOK® SERIES

THE *PASSBOOK® SERIES* has been created to prepare applicants and candidates for the ultimate academic battlefield – the examination room.

At some time in our lives, each and every one of us may be required to take an examination – for validation, matriculation, admission, qualification, registration, certification, or licensure.

Based on the assumption that every applicant or candidate has met the basic formal educational standards, has taken the required number of courses, and read the necessary texts, the *PASSBOOK® SERIES* furnishes the one special preparation which may assure passing with confidence, instead of failing with insecurity. Examination questions – together with answers – are furnished as the basic vehicle for study so that the mysteries of the examination and its compounding difficulties may be eliminated or diminished by a sure method.

This book is meant to help you pass your examination provided that you qualify and are serious in your objective.

The entire field is reviewed through the huge store of content information which is succinctly presented through a provocative and challenging approach – the question-and-answer method.

A climate of success is established by furnishing the correct answers at the end of each test.

You soon learn to recognize types of questions, forms of questions, and patterns of questioning. You may even begin to anticipate expected outcomes.

You perceive that many questions are repeated or adapted so that you can gain acute insights, which may enable you to score many sure points.

You learn how to confront new questions, or types of questions, and to attack them confidently and work out the correct answers.

You note objectives and emphases, and recognize pitfalls and dangers, so that you may make positive educational adjustments.

Moreover, you are kept fully informed in relation to new concepts, methods, practices, and directions in the field.

You discover that you are actually taking the examination all the time: you are preparing for the examination by "taking" an examination, not by reading extraneous and/or supererogatory textbooks.

In short, this PASSBOOK®, used directedly, should be an important factor in helping you to pass your test.

SCHOOL LUNCH DIRECTOR

DUTIES

Performs administrative duties in planning and directing a very large school lunch program. Plans and directs the preparation and distribution of nutritious lunches. Supervises the preparation of a school lunch program budget. Maintains all financial and business records. Directs the purchase of food, supplies, and equipment, including the preparation of competitive bidding requirements. Interviews and selects school lunch program personnel. Meets with community organizations and individuals to communicate information regarding school lunch program. Performs related work as required.

SCOPE OF THE WRITTEN TEST

The written test will be designed to cover knowledges, skills, and/or abilities in the following areas:
1. Food service management principles and practices;
2. Menu planning principles and practices;
3. Proper food preparation and serving techniques;
4. Sanitary food handling and storage practices;
5. Nutrition and dietetics;
6. Administrative supervision and training; and
7. Understanding and interpreting tabular material.

HOW TO TAKE A TEST

I. YOU MUST PASS AN EXAMINATION

A. WHAT EVERY CANDIDATE SHOULD KNOW

Examination applicants often ask us for help in preparing for the written test. What can I study in advance? What kinds of questions will be asked? How will the test be given? How will the papers be graded?

As an applicant for a civil service examination, you may be wondering about some of these things. Our purpose here is to suggest effective methods of advance study and to describe civil service examinations.

Your chances for success on this examination can be increased if you know how to prepare. Those "pre-examination jitters" can be reduced if you know what to expect. You can even experience an adventure in good citizenship if you know why civil service exams are given.

B. WHY ARE CIVIL SERVICE EXAMINATIONS GIVEN?

Civil service examinations are important to you in two ways. As a citizen, you want public jobs filled by employees who know how to do their work. As a job seeker, you want a fair chance to compete for that job on an equal footing with other candidates. The best-known means of accomplishing this two-fold goal is the competitive examination.

Exams are widely publicized throughout the nation. They may be administered for jobs in federal, state, city, municipal, town or village governments or agencies.

Any citizen may apply, with some limitations, such as the age or residence of applicants. Your experience and education may be reviewed to see whether you meet the requirements for the particular examination. When these requirements exist, they are reasonable and applied consistently to all applicants. Thus, a competitive examination may cause you some uneasiness now, but it is your privilege and safeguard.

C. HOW ARE CIVIL SERVICE EXAMS DEVELOPED?

Examinations are carefully written by trained technicians who are specialists in the field known as "psychological measurement," in consultation with recognized authorities in the field of work that the test will cover. These experts recommend the subject matter areas or skills to be tested; only those knowledges or skills important to your success on the job are included. The most reliable books and source materials available are used as references. Together, the experts and technicians judge the difficulty level of the questions.

Test technicians know how to phrase questions so that the problem is clearly stated. Their ethics do not permit "trick" or "catch" questions. Questions may have been tried out on sample groups, or subjected to statistical analysis, to determine their usefulness.

Written tests are often used in combination with performance tests, ratings of training and experience, and oral interviews. All of these measures combine to form the best-known means of finding the right person for the right job.

II. HOW TO PASS THE WRITTEN TEST

A. NATURE OF THE EXAMINATION

To prepare intelligently for civil service examinations, you should know how they differ from school examinations you have taken. In school you were assigned certain definite pages to read or subjects to cover. The examination questions were quite detailed and usually emphasized memory. Civil service exams, on the other hand, try to discover your present ability to perform the duties of a position, plus your potentiality to learn these duties. In other words, a civil service exam attempts to predict how successful you will be. Questions cover such a broad area that they cannot be as minute and detailed as school exam questions.

In the public service similar kinds of work, or positions, are grouped together in one "class." This process is known as *position-classification*. All the positions in a class are paid according to the salary range for that class. One class title covers all of these positions, and they are all tested by the same examination.

B. FOUR BASIC STEPS

1) Study the announcement

How, then, can you know what subjects to study? Our best answer is: "Learn as much as possible about the class of positions for which you've applied." The exam will test the knowledge, skills and abilities needed to do the work.

Your most valuable source of information about the position you want is the official exam announcement. This announcement lists the training and experience qualifications. Check these standards and apply only if you come reasonably close to meeting them.

The brief description of the position in the examination announcement offers some clues to the subjects which will be tested. Think about the job itself. Review the duties in your mind. Can you perform them, or are there some in which you are rusty? Fill in the blank spots in your preparation.

Many jurisdictions preview the written test in the exam announcement by including a section called "Knowledge and Abilities Required," "Scope of the Examination," or some similar heading. Here you will find out specifically what fields will be tested.

2) Review your own background

Once you learn in general what the position is all about, and what you need to know to do the work, ask yourself which subjects you already know fairly well and which need improvement. You may wonder whether to concentrate on improving your strong areas or on building some background in your fields of weakness. When the announcement has specified "some knowledge" or "considerable knowledge," or has used adjectives like "beginning principles of…" or "advanced … methods," you can get a clue as to the number and difficulty of questions to be asked in any given field. More questions, and hence broader coverage, would be included for those subjects which are more important in the work. Now weigh your strengths and weaknesses against the job requirements and prepare accordingly.

3) Determine the level of the position

Another way to tell how intensively you should prepare is to understand the level of the job for which you are applying. Is it the entering level? In other words, is this the position in which beginners in a field of work are hired? Or is it an intermediate or advanced level? Sometimes this is indicated by such words as "Junior" or "Senior" in the class title. Other jurisdictions use Roman numerals to designate the level – Clerk I, Clerk II, for example. The word "Supervisor" sometimes appears in the title. If the level is not indicated by the title, check the description of duties. Will you be working under very close supervision, or will you have responsibility for independent decisions in this work?

4) Choose appropriate study materials

Now that you know the subjects to be examined and the relative amount of each subject to be covered, you can choose suitable study materials. For beginning level jobs, or even advanced ones, if you have a pronounced weakness in some aspect of your training, read a modern, standard textbook in that field. Be sure it is up to date and has general coverage. Such books are normally available at your library, and the librarian will be glad to help you locate one. For entry-level positions, questions of appropriate difficulty are chosen -- neither highly advanced questions, nor those too simple. Such questions require careful thought but not advanced training.

If the position for which you are applying is technical or advanced, you will read more advanced, specialized material. If you are already familiar with the basic principles of your field, elementary textbooks would waste your time. Concentrate on advanced textbooks and technical periodicals. Think through the concepts and review difficult problems in your field.

These are all general sources. You can get more ideas on your own initiative, following these leads. For example, training manuals and publications of the government agency which employs workers in your field can be useful, particularly for technical and professional positions. A letter or visit to the government department involved may result in more specific study suggestions, and certainly will provide you with a more definite idea of the exact nature of the position you are seeking.

III. KINDS OF TESTS

Tests are used for purposes other than measuring knowledge and ability to perform specified duties. For some positions, it is equally important to test ability to make adjustments to new situations or to profit from training. In others, basic mental abilities not dependent on information are essential. Questions which test these things may not appear as pertinent to the duties of the position as those which test for knowledge and information. Yet they are often highly important parts of a fair examination. For very general questions, it is almost impossible to help you direct your study efforts. What we can do is to point out some of the more common of these general abilities needed in public service positions and describe some typical questions.

1) General information

Broad, general information has been found useful for predicting job success in some kinds of work. This is tested in a variety of ways, from vocabulary lists to questions about current events. Basic background in some field of work, such as sociology or economics, may be sampled in a group of questions. Often these are principles which have become familiar to most persons through exposure rather than through formal training. It is difficult to advise you how to study for these questions; being alert to the world around you is our best suggestion.

2) Verbal ability

An example of an ability needed in many positions is verbal or language ability. Verbal ability is, in brief, the ability to use and understand words. Vocabulary and grammar tests are typical measures of this ability. Reading comprehension or paragraph interpretation questions are common in many kinds of civil service tests. You are given a paragraph of written material and asked to find its central meaning.

3) Numerical ability

Number skills can be tested by the familiar arithmetic problem, by checking paired lists of numbers to see which are alike and which are different, or by interpreting charts and graphs. In the latter test, a graph may be printed in the test booklet which you are asked to use as the basis for answering questions.

4) Observation

A popular test for law-enforcement positions is the observation test. A picture is shown to you for several minutes, then taken away. Questions about the picture test your ability to observe both details and larger elements.

5) Following directions

In many positions in the public service, the employee must be able to carry out written instructions dependably and accurately. You may be given a chart with several columns, each column listing a variety of information. The questions require you to carry out directions involving the information given in the chart.

6) Skills and aptitudes

Performance tests effectively measure some manual skills and aptitudes. When the skill is one in which you are trained, such as typing or shorthand, you can practice. These tests are often very much like those given in business school or high school courses. For many of the other skills and aptitudes, however, no short-time preparation can be made. Skills and abilities natural to you or that you have developed throughout your lifetime are being tested.

Many of the general questions just described provide all the data needed to answer the questions and ask you to use your reasoning ability to find the answers. Your best preparation for these tests, as well as for tests of facts and ideas, is to be at your physical and mental best. You, no doubt, have your own methods of getting into an exam-taking mood and keeping "in shape." The next section lists some ideas on this subject.

IV. KINDS OF QUESTIONS

Only rarely is the "essay" question, which you answer in narrative form, used in civil service tests. Civil service tests are usually of the short-answer type. Full instructions for answering these questions will be given to you at the examination. But in case this is your first experience with short-answer questions and separate answer sheets, here is what you need to know:

1) Multiple-choice Questions

Most popular of the short-answer questions is the "multiple choice" or "best answer" question. It can be used, for example, to test for factual knowledge, ability to solve problems or judgment in meeting situations found at work.

A multiple-choice question is normally one of three types—
- It can begin with an incomplete statement followed by several possible endings. You are to find the one ending which *best* completes the statement, although some of the others may not be entirely wrong.
- It can also be a complete statement in the form of a question which is answered by choosing one of the statements listed.

- It can be in the form of a problem – again you select the best answer.

Here is an example of a multiple-choice question with a discussion which should give you some clues as to the method for choosing the right answer:

When an employee has a complaint about his assignment, the action which will *best* help him overcome his difficulty is to
   A. discuss his difficulty with his coworkers
   B. take the problem to the head of the organization
   C. take the problem to the person who gave him the assignment
   D. say nothing to anyone about his complaint

In answering this question, you should study each of the choices to find which is best. Consider choice "A" – Certainly an employee may discuss his complaint with fellow employees, but no change or improvement can result, and the complaint remains unresolved. Choice "B" is a poor choice since the head of the organization probably does not know what assignment you have been given, and taking your problem to him is known as "going over the head" of the supervisor. The supervisor, or person who made the assignment, is the person who can clarify it or correct any injustice. Choice "C" is, therefore, correct. To say nothing, as in choice "D," is unwise. Supervisors have and interest in knowing the problems employees are facing, and the employee is seeking a solution to his problem.

2) True/False Questions

The "true/false" or "right/wrong" form of question is sometimes used. Here a complete statement is given. Your job is to decide whether the statement is right or wrong.

SAMPLE: A roaming cell-phone call to a nearby city costs less than a non-roaming call to a distant city.

This statement is wrong, or false, since roaming calls are more expensive.

This is not a complete list of all possible question forms, although most of the others are variations of these common types. You will always get complete directions for answering questions. Be sure you understand *how* to mark your answers – ask questions until you do.

V. RECORDING YOUR ANSWERS

Computer terminals are used more and more today for many different kinds of exams.
For an examination with very few applicants, you may be told to record your answers in the test booklet itself. Separate answer sheets are much more common. If this separate answer sheet is to be scored by machine – and this is often the case – it is highly important that you mark your answers correctly in order to get credit.
An electronic scoring machine is often used in civil service offices because of the speed with which papers can be scored. Machine-scored answer sheets must be marked with a pencil, which will be given to you. This pencil has a high graphite content which responds to the electronic scoring machine. As a matter of fact, stray dots may register as answers, so do not let your pencil rest on the answer sheet while you are pondering the correct answer. Also, if your pencil lead breaks or is otherwise defective, ask for another.

Since the answer sheet will be dropped in a slot in the scoring machine, be careful not to bend the corners or get the paper crumpled.

The answer sheet normally has five vertical columns of numbers, with 30 numbers to a column. These numbers correspond to the question numbers in your test booklet. After each number, going across the page are four or five pairs of dotted lines. These short dotted lines have small letters or numbers above them. The first two pairs may also have a "T" or "F" above the letters. This indicates that the first two pairs only are to be used if the questions are of the true-false type. If the questions are multiple choice, disregard the "T" and "F" and pay attention only to the small letters or numbers.

Answer your questions in the manner of the sample that follows:

32. The largest city in the United States is
    A. Washington, D.C.
    B. New York City
    C. Chicago
    D. Detroit
    E. San Francisco

1) Choose the answer you think is best. (New York City is the largest, so "B" is correct.)
2) Find the row of dotted lines numbered the same as the question you are answering. (Find row number 32)
3) Find the pair of dotted lines corresponding to the answer. (Find the pair of lines under the mark "B.")
4) Make a solid black mark between the dotted lines.

VI. BEFORE THE TEST

Common sense will help you find procedures to follow to get ready for an examination. Too many of us, however, overlook these sensible measures. Indeed, nervousness and fatigue have been found to be the most serious reasons why applicants fail to do their best on civil service tests. Here is a list of reminders:

- Begin your preparation early – Don't wait until the last minute to go scurrying around for books and materials or to find out what the position is all about.
- Prepare continuously – An hour a night for a week is better than an all-night cram session. This has been definitely established. What is more, a night a week for a month will return better dividends than crowding your study into a shorter period of time.
- Locate the place of the exam – You have been sent a notice telling you when and where to report for the examination. If the location is in a different town or otherwise unfamiliar to you, it would be well to inquire the best route and learn something about the building.
- Relax the night before the test – Allow your mind to rest. Do not study at all that night. Plan some mild recreation or diversion; then go to bed early and get a good night's sleep.
- Get up early enough to make a leisurely trip to the place for the test – This way unforeseen events, traffic snarls, unfamiliar buildings, etc. will not upset you.
- Dress comfortably – A written test is not a fashion show. You will be known by number and not by name, so wear something comfortable.

- Leave excess paraphernalia at home – Shopping bags and odd bundles will get in your way. You need bring only the items mentioned in the official notice you received; usually everything you need is provided. Do not bring reference books to the exam. They will only confuse those last minutes and be taken away from you when in the test room.
- Arrive somewhat ahead of time – If because of transportation schedules you must get there very early, bring a newspaper or magazine to take your mind off yourself while waiting.
- Locate the examination room – When you have found the proper room, you will be directed to the seat or part of the room where you will sit. Sometimes you are given a sheet of instructions to read while you are waiting. Do not fill out any forms until you are told to do so; just read them and be prepared.
- Relax and prepare to listen to the instructions
- If you have any physical problem that may keep you from doing your best, be sure to tell the test administrator. If you are sick or in poor health, you really cannot do your best on the exam. You can come back and take the test some other time.

VII. AT THE TEST

The day of the test is here and you have the test booklet in your hand. The temptation to get going is very strong. Caution! There is more to success than knowing the right answers. You must know how to identify your papers and understand variations in the type of short-answer question used in this particular examination. Follow these suggestions for maximum results from your efforts:

1) Cooperate with the monitor

The test administrator has a duty to create a situation in which you can be as much at ease as possible. He will give instructions, tell you when to begin, check to see that you are marking your answer sheet correctly, and so on. He is not there to guard you, although he will see that your competitors do not take unfair advantage. He wants to help you do your best.

2) Listen to all instructions

Don't jump the gun! Wait until you understand all directions. In most civil service tests you get more time than you need to answer the questions. So don't be in a hurry. Read each word of instructions until you clearly understand the meaning. Study the examples, listen to all announcements and follow directions. Ask questions if you do not understand what to do.

3) Identify your papers

Civil service exams are usually identified by number only. You will be assigned a number; you must not put your name on your test papers. Be sure to copy your number correctly. Since more than one exam may be given, copy your exact examination title.

4) Plan your time

Unless you are told that a test is a "speed" or "rate of work" test, speed itself is usually not important. Time enough to answer all the questions will be provided, but this does not mean that you have all day. An overall time limit has been set. Divide the total time (in minutes) by the number of questions to determine the approximate time you have for each question.

5) Do not linger over difficult questions

If you come across a difficult question, mark it with a paper clip (useful to have along) and come back to it when you have been through the booklet. One caution if you do this – be sure to skip a number on your answer sheet as well. Check often to be sure that you have not lost your place and that you are marking in the row numbered the same as the question you are answering.

6) Read the questions

Be sure you know what the question asks! Many capable people are unsuccessful because they failed to *read* the questions correctly.

7) Answer all questions

Unless you have been instructed that a penalty will be deducted for incorrect answers, it is better to guess than to omit a question.

8) Speed tests

It is often better NOT to guess on speed tests. It has been found that on timed tests people are tempted to spend the last few seconds before time is called in marking answers at random – without even reading them – in the hope of picking up a few extra points. To discourage this practice, the instructions may warn you that your score will be "corrected" for guessing. That is, a penalty will be applied. The incorrect answers will be deducted from the correct ones, or some other penalty formula will be used.

9) Review your answers

If you finish before time is called, go back to the questions you guessed or omitted to give them further thought. Review other answers if you have time.

10) Return your test materials

If you are ready to leave before others have finished or time is called, take ALL your materials to the monitor and leave quietly. Never take any test material with you. The monitor can discover whose papers are not complete, and taking a test booklet may be grounds for disqualification.

VIII. EXAMINATION TECHNIQUES

1) Read the general instructions carefully. These are usually printed on the first page of the exam booklet. As a rule, these instructions refer to the timing of the examination; the fact that you should not start work until the signal and must stop work at a signal, etc. If there are any *special* instructions, such as a choice of questions to be answered, make sure that you note this instruction carefully.

2) When you are ready to start work on the examination, that is as soon as the signal has been given, read the instructions to each question booklet, underline any key words or phrases, such as *least, best, outline, describe* and the like. In this way you will tend to answer as requested rather than discover on reviewing your paper that you *listed without describing*, that you selected the *worst* choice rather than the *best* choice, etc.

3) If the examination is of the objective or multiple-choice type – that is, each question will also give a series of possible answers: A, B, C or D, and you are called upon to select the best answer and write the letter next to that answer on your answer paper – it is advisable to start answering each question in turn. There may be anywhere from 50 to 100 such questions in the three or four hours allotted and you can see how much time would be taken if you read through all the questions before beginning to answer any. Furthermore, if you come across a question or group of questions which you know would be difficult to answer, it would undoubtedly affect your handling of all the other questions.

4) If the examination is of the essay type and contains but a few questions, it is a moot point as to whether you should read all the questions before starting to answer any one. Of course, if you are given a choice – say five out of seven and the like – then it is essential to read all the questions so you can eliminate the two that are most difficult. If, however, you are asked to answer all the questions, there may be danger in trying to answer the easiest one first because you may find that you will spend too much time on it. The best technique is to answer the first question, then proceed to the second, etc.

5) Time your answers. Before the exam begins, write down the time it started, then add the time allowed for the examination and write down the time it must be completed, then divide the time available somewhat as follows:
    - If 3-1/2 hours are allowed, that would be 210 minutes. If you have 80 objective-type questions, that would be an average of 2-1/2 minutes per question. Allow yourself no more than 2 minutes per question, or a total of 160 minutes, which will permit about 50 minutes to review.
    - If for the time allotment of 210 minutes there are 7 essay questions to answer, that would average about 30 minutes a question. Give yourself only 25 minutes per question so that you have about 35 minutes to review.

6) The most important instruction is to *read each question* and make sure you know what is wanted. The second most important instruction is to *time yourself properly* so that you answer every question. The third most important instruction is to *answer every question*. Guess if you have to but include something for each question. Remember that you will receive no credit for a blank and will probably receive some credit if you write something in answer to an essay question. If you guess a letter – say "B" for a multiple-choice question – you may have guessed right. If you leave a blank as an answer to a multiple-choice question, the examiners may respect your feelings but it will not add a point to your score. Some exams may penalize you for wrong answers, so in such cases *only*, you may not want to guess unless you have some basis for your answer.

7) Suggestions
    a. Objective-type questions
        1. Examine the question booklet for proper sequence of pages and questions
        2. Read all instructions carefully
        3. Skip any question which seems too difficult; return to it after all other questions have been answered
        4. Apportion your time properly; do not spend too much time on any single question or group of questions

5. Note and underline key words – *all, most, fewest, least, best, worst, same, opposite*, etc.
6. Pay particular attention to negatives
7. Note unusual option, e.g., unduly long, short, complex, different or similar in content to the body of the question
8. Observe the use of "hedging" words – *probably, may, most likely*, etc.
9. Make sure that your answer is put next to the same number as the question
10. Do not second-guess unless you have good reason to believe the second answer is definitely more correct
11. Cross out original answer if you decide another answer is more accurate; do not erase until you are ready to hand your paper in
12. Answer all questions; guess unless instructed otherwise
13. Leave time for review

   b. Essay questions
   1. Read each question carefully
   2. Determine exactly what is wanted. Underline key words or phrases.
   3. Decide on outline or paragraph answer
   4. Include many different points and elements unless asked to develop any one or two points or elements
   5. Show impartiality by giving pros and cons unless directed to select one side only
   6. Make and write down any assumptions you find necessary to answer the questions
   7. Watch your English, grammar, punctuation and choice of words
   8. Time your answers; don't crowd material

8) Answering the essay question

Most essay questions can be answered by framing the specific response around several key words or ideas. Here are a few such key words or ideas:

M's: manpower, materials, methods, money, management
P's: purpose, program, policy, plan, procedure, practice, problems, pitfalls, personnel, public relations

   a. Six basic steps in handling problems:
   1. Preliminary plan and background development
   2. Collect information, data and facts
   3. Analyze and interpret information, data and facts
   4. Analyze and develop solutions as well as make recommendations
   5. Prepare report and sell recommendations
   6. Install recommendations and follow up effectiveness

   b. Pitfalls to avoid
   1. *Taking things for granted* – A statement of the situation does not necessarily imply that each of the elements is necessarily true; for example, a complaint may be invalid and biased so that all that can be taken for granted is that a complaint has been registered

2. *Considering only one side of a situation* – Wherever possible, indicate several alternatives and then point out the reasons you selected the best one
3. *Failing to indicate follow up* – Whenever your answer indicates action on your part, make certain that you will take proper follow-up action to see how successful your recommendations, procedures or actions turn out to be
4. *Taking too long in answering any single question* – Remember to time your answers properly

IX. AFTER THE TEST

Scoring procedures differ in detail among civil service jurisdictions although the general principles are the same. Whether the papers are hand-scored or graded by machine we have described, they are nearly always graded by number. That is, the person who marks the paper knows only the number – never the name – of the applicant. Not until all the papers have been graded will they be matched with names. If other tests, such as training and experience or oral interview ratings have been given, scores will be combined. Different parts of the examination usually have different weights. For example, the written test might count 60 percent of the final grade, and a rating of training and experience 40 percent. In many jurisdictions, veterans will have a certain number of points added to their grades.

After the final grade has been determined, the names are placed in grade order and an eligible list is established. There are various methods for resolving ties between those who get the same final grade – probably the most common is to place first the name of the person whose application was received first. Job offers are made from the eligible list in the order the names appear on it. You will be notified of your grade and your rank as soon as all these computations have been made. This will be done as rapidly as possible.

People who are found to meet the requirements in the announcement are called "eligibles." Their names are put on a list of eligible candidates. An eligible's chances of getting a job depend on how high he stands on this list and how fast agencies are filling jobs from the list.

When a job is to be filled from a list of eligibles, the agency asks for the names of people on the list of eligibles for that job. When the civil service commission receives this request, it sends to the agency the names of the three people highest on this list. Or, if the job to be filled has specialized requirements, the office sends the agency the names of the top three persons who meet these requirements from the general list.

The appointing officer makes a choice from among the three people whose names were sent to him. If the selected person accepts the appointment, the names of the others are put back on the list to be considered for future openings.

That is the rule in hiring from all kinds of eligible lists, whether they are for typist, carpenter, chemist, or something else. For every vacancy, the appointing officer has his choice of any one of the top three eligibles on the list. This explains why the person whose name is on top of the list sometimes does not get an appointment when some of the persons lower on the list do. If the appointing officer chooses the second or third eligible, the No. 1 eligible does not get a job at once, but stays on the list until he is appointed or the list is terminated.

X. HOW TO PASS THE INTERVIEW TEST

The examination for which you applied requires an oral interview test. You have already taken the written test and you are now being called for the interview test – the final part of the formal examination.

You may think that it is not possible to prepare for an interview test and that there are no procedures to follow during an interview. Our purpose is to point out some things you can do in advance that will help you and some good rules to follow and pitfalls to avoid while you are being interviewed.

What is an interview supposed to test?

The written examination is designed to test the technical knowledge and competence of the candidate; the oral is designed to evaluate intangible qualities, not readily measured otherwise, and to establish a list showing the relative fitness of each candidate – as measured against his competitors – for the position sought. Scoring is not on the basis of "right" and "wrong," but on a sliding scale of values ranging from "not passable" to "outstanding." As a matter of fact, it is possible to achieve a relatively low score without a single "incorrect" answer because of evident weakness in the qualities being measured.

Occasionally, an examination may consist entirely of an oral test – either an individual or a group oral. In such cases, information is sought concerning the technical knowledges and abilities of the candidate, since there has been no written examination for this purpose. More commonly, however, an oral test is used to supplement a written examination.

Who conducts interviews?

The composition of oral boards varies among different jurisdictions. In nearly all, a representative of the personnel department serves as chairman. One of the members of the board may be a representative of the department in which the candidate would work. In some cases, "outside experts" are used, and, frequently, a businessman or some other representative of the general public is asked to serve. Labor and management or other special groups may be represented. The aim is to secure the services of experts in the appropriate field.

However the board is composed, it is a good idea (and not at all improper or unethical) to ascertain in advance of the interview who the members are and what groups they represent. When you are introduced to them, you will have some idea of their backgrounds and interests, and at least you will not stutter and stammer over their names.

What should be done before the interview?

While knowledge about the board members is useful and takes some of the surprise element out of the interview, there is other preparation which is more substantive. It *is* possible to prepare for an oral interview – in several ways:

1) Keep a copy of your application and review it carefully before the interview

This may be the only document before the oral board, and the starting point of the interview. Know what education and experience you have listed there, and the sequence and dates of all of it. Sometimes the board will ask you to review the highlights of your experience for them; you should not have to hem and haw doing it.

2) Study the class specification and the examination announcement

Usually, the oral board has one or both of these to guide them. The qualities, characteristics or knowledges required by the position sought are stated in these documents. They offer valuable clues as to the nature of the oral interview. For example, if the job involves supervisory responsibilities, the announcement will usually indicate that knowledge of modern supervisory methods and the qualifications of the candidate as a supervisor will be tested. If so, you can expect such questions, frequently in the form of a hypothetical situation which you are expected to solve. NEVER go into an oral without knowledge of the duties and responsibilities of the job you seek.

3) Think through each qualification required

Try to visualize the kind of questions you would ask if you were a board member. How well could you answer them? Try especially to appraise your own knowledge and background in each area, *measured against the job sought*, and identify any areas in which you are weak. Be critical and realistic – do not flatter yourself.

4) Do some general reading in areas in which you feel you may be weak

For example, if the job involves supervision and your past experience has NOT, some general reading in supervisory methods and practices, particularly in the field of human relations, might be useful. Do NOT study agency procedures or detailed manuals. The oral board will be testing your understanding and capacity, not your memory.

5) Get a good night's sleep and watch your general health and mental attitude

You will want a clear head at the interview. Take care of a cold or any other minor ailment, and of course, no hangovers.

What should be done on the day of the interview?

Now comes the day of the interview itself. Give yourself plenty of time to get there. Plan to arrive somewhat ahead of the scheduled time, particularly if your appointment is in the fore part of the day. If a previous candidate fails to appear, the board might be ready for you a bit early. By early afternoon an oral board is almost invariably behind schedule if there are many candidates, and you may have to wait. Take along a book or magazine to read, or your application to review, but leave any extraneous material in the waiting room when you go in for your interview. In any event, relax and compose yourself.

The matter of dress is important. The board is forming impressions about you – from your experience, your manners, your attitude, and your appearance. Give your personal appearance careful attention. Dress your best, but not your flashiest. Choose conservative, appropriate clothing, and be sure it is immaculate. This is a business interview, and your appearance should indicate that you regard it as such. Besides, being well groomed and properly dressed will help boost your confidence.

Sooner or later, someone will call your name and escort you into the interview room. *This is it.* From here on you are on your own. It is too late for any more preparation. But remember, you asked for this opportunity to prove your fitness, and you are here because your request was granted.

What happens when you go in?

The usual sequence of events will be as follows: The clerk (who is often the board stenographer) will introduce you to the chairman of the oral board, who will introduce you to the other members of the board. Acknowledge the introductions before you sit down. Do not be surprised if you find a microphone facing you or a stenotypist sitting by. Oral interviews are usually recorded in the event of an appeal or other review.

Usually the chairman of the board will open the interview by reviewing the highlights of your education and work experience from your application – primarily for the benefit of the other members of the board, as well as to get the material into the record. Do not interrupt or comment unless there is an error or significant misinterpretation; if that is the case, do not hesitate. But do not quibble about insignificant matters. Also, he will usually ask you some question about your education, experience or your present job – partly to get you to start talking and to establish the interviewing "rapport." He may start the actual questioning, or turn it over to one of the other members. Frequently, each member undertakes the questioning on a particular area, one in which he is perhaps most competent, so you can expect each member to participate in the examination. Because time is limited, you may also expect some rather abrupt switches in the direction the questioning takes, so do not be upset by it. Normally, a board member will not pursue a single line of questioning unless he discovers a particular strength or weakness.

After each member has participated, the chairman will usually ask whether any member has any further questions, then will ask you if you have anything you wish to add. Unless you are expecting this question, it may floor you. Worse, it may start you off on an extended, extemporaneous speech. The board is not usually seeking more information. The question is principally to offer you a last opportunity to present further qualifications or to indicate that you have nothing to add. So, if you feel that a significant qualification or characteristic has been overlooked, it is proper to point it out in a sentence or so. Do not compliment the board on the thoroughness of their examination – they have been sketchy, and you know it. If you wish, merely say, "No thank you, I have nothing further to add." This is a point where you can "talk yourself out" of a good impression or fail to present an important bit of information. Remember, *you close the interview yourself.*

The chairman will then say, "That is all, Mr. _____, thank you." Do not be startled; the interview is over, and quicker than you think. Thank him, gather your belongings and take your leave. Save your sigh of relief for the other side of the door.

How to put your best foot forward
Throughout this entire process, you may feel that the board individually and collectively is trying to pierce your defenses, seek out your hidden weaknesses and embarrass and confuse you. Actually, this is not true. They are obliged to make an appraisal of your qualifications for the job you are seeking, and they want to see you in your best light. Remember, they must interview all candidates and a non-cooperative candidate may become a failure in spite of their best efforts to bring out his qualifications. Here are 15 suggestions that will help you:

1) Be natural – Keep your attitude confident, not cocky
If you are not confident that you can do the job, do not expect the board to be. Do not apologize for your weaknesses, try to bring out your strong points. The board is interested in a positive, not negative, presentation. Cockiness will antagonize any board member and make him wonder if you are covering up a weakness by a false show of strength.

2) Get comfortable, but don't lounge or sprawl
Sit erectly but not stiffly. A careless posture may lead the board to conclude that you are careless in other things, or at least that you are not impressed by the importance of the occasion. Either conclusion is natural, even if incorrect. Do not fuss with your clothing, a pencil or an ashtray. Your hands may occasionally be useful to emphasize a point; do not let them become a point of distraction.

3) Do not wisecrack or make small talk
This is a serious situation, and your attitude should show that you consider it as such. Further, the time of the board is limited – they do not want to waste it, and neither should you.

4) Do not exaggerate your experience or abilities

In the first place, from information in the application or other interviews and sources, the board may know more about you than you think. Secondly, you probably will not get away with it. An experienced board is rather adept at spotting such a situation, so do not take the chance.

5) If you know a board member, do not make a point of it, yet do not hide it

Certainly you are not fooling him, and probably not the other members of the board. Do not try to take advantage of your acquaintanceship – it will probably do you little good.

6) Do not dominate the interview

Let the board do that. They will give you the clues – do not assume that you have to do all the talking. Realize that the board has a number of questions to ask you, and do not try to take up all the interview time by showing off your extensive knowledge of the answer to the first one.

7) Be attentive

You only have 20 minutes or so, and you should keep your attention at its sharpest throughout. When a member is addressing a problem or question to you, give him your undivided attention. Address your reply principally to him, but do not exclude the other board members.

8) Do not interrupt

A board member may be stating a problem for you to analyze. He will ask you a question when the time comes. Let him state the problem, and wait for the question.

9) Make sure you understand the question

Do not try to answer until you are sure what the question is. If it is not clear, restate it in your own words or ask the board member to clarify it for you. However, do not haggle about minor elements.

10) Reply promptly but not hastily

A common entry on oral board rating sheets is "candidate responded readily," or "candidate hesitated in replies." Respond as promptly and quickly as you can, but do not jump to a hasty, ill-considered answer.

11) Do not be peremptory in your answers

A brief answer is proper – but do not fire your answer back. That is a losing game from your point of view. The board member can probably ask questions much faster than you can answer them.

12) Do not try to create the answer you think the board member wants

He is interested in what kind of mind you have and how it works – not in playing games. Furthermore, he can usually spot this practice and will actually grade you down on it.

13) Do not switch sides in your reply merely to agree with a board member

Frequently, a member will take a contrary position merely to draw you out and to see if you are willing and able to defend your point of view. Do not start a debate, yet do not surrender a good position. If a position is worth taking, it is worth defending.

14) Do not be afraid to admit an error in judgment if you are shown to be wrong

The board knows that you are forced to reply without any opportunity for careful consideration. Your answer may be demonstrably wrong. If so, admit it and get on with the interview.

15) Do not dwell at length on your present job

The opening question may relate to your present assignment. Answer the question but do not go into an extended discussion. You are being examined for a *new* job, not your present one. As a matter of fact, try to phrase ALL your answers in terms of the job for which you are being examined.

Basis of Rating

Probably you will forget most of these "do's" and "don'ts" when you walk into the oral interview room. Even remembering them all will not ensure you a passing grade. Perhaps you did not have the qualifications in the first place. But remembering them will help you to put your best foot forward, without treading on the toes of the board members.

Rumor and popular opinion to the contrary notwithstanding, an oral board wants you to make the best appearance possible. They know you are under pressure – but they also want to see how you respond to it as a guide to what your reaction would be under the pressures of the job you seek. They will be influenced by the degree of poise you display, the personal traits you show and the manner in which you respond.

ABOUT THIS BOOK

This book contains tests divided into Examination Sections. Go through each test, answering every question in the margin. We have also attached a sample answer sheet at the back of the book that can be removed and used. At the end of each test look at the answer key and check your answers. On the ones you got wrong, look at the right answer choice and learn. Do not fill in the answers first. Do not memorize the questions and answers, but understand the answer and principles involved. On your test, the questions will likely be different from the samples. Questions are changed and new ones added. If you understand these past questions you should have success with any changes that arise. Tests may consist of several types of questions. We have additional books on each subject should more study be advisable or necessary for you. Finally, the more you study, the better prepared you will be. This book is intended to be the last thing you study before you walk into the examination room. Prior study of relevant texts is also recommended. NLC publishes some of these in our Fundamental Series. Knowledge and good sense are important factors in passing your exam. Good luck also helps. So now study this Passbook, absorb the material contained within and take that knowledge into the examination. Then do your best to pass that exam.

EXAMINATION SECTION

EXAMINATION SECTION
TEST 1

DIRECTIONS: Each question or incomplete statement is followed by several suggested answers or completions. Select the one that BEST answers the question or completes the statement. *PRINT THE LETTER OF THE CORRECT ANSWER IN THE SPACE AT THE RIGHT.*

1. In food service operations, the supervisor usually can arrive at a decision concerning an operations problem by considering the following steps to a solution:
    I. Analysis of available information
    II. Definition of problem
    III. Development of alternate solutions
    IV. Selection of decision
   In which of the following options are the steps given in PROPER sequence?

    A. II, I, III, IV
    B. I, III, II, IV
    C. I, II, III, IV
    D. III, I, II, IV

    1.____

2. The one of the following which is MOST important for improvement of the productivity of food-service employees is the

    A. use of convenience foods
    B. posting of food preparation schedules for employees
    C. adoption and implementation of a program of task analysis and work measurement
    D. advance preparation of as much food as possible

    2.____

3. Assume that all of the following problems are occurring in a kitchen under your supervision: production is slow in terms of food preparation; housekeeping is lax; the quality of the food prepared is very poor; morale is low.
   Of these four problems, the one that is *most likely* the cause of all the others and should probably be attended to FIRST is

    A. slow production
    B. lax housekeeping
    C. poorly prepared food
    D. low morale

    3.____

4. A common problem in food-service supervision is that improper supervisory practices can lead to situations in which subordinates disobey direct orders given to them by their superior.
   Which of the following supervisors would be *most likely* to promote such a situation? A supervisor who

    A. does not delegate authority
    B. does not make a decision without consulting his or her entire staff
    C. is unwilling to punish any employee for an infraction of the rules
    D. rarely holds meetings with his or her staff

    4.____

5. While reviewing kitchen operations, you notice that a recently-hired employee is using too large a scoop for serving mashed potatoes. Since you personally instructed this individual in the proper utilization of serving utensils, you believe that this employee should be reprimanded.
   In this situation, the *most appropriate* of the following actions would be to

    5.____

1

A. call the employee aside, inform him of his mistake, and plan for additional instruction
B. inform the employee of his mistake in the presence of the other employees
C. remove the employee from his work station and assign him to some less desirable tasks
D. assign another employee to serve the mashed potatoes with the appropriate size scoop and have the recently-hired employee observe

6. Assume that you are approached individually by two employees who work together in food preparation. Each employee registers her complaint against working with the other. Which one of the following would be the MOST effective action to take in order to handle this problem?   6._____

    A. At the next regularly scheduled staff meeting, mention the importance of good working relationships.
    B. Ask your superior to make a judgment in this case, instead of deciding what to do yourself.
    C. Reassign one employee to a suitable job where she will not have to work with the other employee.
    D. Write a report to your superior detailing the problem and requesting transfers for both of the employees.

7. Suppose that, as a supervisor, you have an idea for changing the way a certain task is performed by your staff so that it will be less tedious and get done faster.   7._____
Of the following, the MOST advisable action for you to take regarding this idea is to

    A. issue a written memorandum, explaining the new method and giving reasons why it is to replace the old one
    B. discuss it with your staff to get their reactions and suggestions
    C. set up a training class in the new method for your staff
    D. try it out on an experimental basis on half the staff

8. In preparing work schedules for food-service employees, the one of the following considerations to which the supervisor should give LEAST priority is the   8._____

    A. work skills of the employees
    B. jobs to be done
    C. physical set-up of the work area and equipment available
    D. preferences of the employees

9. A new employee complains to you that she thinks the current method of serving meals is very ineffective. This employee strongly insists that another method is much better. However, the suggested method had been tried in the past with very unsatisfactory results. Of the following, the BEST way for you to handle the situation would be to   9._____

    A. assign the employee to a different work area to avoid conflict
    B. try out the suggested method for one or two days to demonstrate why it doesn't work
    C. briefly tell the employee that her suggested method will not work
    D. discuss with the employee the reasons why the present method has proven to be more successful than her suggested method

10. Assume that you find it necessary to discipline two subordinates, Mr. Tate and Mr. Sawyer, for coming to work late on several occasions. Their latenesses have had disruptive effects on the work schedule, and you have given both of them several verbal warnings. Mr. Tate has been in your work unit for many years, and his work has always been satisfactory. Mr. Sawyer is a probationary employee who has had some problems in learning your procedures. You decide to give Mr. Tate one more warning, in private, for his latenesses.
According to good supervisory practice, which one of the following disciplinary actions should you take with regard to Mr. Sawyer?

    A. Give him a reprimand in front of his co-workers to make a lasting impression.
    B. Recommend dismissal since he has not yet completed his probationary period.
    C. Give him one more warning, in private, for his latenesses.
    D. Recommend a short suspension or payroll deduction to impress on him the importance of coming to work on time.

10.____

11. Assume that you have delegated a very important work assignment to Johnson, one of your most experienced subordinates. Prior to completion of the assignment, your superior accidentally discovers that the assignment is being carried out incorrectly and tells you about it.
Which one of the following responses is *most appropriate* for you to give to your superior?

    A. "I take full responsibility, and I will see to it that the assignment is carried out correctly."
    B. "Johnson has been with us for many years now and should know better."
    C. "It really isn't Johnson's fault, rather it is the fault of the ancient equipment we have to do the job."
    D. "I think you should inform Johnson since he is the one at fault, not I."

11.____

12. Assume that you observe that one of your employees is talking excessively with other employees, quitting early and taking unusually long rest periods. Despite these abuses, she is one of your most productive employees, and her work is usually of the highest quality.
Of the following, the *most appropriate* action to take with regard to this employee is to

    A. ignore these infractions since she is one of your best workers
    B. ask your superior to reprimand her so that you can remain on the employee's good side
    C. reprimand her since not doing so would lower the morale of the other employees
    D. ask another of your subordinates to mention these infractions to the offending employee and suggest that she stop breaking rules

12.____

13. Assume that you have noticed that an employee whose attendance had been quite satisfactory is now showing marked evidence of a consistent pattern of absences.
Of the following, the BEST way to cope with this problem is to

    A. wait several weeks to see whether this pattern continues
    B. meet with the employee to try to find out the reasons for this change
    C. call a staff meeting and discuss the need for good attendance
    D. write a carefully worded warning to the employee

13.____

14. It is generally agreed that the successful supervisor must know how to wisely delegate work to her subordinates since she cannot do everything herself.
Which one of the following practices is *most likely* to result in INEFFECTIVE delegation by a supervisor?

    A. Establishment of broad controls to assure feedback about any deviations from plans
    B. Willingness to let subordinates use their own ideas about how to get the job done, where appropriate
    C. Constant observance of employees to see if they are making any mistakes
    D. Granting of enough authority to make possible the accomplishment of the delegated work

15. Suppose that, in accordance with grievance procedures, an employee brings a complaint to you, his immediate supervisor.
In dealing with his complaint, the one of the following which is MOST important for you to do is to

    A. talk to the employee's co-workers to learn whether the complaint is justified
    B. calm the employee by assuring him that you will look into the matter as soon as possible
    C. tell your immediate superior about the employee's complaint
    D. give the employee an opportunity to tell the full story

16. The successful application by a supervisor of work simplification techniques to food preparation and service work is *most likely* to result in which one of the following?

    A. Employees working harder than before
    B. Food products of higher nutritional value
    C. Better employee attendance
    D. Elimination of unnecessary parts of jobs

17. Holding staff meetings at regular intervals is generally considered to be a good supervisory practice.
Which one of the following subjects is LEAST desirable for discussion at such a meeting?

    A. Revisions in agency personnel policies
    B. Violation of an agency rule by one of the employees present
    C. Problems of waste and breakage in the work area
    D. Complaints of employees about working conditions

18. Suppose that you are informed that your staff is soon to be reduced by one-third due to budget problems.
Which one of the following steps would be LEAST advisable in your effort to maintain a quality service with the smaller number of employees?

    A. Directing employees to speed up operations
    B. Giving employees training or retraining
    C. Rearranging the work area
    D. Revising work methods

19. Of the following, which action on the part of the supervisor is LEAST likely to contribute to upgrading the skills of her subordinates? 19.____

    A. Providing appropriate training to subordinates
    B. Making periodic evaluations of subordinates and discussing the evaluations with the subordinates
    C. Consistently assigning subordinates to those tasks with which they are familiar
    D. Giving increased responsibility to appropriate subordinates

20. Suppose that a new employee on your staff has difficulty in performing his assigned tasks, after having been given training. 20.____
    Of the following courses of action, the one which would be BEST for you, his supervisor, to take FIRST is to

    A. change his work assignment
    B. give him a poor evaluation since he is obviously unable to do the work
    C. give him the training again
    D. have him work with an employee who is more experienced in the tasks for a short while

21. To insure the safety of employees who must retrieve items from a food storeroom, the supervisor should direct that 21.____

    A. bulky items be put on the floor near the storeroom door
    B. newly-received items be put on the shelves in front of previously-received items
    C. ladders or step-stools be used to reach upper shelves
    D. frequently-requisitioned items be piled up just outside the entrance to the storeroom

22. Suppose that a cook receives a minor burn, which causes a blister on his hand, while handling a hot pan of food. After seeing that the employee gets proper treatment for the burn, the MOST advisable of the following actions for the supervisor to take is to 22.____

    A. send the employee home
    B. tell the employee to return to his work station
    C. help the employee to finish the day's food preparation
    D. temporarily assign the employee to a task other than handling food

23. Of the following, the FIRST step which should be taken by you, the supervisor, in the orientation of a new food-service employee is to 23.____

    A. include the new employee in the next regularly-scheduled staff conference
    B. discuss with the new employee the many problems which the kitchen staff faces daily
    C. give the new employee a task to see how well he can perform
    D. have a conference with the new employee and discuss what his duties will be

24. Assume that, as part of a step-by-step training process, the supervisor explained and demonstrated a food preparation task to a new employee. As a last step, the supervisor told the employee to perform the task himself. 24.____
    The training given by this supervisor was

A. *good;* by putting the employee on his own, the supervisor indicated confidence in the employee
B. *poor;* he didn't ask whether the employee understood how to perform the task
C. *good;* he employed the technique of demonstration
D. *poor;* more than one instructor is required to make this method of training effective

25. Of the following, the BEST way to follow-up immediately after giving a new employee training in food preparation tasks is to

    A. have the new employee observe more experienced employees performing their tasks
    B. give the new employee an overall view of all the food service operations
    C. allow the new employee to perform the tasks herself under careful supervision
    D. have the new employee write a report on what she has learned

26. If one of your kitchen staff performs a particularly important task incorrectly, the one of the following times which is BEST for teaching her the proper procedure so that she will remember it is

    A. later on in the day after she has had time to think about the task
    B. immediately so that she can correct her error
    C. after the workday ends so you may speak to her with less distraction
    D. during the next regularly-scheduled staff training session

27. Assume that you are approached by a cook who is upset and who wants to give you her explanation as to why the day's food preparation went wrong.
    In order to be an understanding listener, you should do ALL of the following EXCEPT

    A. carefully question the worker
    B. make a value judgment so you can take a definite position on the matter
    C. try to find out the meaning of the emotions behind the cook's statements
    D. restate the cook's position to assure that you comprehend what she is telling you

28. A troubled subordinate privately approaches his supervisor in order to talk about a problem on the job.
    In this situation, the one of the following actions that is NOT desirable on the part of the supervisor is to

    A. ask the subordinate pertinent questions to help develop points further
    B. close his office door during the talk to block noisy distractions
    C. allow sufficient time to complete the discussion with the subordinate
    D. take over the conversation so the employee won't be embarrassed

29. Suppose that one of your goals as a supervisor is to foster good working relationships between yourself and your employees, without undermining your supervisory effectiveness by being too friendly.
    Of the following, the BEST way to achieve this goal when dealing with employees' work problems is to

    A. discourage individual personal conferences by using regularly scheduled staff meetings to discuss work problems
    B. try to resolve work problems within a relatively short period of time

C. insist that employees put all work problems into writing before seeing you
D. maintain an open-door policy, allowing employees complete freedom of access to you without making appointments to discuss work problems

30. Of the following duties, the one that may be performed by a designated employee instead of the manager is 30._____

   A. preparing work schedules for each job in the kitchen
   B. placing all orders for food
   C. checking, counting, and weighing supplies received
   D. tasting all cooked foods, salads, sandwich and dessert mixtures

---

KEY (CORRECT ANSWERS)

1. A	11. A	21. C
2. C	12. C	22. D
3. D	13. B	23. D
4. C	14. C	24. B
5. A	15. D	25. C
6. C	16. D	26. B
7. B	17. B	27. B
8. D	18. A	28. D
9. D	19. C	29. B
10. C	20. D	30. C

EXAMINATION SECTION
TEST 1

DIRECTIONS: Each question or incomplete statement is followed by several suggested answers or completions. Select the one that BEST answers the question or completes the statement. *PRINT THE LETTER OF THE CORRECT ANSWER IN THE SPACE AT THE RIGHT.*

1. The one of the following entrees which offers the LEAST variation in texture is   1.____

   A. turkey, cranberry sauce, fried golden brown potatoes, peas
   B. chopped sirloin, mushroom gravy, French fried potatoes broccoli spears
   C. oven-fried chicken, baked potato, peas and carrots, salad
   D. meat loaf, mashed potatoes, creamed spinach, white bread

2. In planning a menu, the FIRST item which should be chosen is the   2.____

   A. vegetable   B. salad   C. entree   D. dessert

3. Of the following, the BEST method of tenderizing cuts of meat which are less tender is by   3.____

   A. broiling   B. stewing   C. baking   D. deep-frying

4. Which one of the following statements regarding proteins is CORRECT?   4.____

   A. The amount of protein in the body is a constant.
   B. The presence of nitrogen distinguishes protein from carbohydrates and fat.
   C. Protein provides more calories per gram than carbohydrates or fat.
   D. Protein provides the principal source of glucose to brain tissue.

5. The one of the following foods that provides MORE vitamin C per serving than the others is   5.____

   A. brussels sprouts   B. cabbage
   C. tomatoes   D. turnips

6. Liver is a PRIMARY source of which one of the following vitamins?   6.____

   A. A   B. B_6 C. C   D. D

7. Vitamin A is a fat soluble vitamin essential in an adequate diet for children and adults. Which one of the following statements concerning vitamin A is TRUE?   7.____

   A. The Recommended Daily Allowance for vitamin A for the adult male and female 10 years of age and older is the same.
   B. The Recommended Daily Allowance for vitamin A is expressed in terms of U.S.P. units.
   C. Vegetables have vitamin A activity equal to vitamin A in animal foods.
   D. Excessive amounts of vitamin A are well tolerated by adults.

8. Iron is a mineral required for growth and to keep the body functioning properly. Of the following, the combination of foods that will provide the BEST intake of iron is   8.____

   A. green peas, liver, enriched bread, dried potatoes
   B. cheese, oranges, liver, butter

C. peanut butter, milk, carrots, liver
D. liver, ice cream, chicken, peaches

9. Calcium and phosphorous account for approximately three-fourths of the mineral elements in the body. Their intake is important for adequate nutrition.
Which one of the following statements is CORRECT about both minerals?

   A. For children and young adults, the Recommended Daily Allowance for calcium is twice that for phosphorous.
   B. Their absorption and utilization are enhanced by the presence of vitamin E.
   C. They are not found in soft tissues.
   D. They constitute an important buffer system in the regulation of body neutrality.

10. When a menu is being planned for a specific holiday, the one of the following which is LEAST appropriate is to

    A. ask for suitable menu possibilities from the staff
    B. choose only foods which are familiar to those who will be served
    C. test acceptability of possible holiday items by serving one or two items at earlier meals
    D. include traditional foods associated with the holiday, if available

11. When a No. 8 scoop is used to serve mashed potatoes, the portion served should be _____ cup.

    A. 2/5   B. 1/3   C. 1/2   D. 2/3

12. A six-ounce ladle is equal to APPROXIMATELY _____ cup(s).

    A. 1/2   B. 1   C. 3/4   D. 1 1/4

13. The MOST accurate measurement of food is by

    A. volume
    B. weight
    C. can size
    D. number of pieces per container

14. Deep fat frying is BEST accomplished at which one of the following temperatures?

    A. 300° F   B. 350° F   C. 400° F   D. 450° F

15. When you are roasting beef, the indication that a well-done and palatable product has been achieved is an interior temperature in the range of

    A. 110° to 130° F   B. 131° to 150° F
    C. 151° to 170° F   D. 171° to 190° F

16. Of the following methods of roasting beef, the one that causes the LEAST amount of shrinkage is cooking at

    A. high temperature during the first half of the cooking time and at low temperature during the other half
    B. high temperature during the entire cooking time

C. moderate temperature during the first half of the cooking time and at high temperature during the other half
D. low temperature during the entire cooking time

17. The method of meat preparation that calls for cutting the meat into small pieces, covering with hot liquid, and cooking at about 185° F is known as

A. boiling B. stewing C. roasting D. broiling

17.____

18. Of the following pressure ranges, the one in which three compartment steamers operate is the _____ lb. range.

A. 1-5 B. 5-15 C. 15-30 D. 30-50

18.____

19. When vegetables are cooked for large numbers of people, the BEST results are obtained by *batch cooking*.
This kind of cooking is done in order to

A. have high-quality vegetables available during the entire serving period
B. prepare more vegetables using less staff
C. use less equipment
D. prepare several batches of vegetables at the same time

19.____

20. The one of the following procedures that could cause food poisoning is

A. allowing cooked poultry to stand for an hour, slicing it, and covering it with broth, and holding it at room temperature for several hours
B. keeping food mixtures on cafeteria counters for one hour
C. cooking left-over food mixtures quickly by frequent stirring and then refrigerating in shallow pans
D. chilling all ingredients for salads for at least one hour before preparation

20.____

21. When large numbers of people are to be served in a cafeteria setting, an estimate should be made each day of the quantity of food to be prepared and cooked.
This is BEST done by which one of the following ways?

A. Having the cook make a list of the previous day's leftovers.
B. Considering previous sales of the same menu combinations, as well as the weather and any special events.
C. Cooking as much food as the staff and equipment allow so as not to be caught short.
D. Using the capacity of the seating area as a base.

21.____

22. Which one of the following statements concerning frozen pre-cooked foods is NOT correct?

A. Certain pre-cooked foods are excellent when freshly prepared, but deteriorate rapidly in an ordinary freezer.
B. Some pre-cooked foods are so greatly changed by freezing and subsequent reheating that they become unpalatable.
C. All food items which are carefully cooked, rapidly frozen, and then held at low temperature until used, are satisfactory products when served.
D. Many foods may be frozen, stored in an appropriate type of freezer, and thawed without marked change in nutritional and esthetic value.

22.____

23. Of the following, the one which is NOT a method of controlling food costs in an institutional food service is

    A. avoiding the use of *leftover* foods since they are usually unpopular items
    B. maintaining an accurate food inventory
    C. knowing what yield can be obtained from various sizes, counts, and amounts of food
    D. ensuring the food-service employees use standardized recipes and portions

24. The direct labor cost involved in the preparation of meals includes wages paid to cooks, bakers, salad makers, counter workers, etc. and is MOST accurately determined by which one of the following methods?

    A. Making studies of the amount of time spent by employees in actual meal preparation tasks.
    B. Checking employees' time cards to determine total absence time.
    C. Dividing the number of meals served each week by the number of employees.
    D. Determining how much time is lost because of equipment breakdown and adding the value of this time to the cost of employees' wages.

25. Which one of the following would MOST likely enable the supervisor of a food service to attain better cost control over operations?

    A. *Increasing* the output of individual staff members.
    B. *Increasing* the size of the staff.
    C. *Reducing* the amount of time scheduled for food preparation tasks.
    D. *Reducing* the amount of time spent on training staff members.

KEY (CORRECT ANSWERS)

1.	D	11.	C
2.	C	12.	C
3.	B	13.	B
4.	B	14.	B
5.	A	15.	D
6.	A	16.	D
7.	A	17.	B
8.	A	18.	B
9.	D	19.	A
10.	B	20.	A

21. B
22. C
23. A
24. A
25. A

TEST 2

DIRECTIONS: Each question or incomplete statement is followed by several suggested answers or completions. Select the one that BEST answers the question or completes the statement. *PRINT THE LETTER OF THE CORRECT ANSWER IN THE SPACE AT THE RIGHT.*

1. Of the following, the FIRST step in the control of food costs in an institution should be to 1.____

    A. make sure the delivery of foods is in accordance with the order
    B. store foods under tight security as soon as they are received
    C. follow purchase specifications in obtaining food products
    D. get the correct amount of raw food to the cook

2. Of the following, the area in which recipe costing aids are of MOST value is 2.____

    A. making yield studies
    B. planning menus
    C. taking inventories
    D. determining the cost of wasted foods

3. Control records of both the physical and cost aspects of food storage are MOST useful as a basic guide in which one of the following areas? 3.____

    A. Receiving food deliveries
    B. Issuing food to the kitchen
    C. Ordering food
    D. Controlling food theft

4. The one of the following which indicates actual control over food costs in a food service is that 4.____

    A. recipe costing is done
    B. waste is eliminated
    C. yield studies are made
    D. food cost data are regularly analyzed

5. The one of the following which is the MAJOR purpose of a perpetual inventory in the food storage area of a kitchen or other dietary unit is to 5.____

    A. facilitate removal of shelf items that are needed for quick use
    B. reduce breakage and spoilage of liquified foods
    C. act as a control in the area of food purchasing
    D. facilitate the planning of balanced diets and menus

6. Walk-in storage refrigerators can be a very important aspect of a well-equipped kitchen in a food service. 6.____
   Of the following, the MOST desirable location for a walk-in refrigerator is near the

    A. receiving and preparation areas
    B. tray delivery area
    C. cafeteria
    D. dishwashing area

7. Food specifications are precise statements of quality and other commodity requirements. All food should be purchased according to specifications.
   Of the following, the LEAST important aspect of a food specification is the

   A. quantity required in a case, pound, carton, etc.
   B. federal grade desired
   C. size of the container
   D. picture of the item

8. The aim in buying food is to obtain the best value for the money spent.
   Of the following, the practice which is LEAST likely to accomplish that aim is

   A. buying the cheapest item
   B. purchasing by specification
   C. purchasing only the quantities required for the menus planned
   D. checking all purchases on delivery

9. When deciding whether to select a particular piece of equipment for a kitchen or other dietary area, the one of the following which would be LEAST important for you to take into consideration is

   A. whether there is space for it
   B. whether it is easily cleaned and maintained
   C. whether there is an employee currently on staff who knows how to operate it
   D. how well it has worked in other institutions

10. Of the following foods, the type that is MOST likely to cause staph food poisoning if improperly prepared or handled is _____ food.

    A. sugar-coated   B. dried
    C. pickled   D. cream-filled

11. Harmful bacteria are MOST often introduced into foods prepared in a food service operation by

    A. insects   B. rodents   C. employees   D. utensils

12. When planning menus for secondary school students, it is desirable for the manager to do all of the following EXCEPT to

    A. stay within the school's food budget
    B. include familiar ethnic foods
    C. include many food choices
    D. consider the size of the food service staff

13. Of the following, the manager's BEST evidence for a shortage claim on surplus food delivered to a school is

    A. her written report of the shortage claim
    B. the delivery receipt from the truck driver
    C. the container the food was delivered in
    D. an old container of the same item

14. The manager should prepare school lunch menus for a MINIMUM of _____ week(s) at a time.   14._____

    A. one B. two C. three D. four

15. The manager must keep monthly inventories of all of the following EXCEPT   15._____

    A. paper goods B. food items
    C. serving utensils D. cleaning supplies

16. In the Type A lunch pattern for 10- to 12-year-old children, all of the following fulfill the *meat or meat alternate* requirement EXCEPT   16._____

    A. two ounces of cheese
    B. one-half cup of fresh carrots
    C. four tablespoons of peanut butter
    D. one-half cup of cooked dry peas

17. A manager is planning to use tuna fish salad to comply with the guideline for the *meat or meat alternate* requirement of the Type A lunch for secondary school students. How much tuna fish will she need in order to serve 400 secondary school students? _____ pounds.   17._____

    A. $37\frac{1}{2}$ B. 50 C. 75 D. 100

Questions 18-25.

DIRECTIONS: Answer Questions 18 through 25 SOLELY on the basis of information presented in the charts below.

STUDENT SALES COUNTER SHEET
March 4, 2005

Item	Price per Item	No. Items Offered for Sale	No. Items Unsold	Total Cash Received for Items Sold
Hot lunch	$2.25	250	75	
Milk	$0.60	525		$285.00
Soda	$0.75	300	163	$102.75
Ice Cream Bars	$0.45	181	59	$54.90
Buttered Roll	$0.15	200	150	
Cooked Vegetable	$0.90	325	40	$256.50
Pudding	$0.45	565	30	$240.75
Potato Chips	$0.30	610	50	$168.00

STUDENT SALES COUNTER SHEET
March 5, 2005

Item	Price per Item	No. Items Offered for Sale	No. Items Unsold	Total Cash Received for Items Sold
Hot lunch	$2.25	300		$585.00
Milk	$0.60	450		$255.00
Soda	$0.75	275	207	
Ice Cream Bars	$0.45	250	100	
Buttered Roll	$0.15	175	25	
Cooked Vegetable	$0.90	300	62	$214.20
Pudding	$0.45	490	47	
Potato Chips	$0.30	595	45	

18. Hot lunches accounted for APPROXIMATELY what percentage of all cash received for March 4, 2005?

    A. 10%   B. 15%   C. 20%   D. 25%

19. Which one of the following items was sold LEAST on March 4, 2005 and March 5, 2005, combined?

    A. Soda
    C. Buttered roll
    B. Ice cream bars
    D. Cooked vegetable

20. The number of milk containers which were unsold on March 4, 2005 is

    A. 30   B. 50   C. 75   D. 95

21. How many fewer containers of pudding and soda were sold on March 5, 2005 than were sold on March 4, 2005?

    A. 19   B. 81   C. 105   D. 161

22. Which single item, besides hot lunches, accounted for the GREATEST number of items sold on March 4, 2005?

    A. Cooked vegetable
    C. Ice cream bars
    B. Pudding
    D. Soda

23. How many hot lunches were sold on March 4, 2005 and March 5, 2005, combined?

    A. 435   B. 550   C. 625   D. 665

24. Of the following, the item that was bought MOST by the students on both March 4, 2005 and March 5, 2005 is

    A. soda
    C. pudding
    B. buttered roll
    D. potato chips

25. The cumulative total of money received for all the soda, ice cream bars, buttered rolls, and pudding sold on March 4, 2005 is

    A. $165.15   B. $405.90   C. $858.90   D. $1252.65

KEY (CORRECT ANSWERS)

1. C
2. B
3. C
4. B
5. C

6. A
7. D
8. A
9. C
10. D

11. C
12. C
13. C
14. D
15. C

16. B
17. C
18. D
19. C
20. B

21. D
22. B
23. A
24. D
25. B

EXAMINATION SECTION
TEST 1

DIRECTIONS: Each question or incomplete statement is followed by several suggested answers or completions. Select the one that BEST answers the question or completes the statement. *PRINT THE LETTER OF THE CORRECT ANSWER IN THE SPACE AT THE RIGHT.*

1. Foods which are left over may be used by the menu planner CHIEFLY to   1.____

    A. baste meats
    B. stock the freezer with emergency supplies
    C. provide more variety in the next day's menu
    D. add minerals to the diet

2. When a recipe calls for cooking in a hot oven, it is MOST desirable to set the thermostat at a Fahrenheit temperature of   2.____

    A. 300° B. 350° C. 425° D. 525°

3. Of the following, the MOST satisfactory method for cooking the less tender cuts of meat is by   3.____

    A. roasting B. broiling C. dry heat D. moist heat

4. A two-pound chicken is BEST prepared by   4.____

    A. broiling B. stewing C. baking D. roasting

5. Fats are used in food preparation, *not only* as emulsifiers, *but also* as   5.____

    A. shortening agents   B. leavening agents
    C. catalysts   D. sweetening agents

6. Baking powder is used in cake mixtures CHIEFLY in order to   6.____

    A. improve the flavor
    B. increase the acidity
    C. lighten the cake and increase its volume
    D. hold the other ingredients together

7. When making a sponge cake, it is important to remember to   7.____

    A. beat the batter until it doubles in bulk
    B. bake the cake in an ungreased tube pan
    C. bake the cake in a hot oven
    D. remove the cake from the pan as soon as it is baked

8. When making pastry, the fat should be   8.____

    A. creamed with the flour
    B. first melted and then creamed with the flour
    C. cut into the flour
    D. added to the flour after the water is stirred in

9. Of the following, the procedure which is MOST advisable when cooking dried prunes is to

   A. soak the fruit in hot water to seal in the juices
   B. keep the uncooked fruit under refrigeration at all times
   C. simmer the fruit slowly until it is tender
   D. add sugar to the fruit to improve the flavor

10. Assume that you plan to serve a gelatin dessert for dinner. You have found that gelatin made in the usual way softens in hot weather.
    Of the following, the procedure which is MOST advisable to follow on a warm day is to

    A. thicken the gelatin with cornstarch
    B. substitute a non-gelatin dessert
    C. use fruit juice in the mixture
    D. use less water than usual

11. When preparing cream of tomato soup, it is MOST advisable to

    A. add hot milk slowly to cold tomato juice
    B. mix milk and tomato juice and then heat
    C. add cold tomato juice slowly to hot milk
    D. add cold milk slowly to hot tomato juice

12. In order to prevent cornstarch from lumping in cooking, it is MOST advisable to

    A. mix the starch with cold liquid before heating
    B. add hot liquid immediately to the starch
    C. brown the starch and add hot liquid
    D. heat the starch in a double boiler

13. Of the following, the LEAST desirable way to dry bread is to place it in

    A. uncovered pans on top of heated ovens
    B. paper bags which are suspended over the stoves
    C. deep pans in a warm oven
    D. cabinets which have slow heat

14. Of the following, the one which is a mollusk used in the preparation of soup is

    A. crab   B. oyster   C. lobster   D. cod

15. Whole dry milk is preferable to evaporated milk for use as a beverage CHIEFLY because it

    A. takes less time to prepare
    B. contains more vitamins
    C. can be made to look and taste more like whole milk
    D. contains more calories

16. The one of the following which is a RESIDUE-FREE food is

    A. milk   B. grapefruit sections
    C. lettuce   D. lemon gelatin

17. The one of the following which is NOT a legume is 17.____

    A. peanuts   B. okra   C. beans   D. lentils

18. Of the following, the sugar which is SWEETEST is 18.____

    A. lactose   B. fructose   C. sucrose   D. maltose

19. Broths are of value in the diet CHIEFLY because they are 19.____

    A. high in food value
    B. a good source of protein
    C. effective appetite stimulants
    D. a good source of carbohydrates

20. Of the following groups, the one which may be served on a SOFT diet is 20.____

    A. cream soup, mashed potato, spinach puree, toast, butter, custard
    B. broiled chicken, mashed potato, buttered peas, toast, milk
    C. vegetable soup, lamp chops, mashed potato, lettuce salad, toast
    D. clear broth, baked potato, tenderloin steak, carrots, apple pie

21. Of the following fruits, those which may be included in a HIGH ACID ash diet are 21.____

    A. prunes   B. oranges   C. bananas   D. pears

22. Of the following statements regarding yeast, the one which is MOST accurate is that yeast 22.____

    A. is generally harmful   B. changes starch to sugar
    C. lives without air   D. requires alcohol to live

23. The souring of milk is due PRIMARILY to the action of bacteria on 23.____

    A. fatty acids   B. proteins   C. amino acids   D. lactose

24. Glycerol, which is an end product of fat metabolism, is further oxidized in the body to 24.____

    A. sucrose   B. galactose   C. levulose   D. glucose

25. Cereals should be included in menus that are planned PRIMARILY to be 25.____

    A. weight reducing   B. low in starch
    C. low in cost   D. high in vitamin C

KEY (CORRECT ANSWERS)

1. C
2. C
3. D
4. A
5. A

6. C
7. B
8. C
9. C
10. D

11. C
12. A
13. A
14. B
15. C

16. D
17. B
18. B
19. C
20. A

21. A
22. B
23. D
24. D
25. C

TEST 2

DIRECTIONS: Each question or incomplete statement is followed by several suggested answers or completions. Select the one that BEST answers the question or completes the statement. *PRINT THE LETTER OF THE CORRECT ANSWER IN THE SPACE AT THE RIGHT.*

1. Of the following, a high blood sugar content is MOST likely to be a symptom of 1.____

    A. anemia
    B. diabetes mellitus
    C. arteriosclerosis
    D. hypertension

2. Trichinosis is a disease which may be caused by 2.____

    A. eating ham which has been overcooked
    B. unsanitary handling of frozen meats
    C. eating food which has been contaminated by infected flies
    D. eating infected pork which has been cooked insufficiently

3. Of the following, the bacteria which causes MOST food poisoning cases is 3.____

    A. botulinum   B. salmonella   C. pneumococci   D. streptococci

4. In the normal diet, liver should be used at least once a week since it is a GOOD source of 4.____

    A. vitamin C   B. phosphorus   C. iron   D. roughage

5. Water is important in the daily intake of the body CHIEFLY because it 5.____

    A. causes the oxidation of food in the body
    B. is a transporting medium for all body substances
    C. cools the air in the lungs
    D. gives off minerals when it is digested

6. Cod liver oil is given to children CHIEFLY in order to aid in 6.____

    A. absorption of calcium
    B. carbohydrate metabolism
    C. prevention of beriberi
    D. regulation of osmotic pressure

7. Of the following statements with respect to the nutritional needs of children, the one which is MOST accurate is that 7.____

    A. a child of four years of age requires a minimum of 2000 calories a day
    B. it is better for a child to be slightly underweight than to be overweight
    C. proportionately, children require more protein per pound of body weight than do adults
    D. a child whose diet is deficient in vitamin D may develop scurvy as a result

8. The one of the following desserts which it is MOST advisable to use in a low protein diet is 8.____

    A. rune soufflé
    B. fruit cup
    C. gelatin
    D. junket

9. The Karell diet is used in the care of 9.___

   A. Addison's disease B. cardiac conditions
   C. diabetes D. jaundice

10. Rowe elimination diets are used in cases involving 10.___

    A. allergy B. lead poisoning
    C. constipation D. nephritis

11. Of the following conditions, the one for which the normal diet is MODIFIED by restricting sodium is 11.___

    A. tuberculosis B. diabetes C. gastritis D. edema

12. The one of the following conditions which may cause jaundice is 12.___

    A. faulty functioning of the kidneys
    B. an obstruction in the common bile duct
    C. a deficiency of vitamin C
    D. the presence of the yeast spore

13. It is GENERALLY accepted that exophthalmic goiter may result from 13.___

    A. the inability of the body to metabolize purines
    B. injury to the pancreas
    C. a diet deficient in iodine
    D. lack of sufficient sunlight and milk

14. Faulty ossification of the legs, ribs, and cranial bones are symptoms GENERALLY associated with 14.___

    A. pellagra B. rickets C. neuritis D. encephalitis

15. Of the following diseases, the one which is characterized PRIMARILY by destruction of the liver cells is 15.___

    A. diabetes B. leukemia C. scurvy D. cirrhosis

Questions 16-25.

DIRECTIONS: Column I lists 10 diseases or conditions, numbered 16 to 25, which require dietary treatment. Column II lists the dietary treatments which are generally used for the conditions listed in Column I. In the space at the right, opposite the number preceding each of the conditions in Column I, place the letter preceding the dietary treatment in Column II which is MOST appropriate for the condition in Column I.

COLUMN I

16. Addison's disease
17. cirrhosis
18. diabetes
19. exophthalmic goiter
20. gastric ulcer
21. gout
22. lipoid nephrosis
23. obesity
24. rickets
25. typhoid fever

COLUMN II

A. low carbohydrate diet
B. high caloric, non-stimulating diet
C. non-residue diet, high in protein and acid ash
D. diet high in vitamin C and magnesium
E. high protein, high carbohydrate, low roughage diet
F. high caloric, soft diet, given in small, frequent feedings
G. diet high in carbohydrate and vitamins, low in potassium, with added salt
H. diet with normal or high protein, vitamins, and minerals; low in fat and carbohydrate; low in caloric value
I. high protein and sulphur diet
J. low protein, purine-free diet
K. high protein, low fat diet, with limited sodium
L. diet high in protein and carbohydrate, low in fat, high in vitamin B complex
M. diet high in vitamin D

16. ____
17. ____
18. ____
19. ____
20. ____
21. ____
22. ____
23. ____
24. ____
25. ____

KEY (CORRECT ANSWERS)

1. B
2. D
3. B
4. C
5. B

6. A
7. C
8. B
9. B
10. A

11. D
12. B
13. C
14. B
15. D

16. G
17. L
18. A
19. B
20. F

21. J
22. K
23. H
24. M
25. E

EXAMINATION SECTION
TEST 1

DIRECTIONS: Each question or incomplete statement is followed by several suggested answers or completions. Select the one that BEST answers the question or completes the statement. *PRINT THE LETTER OF THE CORRECT ANSWER IN THE SPACE AT THE RIGHT.*

1. The one of the following which is the MOST important requirement of a good menu is that it

   A. include a large variety of food
   B. list foods which are well-liked
   C. be printed neatly on a clean menu card
   D. be suited to the purpose for which it is planned

   1.____

2. Of the following, the procedure which is MOST desirable for proper tray service is to

   A. heat all dishes before placing them on the tray
   B. serve hot food hot, and cold food cold
   C. have all patients elevated in order to permit easier swallowing of food
   D. always serve iced water on the tray

   2.____

3. The PROPER position for the knife on the tray is

   A. above the dinner plate
   B. across the bread and butter plate
   C. to the right of the dinner plate
   D. next to the fork

   3.____

4. For attractive tray service, it is MOST advisable to serve harvard beets

   A. on the plate with the meat
   B. in a small side vegetable dish
   C. on a bed of shredded lettuce
   D. with a very thick, heavy sauce

   4.____

5. The kitchen dietitian can work MOST efficiently if her office is located

   A. away from the kitchen, so she can be free from distractions
   B. in a central position where she may view all that happens
   C. at the entrance to the kitchen where she can see people entering and leaving
   D. next to the pantry, so she can see that no unauthorized person enters

   5.____

6. The PRIMARY purpose of keeping records in the dietary department is to

   A. reduce waste in ordering food and supplies
   B. increase consumption of the most nutritious foods
   C. train subordinates in office techniques
   D. maintain statistical records of retail prices

   6.____

7. A budget is BEST described as a(n)

   A. detailed plan for expenditures
   B. schedule for figuring depreciation of equipment over a period of years
   C. order for necessary equipment
   D. periodic accounting for past expenditures

8. Of the following, the CHIEF reason why a refrigerator door should NOT be left open is that the open door will

   A. stop the motor
   B. cause a drop in room temperature
   C. permit the cold air to rise to the top
   D. permit warm air to enter the refrigerator

9. Ovens with thermostatic heat controls should be

   A. kept closed at all times
   B. opened carefully to prevent jarring
   C. checked periodically for accuracy
   D. disconnected when not in use

10. The term *net weight* means MOST NEARLY the

    A. actual weight of an item
    B. weight of the container when empty
    C. combined weight of an item and its container
    D. estimated weight of the container alone

11. In requisitioning food, it is LEAST necessary for a dietitian to

    A. specify the exact quantity desired
    B. secure the signature of the cashier
    C. know the delivery times and order accordingly
    D. know the sizes in which foods are marketed

12. When receiving an order of food, it is INADVISABLE for the dietitian to

    A. check carefully against the order or requisition
    B. see that all fresh foods are weighed and checked in at the receiving room
    C. check for quality as well as quantity of foods delivered
    D. subtract two pounds tare from the weight of each package delivered in an order

13. Assume that, when inspecting a delivery of vegetables, you find a large amount of sorrel mixed in with a bushel of spinach.
    The one of the following actions which it is MOST advisable for you to take is to

    A. sort the spinach and sorrel in cleaning and cook them separately to allow greater variety in the menu
    B. discard the sorrel as waste
    C. call the purchasing office and arrange to return the spinach as unsatisfactory
    D. place the sorrel in the refrigerator and return it to the driver on his next delivery

14. When purchasing iceberg lettuce, it is ADVISABLE to look for lettuce which is   14._____

    A. loosely headed, with soft curly leaves and a yellow heart
    B. tightly headed, elongated, with coarse green leaves
    C. tightly headed, with medium green outside leaves and a pale green heart
    D. loosely headed, with elongated stalk and rugged curly leaves

15. The term *30-40 prunes* is used to describe the   15._____

    A. number of prunes in a box
    B. particular variety of prunes
    C. brand name of prunes
    D. number of prunes in a pound

16. When ordering chocolate liquor, the dietitian should expect to receive a _____ choco-   16._____
    late.

    A. solid piece of   B. semi-liquid
    C. liquid   D. glass jar of

17. Of the following, the BEST reason for discarding the green part of potatoes is that it con-   17._____
    tains a poison known as

    A. cevitamic acid   B. citric acid
    C. solanine   D. trichinae

18. The number of cans that a standard case of #10 canned apples USUALLY contains is   18._____

    A. 6   B. 12   C. 18   D. 24

19. Of the following, the person MOST closely associated with work in the field of infant   19._____
    behavior and feeding is

    A. H. Pollack   B. A. Gesell
    C. E.J. Stieglitz   D. J.F. Freeman

20. Of the following, the person BEST known for work in the field of diabetes is   20._____

    A. N. Jolliffe   B. H. Sherman
    C. R.M. Wilder   D. F. Stern

21. An egg which is strictly fresh will   21._____

    A. float in cold water
    B. have a thin and watery egg white
    C. have a swollen egg yolk which is easily broken
    D. sink in cold water

22. Cocoa and chocolate are rich in   22._____

    A. glycogen   B. gum   C. cellulose   D. starch

23. The percentage of protein that is usually converted into glucose in the body is MOST   23._____
    NEARLY

    A. 49%   B. 58%   C. 67%   D. 78%

24. Of the following vegetables, the one which gives the LARGEST yield, pound for pound, when pureed is 24.____

    A. fresh celery
    B. frozen peas
    C. frozen asparagus
    D. fresh carrots

25. If the composition of two small rib chops is Protein - 21 grams and Fat - 17 grams, the number of calories in the two chops is MOST NEARLY 25.____

    A. 136   B. 200   C. 237   D. 257

KEY (CORRECT ANSWERS)

1. D
2. B
3. C
4. B
5. B

6. A
7. A
8. D
9. C
10. A

11. B
12. D
13. C
14. C
15. D

16. C
17. C
18. A
19. B
20. C

21. D
22. D
23. B
24. D
25. C

TEST 2

DIRECTIONS: Each question or incomplete statement is followed by several suggested answers or completions. Select the one that BEST answers the question or completes the statement. *PRINT THE LETTER OF THE CORRECT ANSWER IN THE SPACE AT THE RIGHT.*

1. An APPROPRIATE substitute for sucrose for a patient on a low carbohydrate diet is   1.____

    A. saccharin   B. casec   C. lactose   D. protinol

2. Of the following, the vegetables which are high in protein and, therefore, sometimes substituted for meat are   2.____

    A. green leafy vegetables   B. legumes
    C. root vegetables   D. gourds

3. When planning menus, it is *advisable* to use fish at least once a week because it is a GOOD source of   3.____

    A. iron   B. vitamin C   C. zinc   D. iodine

4. Of the following, the one which is a *non-nutritive* beverage is   4.____

    A. clear tea   B. orangeade
    C. oatmeal gruel   D. cream soda

5. Macaroni is *usually* used as a substitute for   5.____

    A. salad   B. meat   C. potato   D. dessert

6. Bread is dextrinized by   6.____

    A. toasting   B. chopping
    C. drying in open air   D. soaking in hot water

7. Baked custard is used on the menu CHIEFLY   7.____

    A. as a source of vitamin C
    B. because of its high protein content
    C. to add color
    D. as a source of starch

8. The one of the following which is a *non-irritating* food is   8.____

    A. cabbage   B. pickles   C. spaghetti   D. celery

9. Leaves of rhubarb and beets, when boiled in an aluminum container, will clean the container because they contain   9.____

    A. sulphuric acid   B. oxalic acid
    C. ammonia   D. alkali

10. When refinishing a refrigerator ice cube tray, the one of the following which should NOT be used as a coating material is   10.____

    A. aluminum   B. cadmium   C. tin   D. nickel

11. The Department of Health requires the sterilization of eating utensils by 11.____

    A. hot air sterilizers
    B. ultraviolet rays
    C. chemical solutions
    D. water at 180° F

12. Suppose that the dishwashing machine has become clogged with food particles. 12.____
    Of the following, the action which would be MOST advisable for the dietitian to take *first* is to

    A. call the service man to disassemble and clean the machine
    B. instruct the employees assigned to washing dishes about proper scraping of dishes
    C. order the employees to prerinse all dishes in order to prevent clogging
    D. remove the strainer tray

13. The one of the following which is the MOST effective way to rid a food storeroom of mice 13.____
    is to

    A. cement tight all holes which permit invasion
    B. set traps to catch the mice
    C. spread poison around the floor
    D. burn a sulphur candle in the storeroom

14. Black stoves are cleaned BEST by 14.____

    A. polishing with an oiled cloth
    B. rubbing with a piece of wax paper
    C. scrubbing with soap and water
    D. heating until they are red hot

15. Of the following, the BEST procedure for cleaning a red quarry tile floor in a hospital 15.____
    kitchen is to

    A. scrub it, then wax the floor
    B. hose it down with steam
    C. wash it with a strong soap
    D. wash it with a lye

16. After making ice cream, it is MOST important that the machine be 16.____

    A. rinsed thoroughly in cold water
    B. sterilized
    C. soaked in soap solution
    D. scrubbed with a brush

17. A dietitian assigned to work with clinic patients should have a basic knowledge of the 17.____
    foods of foreign-born people.
    Of the following, the MOST important reason for this is that

    A. it is interesting and exciting to eat the exotic dishes of foreign lands
    B. such knowledge would prove beyond doubt that poor diet is the cause of poor health among the foreign-born

C. such knowledge would help the dietitian to plan the patient's prescribed diet around familiar foods
D. many foreign dishes are more nutritious than American foods

18. The clinic dietitian meets several problems of the aging. The one of the following for which she is LEAST responsible is the

    A. detection of the onset of chronic degenerative diseases
    B. conservation of the health of the individual
    C. re-evaluation of the caloric requirements of aged patients
    D. overcoming of superstitions and food fallacies

19. When advising on methods of economizing, the clinic dietitian should instruct patients to AVOID buying

    A. foods in quantity, even though storage space permits
    B. foods that are in season and in abundance on the market
    C. less expensive cuts of meat
    D. butter, since there are less expensive substitutes on the market

20. The one of the following services which is the LEAST basic function of a nutrition clinic is to

    A. serve as a teaching center for students
    B. provide educational programs for patients of all ages
    C. follow up the nutritional status of individual patients
    D. secure diet histories of patients for the correction of undesirable food habits

21. Time and motion studies in the field of dietetics are used PRIMARILY to

    A. check on lateness and absence records of employees
    B. reduce effort and increase efficiency in performing particular tasks
    C. prepare estimates of time required between requisition and delivery dates
    D. schedule the daily work assignments for the entire staff

22. The PRIMARY purpose of using standardized recipes is to

    A. aid in controlling food costs
    B. encourage the cooks to try out new foods
    C. prepare large quantities of food
    D. determine the caloric values of foods

23. The CHIEF advantage of keeping a perpetual inventory of stock items is that

    A. supplies may be stored more easily
    B. there will be less breakage and loss of stock
    C. it makes it unnecessary to order replacements for stock supplies
    D. the balance on hand at any time is easily determined

24. In order to prevent the loss of vitamins in cooking, it is HOST advisable to

    A. cover the food completely with water while cooking and boil it rapidly
    B. peel and soak vegetables in cold water before cooking

C. dice vegetables into small pieces and boil them in an open pot
D. cook vegetables in the shortest possible time in a covered pot containing little water

25. To marinate is to 25.____
   A. let foods stand in a specially prepared liquid to add flavor or to tenderize them
   B. cook food in liquid just below the boiling point
   C. moisten food while cooking by pouring over it drippings or other liquids
   D. cook food in water at boiling temperature

KEY (CORRECT ANSWERS)

1. A
2. B
3. D
4. A
5. C

6. A
7. B
8. C
9. B
10. B

11. D
12. A
13. A
14. C
15. B

16. B
17. C
18. A
19. D
20. A

21. B
22. A
23. D
24. D
25. A

EXAMINATION SECTION
TEST 1

DIRECTIONS: Each question or incomplete statement is followed by several suggested answers or completions. Select the one that BEST answers the question or completes the statement. *PRINT THE LETTER OF THE CORRECT ANSWER IN THE SPACE AT THE RIGHT.*

1. The one of the following groups of garnishes or accompaniments which is MOST appropriate for the entree designated is

    A. boiled beef; horseradish sour cream sauce, mixed pickles, beet and onion relish, lemon wedge
    B. roast veal; cranberry sauce, fried apple ring, parsley, French fried onion ring
    C. broiled fish; lemon wedge, tartar sauce, chopped parsley, lemon butter
    D. hamburger; sliced onion, catsup, French fried onion rings, Hollandaise sauce

    1.____

2. Assume that the following menu has been submitted: chicken fricasee, mashed potatoes, cauliflower, bread and butter, applesauce, coffee, tea, milk.
The CHIEF defect of this menu is that it is

    A. inadequate in protein content
    B. lacking in color and texture contrast
    C. improperly balanced as to nutrient content
    D. too high in calories

    2.____

3. Assume that the following menu has been submitted for lunch: baked ham, pan browned parsnips, baked sweet potato, cornbread and butter, Apple Brown Betty with whipped topping.
This menu is NOT well-planned primarily because

    A. there are too many calories
    B. there are no vitamin C foods
    C. there is not enough variety in texture of the foods
    D. the workload is not well distributed for the kitchen's cooking equipment

    3.____

4. If a patient on a diabetic diet dislikes milk, he may exchange the milk with one

    A. bread exchange, one meat exchange, and one fat exchange
    B. fruit exchange
    C. bread exchange, one beverage, and one fat exchange
    D. meat exchange and one fruit exchange

    4.____

5. The one of the following foods which can be used by a diabetic patient as a substitute in a meat exchange is

    A. ice cream
    B. cheddar cheese
    C. lima beans
    D. blackeye peas

    5.____

6. Of the following foods, the one which should NOT be included in a clear liquid diet is

    A. milk
    B. fat-free broth
    C. fruit or vegetable juice
    D. carbonated beverages

    6.____

35

7. The one of the following which is permitted on a 500 mg. sodium diet is

   A. cornflakes
   B. rice krispies
   C. puffed wheat
   D. wheat flakes

8. The one of the following statements which is INCORRECT is that riboflavin

   A. helps the cells utilize oxygen
   B. helps keep vision clear
   C. prevents cracking of mouth corners
   D. helps the body absorb calcium

9. The one of the following which is NOT concerned with the digestion of fat is

   A. cholecystokinin
   B. lipase
   C. bile
   D. ptyalin

10. The diet which should be given to a patient who has chronic kidney disease with nitrogen retention is

    A. high protein, low carbohydrate
    B. low protein
    C. low calcium, low phosphorus
    D. low purine

11. The diet MOST likely to be ordered for the pernicious vomiting of pregnancy is

    A. high carbohydrate, low fat
    B. high carbohydrate, high fat, high protein
    C. low carbohydrate, low fat, high protein
    D. high protein, low sodium

12. In the treatment of hemorrhagic and nutritional anemias, the MOST important nutrients to stress are iron and

    A. protein   B. vitamin A   C. iodine   D. vitamin E

13. The USUAL diet for a patient with acute gallbladder is a _____ diet.

    A. low fat
    B. 1000 mg. sodium
    C. high protein
    D. low cholesterol

14. Assume that a leukemia patient has difficulty swallowing the foods prescribed for her. In order to provide a diet which is nutritionally adequate, it is LEAST advisable to recommend

    A. a liquid diet emphasizing high caloric liquids and protein supplements
    B. nasal tube feeding in order to meet all nutritional requirements and to avoid the problem of swallowing
    C. a diet on which the meat is minced and all fruits and vegetables are pureed
    D. a diet similar to the one prescribed for her except that each item is pureed

15. The diet MOST likely to be prescribed for a patient who has renal stones is a(n) _____ diet.

    A. elimination
    B. low oxalate
    C. low cholesterol
    D. high carbohydrate, low protein, low fat

16. A rice diet is USUALLY prescribed for patients who

    A. have high blood pressure
    B. have a food allergy
    C. are recovering from a gallbladder operation
    D. require a high caloric intake

17. Patients suffering severe burns are MOST likely to have

    A. loss of serum protein   B. steatorrhea
    C. polyneuritis   D. stomatitis

18. Of the following statements concerning phenylketonuria, the one that is NOT correct is that it

    A. is caused by an enzyme deficiency
    B. leads to mental retardation
    C. is treated by the restriction of carbohydrates
    D. must be detected in the first few months of life in order to be treated

19. During all periods of growth, vitamin D is essential for efficient absorption and utilization of

    A. calcium and potassium   B. potassium and iron
    C. magnesium and calcium   D. phosphorus and calcium

20. In the treatment of urinary calculi, the one of the following which will assist in maintaining an acid urine is

    A. cranberry juice   B. peas
    C. cabbage   D. corn oil

21. Of the following, the food containing the HIGHEST amount of thiamine per 100 gram portion is

    A. fresh green peas   B. fresh pork
    C. fresh spinach   D. ground beef

22. The one of the following foods which is the POOREST source of niacin per 100 gram portion is

    A. lean meats   B. peanuts
    C. whole grain cereals   D. green leafy vegetables

23. Of the following lists of foods, the one which will contribute MOST to the ascorbic acid content of a diet is

    A. potatoes, green peppers, raw cabbage
    B. enriched bread, pork, turnips
    C. whole wheat bread, potatoes, prunes
    D. apples, dates, plums

24. Of the following foods, the content of unsaturated fatty acids is GREATEST in

    A. butter   B. corn oil
    C. beef suet   D. lard

25. Of the following, the one with the LOWEST vitamin C content per 4 oz. portion is _____ juice.

    A. orange
    B. lemon
    C. tomato
    D. grapefruit

25.____

KEY (CORRECT ANSWERS)

1. C		11. A	
2. B		12. A	
3. D		13. A	
4. A		14. C	
5. B		15. B	
6. A		16. A	
7. C		17. A	
8. D		18. C	
9. D		19. D	
10. B		20. A	

21. B
22. D
23. A
24. B
25. C

TEST 2

DIRECTIONS: Each question or incomplete statement is followed by several suggested answers or completions. Select the one that BEST answers the question or completes the statement. *PRINT THE LETTER OF THE CORRECT ANSWER IN THE SPACE AT THE RIGHT.*

1. When roasting meat, the GREATEST yield of finished product may be expected when

   A. it is quickly seared on both sides at the beginning
   B. a high temperature is used throughout the roasting period
   C. a small quantity of water is added during roasting
   D. a low temperature is used throughout the roasting process

2. Of the following, the meat which is LEAST suitable for roasting is

   A. loin of pork   B. corned brisket
   C. rump of veal   D. leg of lamb

3. The loss of weight which results from braising boneless bottom round of beef, when proper techniques are used, is

   A. negligible   B. about 10%
   C. about 25%   D. over 50%

4. Of the following, the one which gives the MOST appropriate cooking temperature for the food indicated is

   A. beef loaf - 450° F   B. baked potatoes - 250° F
   C. caramel custard - 325° F   D. gingerbread - 475° F

5. In teaching a *cook trainee* how to deep fat fry various items of food, one should NOT instruct him to

   A. lower the food into the fat quickly
   B. make uniform portions of food for frying in the same load
   C. fill frying baskets to no more than 2/3 of capacity
   D. drain raw wet foods well before frying

6. Foods cooked incorrectly often lose flavor.
   When cooking beans or carrots, it is LEAST advisable to

   A. boil them in a small amount of water
   B. cook them in a steamer
   C. cook them in a pressure cooker
   D. cook them in an uncovered kettle

7. Of the following, the one which would make the LEAST satisfactory thickening agent in a casserole is

   A. wheat flour   B. rice
   C. cornstarch   D. tapioca

8. If baking powder biscuits do not rise to the proper height, the MOST probable cause is too

   A. *little* shortening   B. *much* handling of dough
   C. *little* flour   D. *much* baking powder

9. A soggy bottom crust in a lemon meringue pie is MOST probably caused by 9.___
   A. handling the crust too much
   B. baking at too high a temperature
   C. refrigeration of the crust prior to baking
   D. pouring in the filling when the pie is hot

10. The MOST appropriate type of poultry to purchase for chicken a la king is 10.___

    A. fowl   B. roasters   C. fryers   D. broilers

11. Of the following, Grade B eggs may be used MOST satisfactorily for 11.___
    A. poaching   B. scrambling
    C. frying   D. coddling

12. Considering both quality and economy, the BEST choice of the following grades to be specified when ordering apples for sauce is 12.___
    A. fancy   B. extra fancy
    C. utility   D. U.S. #1

13. When submitting requisitions, the dietitian should give correct specifications for each item. 13.___
    Of the following items, the one which is CORRECTLY specified is
    A. celery - fresh, Grade A, trimmed, in boxes, 140 pounds
    B. oranges - fresh, commercial grade, size 75 to the half crate, 225 pounds
    C. salad greens - romaine, fresh, Grade A, trimmed, 30 pounds
    D. onions - dry, Grade A, in sacks, 200 pounds

14. The one of the following specifications which is INCOMPLETE is 14.___
    A. 200 lbs. of ham, 10 to 12 lbs. each, U.S. #1
    B. 120 lbs. fresh bottom rounds, 20 to 30 lbs. each, Choice
    C. 250 lbs. of boneless corned brisket, deckel removed, 10 to 12 lbs. each, Good
    D. 225 lbs. double veal legs, cut short, 40 to 48 lbs. each, Choice

15. Of the following food items, the one which does NOT have the correct varieties listed for it is 15.___
    A. melon - Honeydew, Cantaloupe, Persian, Casaba
    B. potatoes - Idaho, Cobbler, Russet, Yam
    C. onions - Spanish, Bermuda, Yellow, Red
    D. apples - McIntosh, Emperor, Delicious, Concord

16. Assume that you plan to serve 500 portions of beef stew, with 3 ounces of cooked meat in each portion. 16.___
    To provide this, you would need _____ lbs. _____ beef chuck.
    A. 95; boneless   B. 100; whole
    C. 125; boneless   D. 175; whole

17. You are serving buttered carrot rings on a menu for which you need 750 servings. The number of pounds of topped carrots you should order is MOST NEARLY _____ lbs.

    A. 50 B. 75 C. 150 D. 300

18. Frozen broccoli is on the menu for dinner and you require 260 servings. The number of 2 1/2 lb. packages you would need is MOST NEARLY

    A. 10 B. 25 C. 50 D. 100

19. You wish to serve canned peas to 300 patients on the regular diet, 50 patients on bland diet, 35 patients on low fat diet, and 65 patients on light diet. Peas are supplied in #10 cans, and these are ordered by the case only.
    The number of cases you would need is

    A. 1 B. 2 C. 3 D. 4

20. In order to ensure a minimum of leftover when you plan to serve 3 oz. portions of mashed potatoes to 500 persons, it would be BEST to order _____ potatoes.

    A. 40 lbs. instant
    B. 50 lbs. peeled
    C. 2 cases #10 cans of whole
    D. one 100 lb. sack of

21. The one of the following amounts which is MOST likely to yield 100 average servings is

    A. dry prunes, 25 lbs.
    B. bacon, sliced, rind removed (2 slices per serving), 20 lbs.
    C. coffee, ground for drip, percolator or silex, 2 lbs.
    D. egg noodles, buttered, 18 lbs.

22. The one of the following which would be INCORRECT to order when serving 200 persons is

    A. 8 #10 cans of applesauce
    B. 1 1/2 cases of #5 cans of tomato juice
    C. 100 lbs. of eviscerated fowl
    D. 20 lbs. of rice

23. To ensure that foods are relatively free of contamination when served in a cafeteria during a three hour meal period, it would be MOST advisable to

    A. stagger periods of preparation and service to the counter
    B. maintain a steam table temperature of 120° F
    C. reheat foods when they cool down
    D. eliminate all creamed foods from the menu

24. If egg salad has been prepared in a safe and sanitary manner, the criterion to be used to determine if it may be served one day later is that it

    A. still tastes good
    B. has a satisfactory general appearance
    C. still smells good
    D. has been continuously refrigerated

25. The one of the following statements concerning proper storage which is INCORRECT is that   25._____

   A. crates of eggs should be stored upright, never on ends or sides, because eggs are packed with the small end down
   B. crates of lettuce or fruit should not be stacked upright but on the side and should be cross-stacked to provide for air circulation
   C. fresh raw meat such as veal carcass should be carefully wrapped when stored to prevent contamination
   D. onions and potatoes do not require refrigeration; they are best stored in a dark, well-ventilated room at a temperature of 50° to 60° F

KEY (CORRECT ANSWERS)

1. D
2. B
3. C
4. C
5. A

6. D
7. C
8. B
9. D
10. A

11. B
12. C
13. C
14. A
15. D

16. C
17. C
18. B
19. C
20. D

21. C
22. D
23. A
24. D
25. C

TEST 3

DIRECTIONS: Each question or incomplete statement is followed by several suggested answers or completions. Select the one that BEST answers the question or completes the statement. *PRINT THE LETTER OF THE CORRECT ANSWER IN THE SPACE AT THE RIGHT.*

1. Of the following, the one which gives the LEAST desirable temperature for storing the item indicated is

    A. ripe bananas - 60° to 70° F
    B. fresh eggs - 53° to 58° F
    C. salad greens - 40° to 45° F
    D. fresh lamb - 33° to 38° F

    1.____

2. Of the following, the MOST important reason for requiring good ventilation in a storeroom is to prevent

    A. condensation of moisture
    B. roach or rodent infestation
    C. complaints from storekeepers about odors
    D. spoilage of canned goods

    2.____

3. Of the following foods, the one which is LEAST susceptible to insect infestation is

    A. dried beans   B. dried fruits
    C. plain gelatin   D. non-fat dry milk

    3.____

4. Of the following, the MOST effective measure for the elimination of rodents in a hospital kitchen is to

    A. clean the floors every day
    B. spread poison once a month in all allowable areas
    C. eliminate harborages
    D. screen off the slop sinks at all times

    4.____

5. Of the following ways to store food, it is LEAST desirable to place

    A. sacks of dried beans on racks
    B. cans of peas on the floor
    C. packages of cereal on shelves
    D. quarters of lamb on hooks in the refrigerator

    5.____

6. The MOST important reason for NOT overcrowding refrigerators is to

    A. make cleaning easier
    B. allow air circulation to reach all foods
    C. prevent waste resulting from overlooked foods
    D. reduce opportunities for pilferage of food

    6.____

7. Cooked foods should be cooled and refrigerated quickly, PRIMARILY to

    A. *prevent* growth and development of bacteria
    B. *preserve* food nutrients

    7.____

43

C. *prevent* loss of moisture content
D. *preserve* a *fresh cooked* appearance

8. In planning the layout of a kitchen, it is MOST important to arrange for

   A. grouping together of large pieces of equipment
   B. a separate work area for each cook
   C. a smooth and orderly flow of work
   D. separation of *wet* and *dry* areas

9. Of the following, the MOST satisfactory work surface for a cook's work table is

   A. hardwood 4" thick
   B. heavy gauge stainless steel
   C. heavy duty galvanized iron
   D. heavy gauge aluminum

10. Of the following, the practice which is LEAST advisable in the operation and maintenance of a food grinder is to

    A. hold the knife and plate in place by screwing the adjustment ring as tight as possible
    B. use a mallet to push pieces of food into the grinder
    C. remove the grinder plate and clean it thoroughly with a brush after each use
    D. remove the grinder head at the end of the day and clean all loose parts before storing them

11. The MAIN reason for selecting a cafeteria counter of standard fabricated units rather than a custom-built counter of the same quality is the

    A. lower initial cost
    B. easier cleaning
    C. greater flexibility for change and expansion
    D. lower maintenance costs

12. Of the following, the MOST suitable steam equipment for a main kitchen in a 100 bed hospital is

    A. one compartment steamer, one 80 gallon jacketed kettle, and one 60 gallon jacketed kettle
    B. two 30 gallon jacketed kettles and one 20 gallon jacketed kettle
    C. one 3 compartment steamer and two 30 gallon jacketed kettles
    D. two 2 compartment steamers and one 20 gallon jacketed kettle

13. The BEST choice for the top of a kitchen work table is

    A. 2 inch solid wood
    B. 12 gauge monel metal
    C. 20 gauge stainless steel
    D. galvanized metal

14. For equipment such as steam tables which require a water supply, it is MOST important to

    A. make sure there are no submerged inlets
    B. specify all stainless steel construction
    C. provide a heat booster
    D. supply both hot and cold water

14.____

15. In requisitioning a steam jacketed kettle, the LEAST important specification is that the

    A. draw off tube should be as close to the kettle as possible
    B. bottom should be pitched to facilitate run-off of contents
    C. kettle should be wall hung for easier cleaning
    D. draw off valve should be easily removable

15.____

16. The MAIN factor to consider when purchasing a slicing machine is the

    A. ease of cleaning
    B. adequacy of the safety guard for the cutting edge
    C. size of the machine in relation to the volume of slicing
    D. availability of replacement parts

16.____

17. In submitting your annual budget, you have requested a 2 drawer work table of complete stainless steel construction.
If you are told that you must request a less expensive model, the MOST acceptable compromise for you to make would be to

    A. substitute ducoed legs with stainless steel feet
    B. substitute drawers of galvanized metal with stainless steel fronts
    C. specify a lighter weight stainless steel
    D. reduce the size of the table

17.____

18. The one of the following which is MOST likely to yield 100 average servings is

    A. fish filet - 30 pounds
    B. cream for coffee - 6 quarts
    C. oatmeal (rolled oats) - 5 pounds
    D. frozen spinach - 10 pounds

18.____

19. The one of the following requisitions which is NOT correct for 600 servings is

    A. 15 lbs. of ground coffee
    B. 9 lbs. of margarine chips for toast
    C. 3 #10 cans of jelly
    D. 60 lbs. of granulated sugar for cereal

19.____

20. You have requisitioned 8000 lbs. of beef carcass (650 to 700 lbs. per carcass). This will yield tender steaks, tender roasts, and less tender cuts for roasting, stewing, and chopping.
Taking into account loss from trim, bones, and fat when the carcasses are processed, the amount of edible meat these carcasses should yield is MOST NEARLY _____ lbs.

    A. 4500   B. 5360   C. 6500   D. 7120

20.____

21. Analysis of the distribution of the average food dollar in a hospital can be of assistance to the dietitian in planning for and checking on the expenditure of funds.
Of the following, the MOST advisable distribution of funds for categories of food is: meat, poultry, and fish _____%; dairy products _____%; fruits and vegetables _____%; bread and cereal _____%; miscellaneous _____%.

    A. 40; 20; 20; 10; 10
    B. 50; 10; 10; 10; 20
    C. 20; 20; 20; 20; 20
    D. 30; 30; 30; 5; 5

22. When planning a nutrition curriculum for the clinical instruction of student nurses, the factor which deserves the LEAST consideration is the

    A. educational purposes which the school of nursing seeks to attain
    B. educational experiences which are likely to meet the school's objectives
    C. service needs of the dietary department of the hospital
    D. methods of determining if the educational objectives have been attained

23. The current trend in the teaching of nutrition and diet therapy to student nurses emphasizes

    A. role playing and discussion groups as the most significant teaching devices
    B. instruction in food laboratories on preparation of foods
    C. instruction in food preparation and service to patients in the wards
    D. the clinical importance of diet therapy in a patient-centered plan of teaching

24. Suppose that the electric slicer used in the main kitchen is frequently out of order because of a short in the motor. The repair mechanic has demonstrated that this happens because excessive moisture is being used to flush out debris when cleaning the machine.
To prevent repetition of this breakdown, it would be MOST advisable to

    A. issue detailed written instructions on maintenance procedures to all cooks and kitchen employees who might have occasion to use or clean this slicer
    B. issue an order to all employees that no water is to
    C. be used when cleaning this slicer, only clean dry rags
    D. replace the slicer with a manual one that does not have a motor and, therefore, does not require electric current
    E. instruct two employees on each shift on the procedures to be used in cleaning the machine and restrict the use of the machine to them

25. Assume that a dietitian had instructed the kitchen helpers on how to minimize waste when preparing food for cooking. It would be MOST reasonable to conclude that such waste had been reduced subsequently if

    A. on a spot check, the employees observed were preparing the food as instructed
    B. operating costs for the dietary division during the next month were reduced
    C. the amount of food prepared during the next month decreased on a per capita basis
    D. requisitions of food supplies during the next month decreased

KEY (CORRECT ANSWERS)

1.	B	11.	C
2.	A	12.	C
3.	C	13.	B
4.	C	14.	A
5.	B	15.	C
6.	B	16.	B
7.	A	17.	A
8.	C	18.	A
9.	B	19.	D
10.	A	20.	B

21. A
22. C
23. D
24. D
25. C

EXAMINATION SECTION
TEST 1

DIRECTIONS: Each question or incomplete statement is followed by several suggested answers or completions. Select the one that BEST answers the question or completes the statement. *PRINT THE LETTER OF THE CORRECT ANSWER IN THE SPACE AT THE RIGHT.*

1. The Federal and State grades of food are dependent upon

    A. appearance and freedom from defects
    B. maturity or freshness
    C. variety
    D. shape, color, and size
    E. color, flavor, and size

    1.____

2. Select vegetables and fruits are

    A. wilted or withered
    B. ripe and well-colored
    C. picked over
    D. plump, well-colored, and ripe, firm without decay
    E. well-colored, plump, firm, and top grade

    2.____

3. All perishable vegetables need to be

    A. refrigerated
    B. washed and wrapped
    C. washed, wrapped, and refrigerated
    D. stored at room temperature
    E. stored in a special compartment in the refrigerator

    3.____

4. Fresh fruits, apples, pears, and peaches should be

    A. washed and wrapped separately
    B. refrigerated
    C. wrapped and stored, unwashed, in the refrigerator or other cool place
    D. kept at room temperature
    E. purchased just as they are needed

    4.____

5. Dried vegetables are

    A. equal to fresh vegetables of the same variety in mineral and cellulose
    B. low-cost sources of protein and energy food
    C. good main dish foods
    D. usually cheaper than fresh vegetables
    E. all of the above

    5.____

6. Commercially canned foods are

    A. economical
    B. convenient
    C. easy to store

    6.____

49

D. available
E. important to family food supply because of economy, convenience, and availability

7. Modern frozen foods are prepared

   A. by lowering the temperature slowly to freezing
   B. by lowering the temperature of a food rapidly to freezing
   C. from average grade food products
   D. at the peak of the seasonal supply
   E. at the sacrifice of vitamins

8. To insure color retention and prevent the spoilage action of bacteria, yeasts, and molds, frozen foods should be kept at _____ degrees F.

   A. 10
   B. 0
   C. just under 32
   D. 20
   E. 25-30

9. The grade stamp on beef, veal, calf, lamb, and mutton is one's guide to

   A. fat content
   B. leanness
   C. freedom from disease
   D. wholesomeness and quality characteristics
   E. price

10. Identity of the cuts of meat is helpful because of

    A. economy
    B. method of cooking
    C. tenderness
    D. all of the above
    E. none of the above

11. One will become a more economical shopper if cost of food is figured in terms of

    A. pounds
    B. quarts
    C. servings
    D. weight or measurement
    E. unit by which food is sold

12. The word poultry is applied to

    A. chickens and turkeys
    B. geese and ducks
    C. guineas and pigeons
    D. any wild bird used for food
    E. all domesticated birds used as food

13. Eggs are graded according to

    A. quality of white
    B. quality of yolk
    C. appearance of shell
    D. size
    E. size and quality of white and yolk

14. Coffee and tea contain   14._____

    A. vitamins   B. nutrients   C. stimulants
    D. all of the above   E. none of the above

15. With higher incomes and larger food budgets, Americans are using   15._____

    A. smaller amounts of cereal products
    B. more bread
    C. less fruits and vegetables
    D. more meat and less poultry
    E. greater amounts of cereal products

16. Prepared mixes   16._____

    A. are convenient
    B. are timesaving
    C. always cost more than homemade products
    D. should be firmly packaged
    E. are convenient and timesaving, and sometimes are economical

17. The well-planned kitchen includes areas for   17._____

    A. storage   B. cleanup   C. preparation
    D. service   E. all of the above

18. The selection of kitchen equipment considers   18._____

    A. materials
    B. construction
    C. design
    D. cost
    E. items well-constructed of durable materials in pleasing designs at reasonable costs

19. One of the MOST important things to remember about the kitchen is   19._____

    A. to keep everything immaculately clean
    B. to keep everything in its place
    C. to get as many labor-saving devices as possible
    D. to use all safety precautions - the kitchen can be a dangerous place
    E. that a great deal of the homemaker's time is spent here

20. Meal patterns vary as to   20._____

    A. cost
    B. kinds of foods
    C. amount of time and skill required for preparation
    D. all of the above
    E. none of the above

21. A distinctive menu includes   21._____

    A. flavor and texture contrast
    B. pleasing colors
    C. basic nutrients

D. family likes and dislikes
E. nutrients in pleasing flavor, texture, and color contrasts

22. The trend in modern meal service is toward

    A. very casual service
    B. traditional service
    C. more casual service with some meals served traditionally
    D. elaborate service
    E. a relaxed atmosphere with a hope that all service turns out well

23. The term flatware refers to

    A. pitchers
    B. trays and flat dishes
    C. knives, forks, and spoons
    D. anything made from stainless steel or silver
    E. teapots

24. A good design for dishes, glassware, and other service should be

    A. functional
    B. ornate
    C. simple
    D. an expression of the hostess' personality
    E. both beautiful and functional

25. The MOST practical choice for every day dinnerware for the family with several small children would be

    A. earthenware
    B. high-silicate porcelain china
    C. semi-vitrified china
    D. durable molded plastic
    E. pottery

KEY (CORRECT ANSWERS)

1. D
2. D
3. C
4. C
5. E

6. E
7. B
8. B
9. D
10. D

11. C
12. E
13. E
14. C
15. A

16. E
17. E
18. E
19. D
20. D

21. E
22. C
23. C
24. E
25. D

TEST 2

DIRECTIONS: Each question or incomplete statement is followed by several suggested answers or completions. Select the one that BEST answers the question or completes the statement. *PRINT THE LETTER OF THE CORRECT ANSWER IN THE SPACE AT THE RIGHT.*

1. The MOST suitable choice for cake and frosting combination is   1._____

    A. angel food cake with thick buttery frosting
    B. buttery frosting on a simple economy cake
    C. light fluffy cooked frosting on a simple cake
    D. angel food cake with a heavy cooked frosting
    E. a simple chocolate cake with a chewy boiled frosting

2. Cookies   2._____

    A. are good with most meals
    B. can be frozen, raw, or baked
    C. are usually inexpensive and easy to store
    D. are easy to prepare
    E. all of the above

3. Hot water and *stir and roll* are nonconventional methods of making   3._____

    A. cake   B. cream puffs   C. bread
    D. pie crust   E. cookies

4. Nutmeats and bits of fruit are coated with flour before mixing them into cakes or cookies to   4._____

    A. help them sink to the bottom of the dough
    B. keep them evenly distributed throughout the dough
    C. keep them on top of the dough
    D. make them more attractive
    E. hold in their flavor

5. Poultry may be safely prepared by   5._____

    A. stuffing and freezing it
    B. stuffing it just before cooking
    C. leaving the stuffing in the cooked bird for a long time
    D. refrigerating poultry and stuffing separately two days before cooking
    E. none of the above

6. Cooked leftover meat, poultry, or fish may be used for   6._____

    A. casseroles
    B. salads
    C. sandwiches
    D. ingredients for main dishes, salads, or sandwiches
    E. none of the above

7. Every person who prepares or serves food should   7.____

   A. know and use ways to prevent food contamination or poisoning
   B. be especially clean and healthy
   C. keep foods very hot or very cold
   D. observe all of the above
   E. observe none of the above

8. A recent trend in entertaining with food service is   8.____

   A. buffet   B. cafeteria
   C. out-of-doors meals   D. teas
   E. coffees

9. The school lunch should be   9.____

   A. attractive, nutritious, and have variety
   B. made up of sandwiches
   C. providing half of the day"s calories
   D. packed in any sort of container
   E. given little planning time

10. Diets for the overweight are made up of   10.____

    A. foods high in calories, vitamins, and minerals
    B. foods low in calories, high in protein, vitamins, and minerals
    C. smaller servings of the regular family meals
    D. foods high in cellulose
    E. foods prepared with plenty of seasoning

11. Mental activity takes   11.____

    A. many calories   B. few calories
    C. much energy   D. more protein
    E. more fat in the diet

12. If the breadwinner works as a factory worker or farmer, he may need   12.____

    A. less food
    B. more iron
    C. more calories, perhaps as snacks
    D. more riboflavin
    E. a greater variety of food

13. In middle life, more _____ are needed to protect the body.   13.____

    A. fruits   B. vegetables
    C. calories   D. proteins
    E. fruits and vegetables

14. Older people need decreased numbers of calories and increased amounts of protein,   14.____
    vitamins, and minerals because

    A. the metabolic rate has slowed
    B. they are not so active
    C. their incomes are less

D. shopping for food is more difficult
E. their bodies are less active and the metabolic rate is slowed

15. It is wise to divide foods fairly evenly among three meals a day for

    A. older people
    B. middle-aged people
    C. teenagers
    D. children
    E. all ages

16. Consideration and thoughtfulness is the MOST important part of

    A. adjusting to special diets
    B. reactions to income increases
    C. reactions to income losses
    D. appreciation of unusual foods
    E. learning to cook

17. The healthier a child is between the years of six and twelve,

    A. the better adult health he will have
    B. the better teeth he will have
    C. the taller he will grow
    D. the better adjustments he will make in adolescence
    E. will not affect his future health

18. Pre-adolescent children need

    A. extra calcium and protein for growth
    B. iodine to help regulate the use of food
    C. quick-acting foods for extra energy
    D. minerals and vitamins for body regulation, protein for growth, and extra foods for quick energy
    E. starches and extras between meals

19. One of the MOST important events in the daily dietary life of each family member is

    A. breakfast
    B. lunch
    C. dinner or supper
    D. snack time
    E. the coffee break

20. It is good to remember to give a small child

    A. large servings
    B. small servings with seconds if he desires
    C. a wide variety of foods at the same meal
    D. several foods which are new to him
    E. food which he must eat

21. Children enjoy

    A. highly spiced foods
    B. very cold foods
    C. rough textures
    D. very hot foods
    E. warm foods of smooth texture and mild flavor

4 (#2)

22. An infant should be fed 22.____

    A. in a relaxed atmosphere
    B. when he is hungry
    C. with a balanced diet
    D. on a definite schedule
    E. in a relaxed way, a balanced diet when he is hungry

23. When meat and low-acid vegetables are canned, it is necessary to use a temperature of 23.____
    _____ to kill bacteria.

    A. 100° F   B. 144° F
    C. 200° F   D. 400° F
    E. higher than boiling

24. Foods satisfactorily preserved by a concentration of sugar are 24.____

    A. meats
    B. fruits
    C. vegetables
    D. fruits and some vegetables
    E. whole fruits, or fruit and vegetable juices

25. It may be necessary to add _____ to fruit pulp or juice to make jelly. 25.____

    A. commercial pectin
    B. apple juice
    C. gelatin
    D. alcohol
    E. commercial pectin or apple juice

26. Good food packaging for freezing 26.____

    A. prevents freezer *burn*
    B. prevents transfer of flavor
    C. prevents transfer of odor
    D. need not be leakproof
    E. prevents loss of flavor, odor, color, and moisture

27. Scalding of vegetables before freezing helps 27.____

    A. retain color
    B. retard enzyme growth
    C. destroys some bacteria
    D. may soften and shrink the vegetables
    E. to do all of the above

28. Overscalding of vegetables before freezing 28.____

    A. causes an increase of sugar
    B. absorbs food values soluble in hot water
    C. destroys vitamins
    D. makes the product too soft
    E. does no harm

29. Darkening of color from enzyme action will take place in _____ unless ascorbic acid is used. 29._____

    A. vegetables
    B. fruits
    C. peaches, apples, and pears
    D. tomatoes
    E. meat

30. Before freezing, remove excess _____ from meat, fish, or poultry. 30._____

    A. fat
    B. bone
    C. skin
    D. membranes
    E. materials which will become rancid or waste space

KEY (CORRECT ANSWERS)

1.	B	11.	B	21.	E
2.	E	12.	C	22.	E
3.	D	13.	E	23.	E
4.	B	14.	E	24.	D
5.	B	15.	E	25.	E
6.	D	16.	A	26.	E
7.	D	17.	A	27.	E
8.	C	18.	D	28.	B
9.	A	19.	A	29.	C
10.	B	20.	B	30.	E

TEST 3

DIRECTIONS: Each question or incomplete statement is followed by several suggested answers or completions. Select the one that BEST answers the question or completes the statement. *PRINT THE LETTER OF THE CORRECT ANSWER IN THE SPACE AT THE RIGHT.*

1. Americans became nutrition-conscious approximately seventy years ago with the isolation of 1.____

    A. carbohydrates B. fats C. proteins
    D. minerals E. vitamins

2. A family food plan should include 2.____

    A. sufficient foods from each basic group
    B. choices which meet all the likes of the family
    C. carbohydrates which are less expensive
    D. an abundance of protein
    E. foods containing delicious fats

3. A food plan made a week in advance 3.____

    A. allows one to shop ahead
    B. makes certain that all nutrients will be included
    C. shows how family needs will be met, amount of food needed, and something of cost
    D. is time consuming
    E. allows one to buy foods at bargain prices

4. A simplified food selection guide for healthful living builds meals around 4.____

    A. dairy foods B. meats
    C. breads and cereals D. vegetables and fruits
    E. all of the above

5. If thought is used in the family menu planning, an adequate supply of protein at a *low* cost may be secured from 5.____

    A. beef and veal
    B. pork and lamb
    C. poultry and fish
    D. dry beans, peas, and nuts
    E. meats and protein substitutes

6. Teenagers, pregnant women, and nursing mothers need LARGER amounts of _____ than do other family members. 6.____

    A. dairy foods B. fruits and vegetables
    C. meats D. breads and cereals
    E. all of the above

7. _____ servings of fruits and vegetables, and, breads and cereals should be included for adequate food intake. 7.____

A. Two	B. Three	C. One
D. Five	E. At least four or more

8. Research studies show the diets of teenagers are *likely* to be

   A. well-balanced
   B. poorly balanced
   C. lacking in protein and vitamins and minerals
   D. high in vitamins and minerals
   E. adequate in fruits and vegetables

9. When the daily caloric requirement is exceeded, that not used is

   A. excreted as waste
   B. stored as muscle protein
   C. stored as fat
   D. used for energy
   E. used for heat

10. The MAIN job of _____ is to build and repair body tissue.

    A. carbohydrates	B. proteins	C. minerals
    D. vitamins	E. fats

11. A unit used to measure the warmth and energy value of a food is the

    A. amino acid	B. calorie	C. kilogram
    D. ounce	E. atom

12. Individual caloric requirements depend upon

    A. age and sex
    B. temperature and kind of food eaten
    C. type and amount of exercise
    D. proportion of one's nonfat body weight
    E. all of the above

13. _____ creates bulk which helps to keep the digestive tract working smoothly.

    A. Water	B. Cellulose
    C. Protein	D. Fat
    E. Carbohydrate

14. _____ cups of liquid should be included in the daily food intake to promote body regulation and elimination.

    A. Four	B. Five	C. Six	D. Seven	E. Eight

15. Good nutrition requires that one be able to

    A. discriminate between fact and fallacy in fad diets of today
    B. spend money for *health foods* and *health aids*
    C. purchase highly advertised brands of foods
    D. all of the above
    E. none of the above

16. One's nutritional health depends not only on the selection of a balanced diet but upon   16._____

    A. how this food has been stored before its use
    B. how it has been prepared
    C. how the body is able to use the nutrients
    D. all of the above
    E. none of the above

17. The MOST important factor in development of malnutrition is   17._____

    A. lack of sleep
    B. too little fresh air and sunshine
    C. fatigue
    D. faulty diet
    E. pressure of social life

18. The FIRST step in a weight-control project is to   18._____

    A. begin a program of strenuous exercise
    B. go on a diet to lose or gain weight
    C. try special diets advertised
    D. go on as one has been doing
    E. have a physical check-up by a doctor

19. Food requires a larger portion of the family income than any other item, using _____ percent of the income varying with the amount of income.   19._____

    A. 25-50   B. 50-75   C. 33   D. 20   E. 60

20. It is possible to have a nutritionally adequate diet on less money than the average family spends by   20._____

    A. gaining more knowledge about nutrition
    B. considering more economical shopping procedures
    C. developing an interest in nutrition, consumer practices, and food habits
    D. changing food habits
    E. altering food habits and buying habits after studying nutrition

21. Good food management is essential to   21._____

    A. help economize while replenishing stored food supplies
    B. alter *expensive* food tastes
    C. develop greater numbers of food likes and fewer dislikes
    D. control meals eaten away from home
    E. meet the rise in the cost of staple goods

22. When one shops for food, it is wise to   22._____

    A. compare the market order with the Basic Four
    B. compare food prices and quality
    C. figure the food budget closely in advance
    D. be a careful, ethical shopper
    E. shop carefully and wisely with a good market order which was made considering the Basic Four, prices, and quality

23. State and Federal laws protect consumers from adulterated foods including 23.____
    A. food that may be injurious to health or in such condition as to be unfit for human food
    B. food that has been packed, packaged, or stored under unsanitary conditions
    C. food that uses coal-tar dyes
    D. food that is falsely labeled or has substitutes
    E. foods or any ingredients that use harmful colors or substitutes, or that may be prepared or stored in unsanitary ways so as to injure humans

24. The Federal Food and Drug Act, created in 1906, helps to safeguard our food supply by 24.____
    A. prohibiting false advertising of food, drugs, and cosmetics
    B. requiring the package label to give weight, measure, and contents
    C. prohibiting the transportation in interstate commerce of adulterated or misbranded foods
    D. all of the above
    E. none of the above

25. The MOST important factors in buying food are 25.____
    A. quality and price
    B. price and convenience
    C. quality and convenience
    D. quality, price, and convenience
    E. price and services available

KEY (CORRECT ANSWERS)

1. E
2. A
3. C
4. E
5. E

6. A
7. E
8. C
9. C
10. B

11. B
12. E
13. B
14. E
15. A

16. D
17. D
18. E
19. A
20. E

21. E
22. E
23. E
24. D
25. D

TEST 4

DIRECTIONS: Each question or incomplete statement is followed by several suggested answers or completions. Select the one that BEST answers the question or completes the statement. *PRINT THE LETTER OF THE CORRECT ANSWER IN THE SPACE AT THE RIGHT.*

1. Centerpieces

   A. require little time and thought to arrange attractively
   B. using very fragrant flowers are good
   C. are expensive
   D. made by careful application of design principles are best
   E. should be high

   1.____

2. A convenient way to serve many people with the MINIMUM amount of assistance and space is _____ service.

   A. compromise   B. plate   C. American
   D. formal   E. buffet

   2.____

3. For the family type meal service, all food is passed

   A. to the left
   B. to the right
   C. either right or left as the family decides
   D. the direction which gives the shortest distance
   E. as the hostess indicates

   3.____

4. The person served FIRST at dinner is *usually* the

   A. hostess
   B. host
   C. gentleman guest
   D. person seated at the right of the host
   E. person seated at the right of the hostess

   4.____

5. Cookery can be fascinating allowing for

   A. creativity
   B. observation
   C. concentration
   D. management skill
   E. keen observation, concentrated management, and unlimited creativity

   5.____

6. To use recipes effectively, it is necessary to

   A. understand terms and measurements
   B. use standard measuring tools
   C. have a knowledge of how substitutions may be made
   D. use correct ingredient combinations
   E. all of the above

   6.____

7. To prevent excessive shrinkage of meat, use _____ roasting temperatures. 7._____

   A. very low - below 275° F
   B. slow - about 325° F
   C. moderate - 350° F
   D. hot - 400° F
   E. very hot - 450° F

8. In conventional cooking, heat is applied to the surface of the food, but by electronic cooking the food is cooked 8._____

   A. by energy
   B. by agitation of molecules
   C. by absorption of microwave energy and the resulting heat
   D. a golden brown
   E. a long time

9. Seasonings are used to _____ natural flavors in foods. 9._____

   A. hide
   B. overpower
   C. bring out
   D. alter
   E. disguise unpleasant

10. All oven temperatures in recipes are 10._____

    A. set when the product is put in the oven
    B. preheated temperatures
    C. set after the product is mixed
    D. approximate temperatures
    E. double-checked by use of a separate oven thermometer

11. Extra time is allowed in addition to time for meat cookery to 11._____

    A. allow the meat to set
    B. make the gravy
    C. carve the meat
    D. make carving easier and prepare gravy
    E. be certain the meat is cooked

12. Eggs and cheese should be cooked at _____ temperatures. 12._____

    A. very high
    B. high
    C. moderate
    D. low to moderate
    E. very low

13. To cook vegetables BEST, 13._____

    A. use little water and cook quickly
    B. cook slowly
    C. use a generous amount of water
    D. pare generously
    E. pour off cooking liquid

14. For BEST results, cook frozen vegetables 14.____

    A. as you would fresh vegetables
    B. the same as fresh vegetables, but reduce the cooking time
    C. in a pressure pan
    D. after thawing completely
    E. in a cup of water

15. Fruit cooked in sugar syrup 15.____

    A. retains its natural raw flavor
    B. loses its shape
    C. loses its vitamin content
    D. does keep its shape, but has a changed flavor
    E. remains unchanged in shape or flavor

16. All-purpose flour is 16.____

    A. a blend of hard and soft wheat flours
    B. not desirable for pastries
    C. whole wheat flour
    D. enriched with gluten
    E. more expensive than other flour

17. The _____ in wheat flour makes it possible to develop an elastic dough from it. 17.____

    A. bran   B. germ   C. vitamin B   D. starch   E. gluten

18. Points to consider when evaluating commercial or homemade mixes with conventional mixing methods are 18.____

    A. cost
    B. time involved
    C. quality of resulting product
    D. convenience
    E. analyses of the quality of final products by cost, time, and convenience

19. Essentials for making a good cup of coffee or tea are 19.____

    A. fresh ingredients
    B. freshly cleaned containers
    C. plenty of beverage to be reheated
    D. good fresh coffee or tea, a clean container, and water of the correct temperature
    E. dated ingredients

20. The BEST time to satisfy the craving for sweets is 20.____

    A. with a dessert at mealtime
    B. by eating candy between meals
    C. by eating desserts between meals as snacks
    D. by eating candy just after a meal
    E. whenever the craving arises

21. To adjust a cake recipe for higher altitudes, it may be necessary to   21._____

    A. increase leavening and sugar
    B. decrease leavening or sugar or both
    C. increase liquid
    D. decrease leavening or sugar and increase liquid
    E. increase the shortening

22. Butter cakes are USUALLY made by the _____ methods.   22._____

    A. conventional   B. one bowl quick
    C. sponge   D. conventional or quick
    E. none of the above

23. The characteristics of good plain pastry are   23._____

    A. light, crisp, tender, flaky crust and golden brown color
    B. firm, smooth golden crust
    C. a tender crumbling crust
    D. shrunken edges
    E. a very pale crust

24. The temperature at which candy is cooked determines   24._____

    A. the texture
    B. the softness
    C. the hardness or brittleness
    D. the desired consistency
    E. flavor

25. The amount of handling candy receives after cooking determines   25._____

    A. the flavor
    B. the texture - crystalline or noncrystalline
    C. hardness
    D. softness
    E. texture and consistency

KEY (CORRECT ANSWERS)

1. D
2. E
3. B
4. D
5. E

6. E
7. B
8. C
9. C
10. B

11. D
12. D
13. A
14. B
15. D

16. A
17. E
18. E
19. D
20. A

21. D
22. D
23. A
24. D
25. B

EXAMINATION SECTION
TEST 1

DIRECTIONS: Each question or incomplete statement is followed by several suggested answers or completions. Select the one that BEST answers the question or completes the statement. *PRINT THE LETTER OF THE CORRECT ANSWER IN THE SPACE AT THE RIGHT.*

1. The MAJOR responsibility of a director is to
   A. make certain that his line supervisors keep proper control of staff activity
   B. see that training is given to his staff according to individual needs
   C. insure that his total organization is coordinated toward agency goals and objectives
   D. work constructively with groups so that programs will reflect their needs

1.____

2. A good organizational chart of a department is an IMPORTANT instrument because it can
   A. make it easier to understand the mission of the department
   B. help new employees become acquainted with department personnel
   C. clarify relationships and responsibilities of the various department components
   D. simplify the task of *going to the top*

2.____

3. Unnecessary and obsolete forms can be eliminated MOST effectively by
   A. appointing a representative committee to review and evaluate all forms in relation to operating procedures
   B. discarding all forms which have not been used during the past year
   C. assembling all forms and destroying those which are duplicates or obsolete
   D. directing office managers to review the forms to determine which should be revised or abolished

3.____

4. The director must adopt methods and techniques to insure that his budgeted allowances are properly spent and that organizational objectives are being reached.
   These responsibilities can be fulfilled BEST by
   A. controlling operations with electronic data processing equipment
   B. shifting caseload controls from caseworkers to clerical staff
   C. installing a work simplification program and establishing controls for crucial areas of operation
   D. assigning employees with special skills and training to perform the more important and specialized jobs

4.____

5. The MOST appropriate technique for making the staff thoroughly familiar with department policies would be to
   A. maintain an up-to-date loose-leaf binder of written policies in a central point in the office
   B. issue copies of all policy directives to the unit supervisors
   C. distribute copies of policy directives to the entire staff and arrange for follow-up discussion on a unit basis
   D. discuss all major policy directives at an office-wide staff meeting

6. When a proposed change in a departmental procedure is being evaluated, the factor which should be considered MOST important in reaching the decision is the
   A. extent of resistance anticipated from members of the staff
   B. personnel needed to execute the proposed change
   C. time required for training staff in the revised procedure
   D. degree of organizational dislocation compared with gains expected from the change

7. A director anticipates that certain aspects of a new departmental procedure will be distasteful to many staff members.
   Assuming that the procedure is basically sound in spite of this drawback, the BEST approach for the director to take with his staff is to
   A. advise them to accept the procedure since it has the support of the highest authorities in the department
   B. point out that other procedures which were resisted initially have come to be accepted in time
   C. challenge staff members to suggest another procedure which will accomplish the same purpose better
   D. ask the staff members to discuss the *pros* and *cons* of the procedure and suggest how it can be improved

8. At a staff meeting at which a basic change in departmental procedure is to be announced, a director begins the discussion by asking the participants for criticisms of the existing procedure. He then describes the new procedure to be employed and explains the improvements that are anticipated.
   The director's method of introducing the change is
   A. *good*, mainly because the participants would be more receptive to the new procedure is they understood the inadequacies of the old one
   B. *good*, mainly because the participants' comments on the old procedure will provide the basis for evaluation of the feasibility of the new one
   C. *bad*, mainly because the participants will realize that the decision for change has been made before the meeting, without consideration of the participants' comments
   D. *bad*, mainly because the discussion is focused on the old procedure, rather than on the procedure being introduced

3 (#1)

9. Assume that you are conducting a staff conference to discuss the development of a procedure implementing a change in state policy. There are twelve participants whose office titles range from unit supervisor to senior supervisor, each of whom has responsibility for some aspect of the program affected by the policy change.
After some introductory remarks, the BEST procedure for you to follow is to call upon the participants in the order of their
   A. titles, with the highest titles first because they are likely to have the most experience and knowledge of the subject
   B. titles, with the lower titles first because they are likely to be less inhibited if they are permitted to give their views before the senior participants speak
   C. places around the table, to promote informality and democratic procedure
   D. specialized knowledge of the subject so that those with the most knowledge and competence may lead the discussion

9.____

10. A staff member has suggested a way of reducing the time required to prepare a monthly report by combining several items of information, separating one item into two part, and generally revising definitions of terms.
The CHIEF disadvantage of such a revision is that
   A. comparison of present with past periods will be more difficult
   B. subordinates who prepare the report will require retraining
   C. forms currently in use will have to be discarded
   D. employees using the records will be confused by the changes

10.____

11. Assume that a director happens to be present at a regular staff conference conducted by a senior supervisor. During the course of the conference, the director frequently takes over the discussion in order to amplify remarks made by the supervisor, to impart information about departmental policies, and to modify or correct possible misinterpretations of the supervisor's remarks.
The director's actions in this situation are
   A. *proper*, mainly because the conference members were given the latest and most accurate information concerning departmental policies
   B. *proper*, mainly because the director has an obligation to assist and support the supervisor
   C. *improper*, mainly because the director did not completely take over the conference
   D. *improper*, mainly because the supervisor was put in a difficult position in the presence of his staff

11.____

12. A center has a serious staff morale problem because of rumors that it will probably be abolished. To handle this situation, the direct adopts a policy of promptly corroborating rumors that he knows to be true and denying false ones.
Although this method of dealing with the situation should have some good results, its CHIEF weakness is that
   A. it chases the rumors instead of forestalling them by giving correct information concerning the center's future

12.____

B. the director may not have the necessary information at hand
C. status is given to the rumors as a result of the attention paid to them
D. the director may inadvertently divulge confidential information

13. Realizing the importance of harmonious staff relationships, one of your supervisors makes a practice of unobtrusively intervening in any conflict situation among staff members. Whenever friction seems to be developing, he attempts to soothe ruffled feelings and remove the source of difficulty by such methods as rescheduling, reassigning personnel, etc. His efforts are always behind the scenes and unknown to the personnel involved.
This practice may produce some good results, but the CHIEF drawback is that it
    A. permits staff to engage in unacceptable practices without correction
    B. violates the principle of chain of command
    C. involves the supervisor in personal relationships which are not properly his concern
    D. requires confidential sources of information about personal relationships within the center

14. Assume that the department adopts a policy of transferring administrative personnel from one center to another after stated periods of service in a center, or in a central office.
Of the following, the MAIN advantage of such a policy is that it helps
    A. prevent the formation of cliques among staff members
    B. key staff members keep abreast of new developments
    C. effect a greater utilization of staff members' special talents
    D. develop a broader outlook and loyalty to the department as a whole, rather than to one center

15. A delegation of union members meets with you in your role as director to discuss obtaining assistance for a group of strikers who live in the neighborhood covered by the center. In the course of discussion, you learn that the strike has been called by the local union against the explicit directive of the national union's leadership.
The MOST appropriate course of action for you to take in this instance is to advise the union committee
    A. of your sympathy and assure them that individual applications from the strikers for assistance will receive priority
    B. that if the strikers are in need, they will be able to receive assistance as long as they are on strike
    C. that since the strike is illegal, none of the workers will be eligible for assistance
    D. that there is no bar to an of the strikers receiving assistance provided they are in need and are ready and willing to accept other employment if offered

16. The quality control system is a management tool used to test the validity of the eligibility caseload.
    This system can be helpful to a director in the following ways, with the EXCEPTION of
    A. obtaining objective data to use in evaluating the performance of specific staff members
    B. identifying the need for policy changes
    C. sorting out the source of errors in determining eligibility
    D. setting up training objectives for his staff

17. As director, you observe that there has been a sharp rise in the number of fair hearings. The increase seems to coincide with the intensified activities of the local recipients' organization.
    The MOST appropriate action under the circumstances is to
    A. determine whether the fair hearing requests result from weaknesses in the center's operation, and remedy the causes, if feasible
    B. disregard the matter for the time being because complaints have been stirred up by an organized client group
    C. emphasize to your staff the importance of meeting client needs promptly in order to avoid fair hearing requests
    D. resolve the grievances with the leaders of the recipients' organization

18. As director, you receive notice of a fair hearing decision from the State Commissioner ordering you to restore assistance to a family. You are appalled by the order because the facts cited by the hearing officer are at complete variance with what actually occurred, according to your personal knowledge of the case.
    Of the following, the MOST appropriate course of action for you to take FIRST is to
    A. point out to central office that the decision should be reconsidered and appropriately modified
    B. comply with the decision under protest because it is patently wrong
    C. recommend to central office that it consider court action through an Article 78 proceeding to correct the erroneous decision
    D. comply with the decision, although an order of the State Commissioner has no force and effect of law

19. In your capacity as director, you have received a copy of the monthly statistical report issued by the department. In reviewing the report, you note that your center is showing a rise in caseload which is substantially higher than the average rise throughout the city.
    Which of the alternatives listed below would be MOST appropriate in order to deal with this situation?
    A. Make plans to discuss the situation with central office so that appropriate corrective action can be taken on the basis of your consultation
    B. Collect necessary information and data about the operations of your center and the area it serves to determine the cause of the trend, and plan appropriate action on the basis of your findings

C. Call a meeting of your unit supervisors in order to impress upon them the importance of more diligent efforts to assist clients
D. Assume that the rise in caseload is an inevitable result of the substantial increase in unemployment, and take no immediate action

20. Of the following phases of a training program for administrative personnel, the one which is usually the MOST difficult to formulate is the
    A. selection of training methods for the program
    B. obtaining of frank opinions of the participants as to the usefulness of the program
    C. chief executive officer's judgment as to the need for such a program
    D. evaluation of the effectiveness of the program

21. Assume that you are conducting a conference dealing with problems of the center of which you are the director. The problem being discussed is one with which you have had no experience. However, two of the participants, who have had considerable experience with it, carry on an extended discussion, showing that they understand the problem thoroughly. The others are very much interested in the discussion and are taking notes on the material presented.
    To permit the two staff members to continue for the length of time allowed for discussion of the problem is
    A. *desirable*, chiefly because introduction of the material by the two participants themselves may encourage others to contribute their work experience
    B. *desirable*, chiefly because their discussion may be more meaningful to the others than a discussion which is not based on work experience
    C. *undesirable*, chiefly because they are discussing material only in light of their own experience rather than in general terms
    D. *undesirable*, chiefly because it would reveal your own lack of experience with the problem and undermine your authority with the staff

22. In dealing with staff members, it is a commonly accepted principle that individual differences exist, suggesting that employees should be treated in an unlike manner in order to achieve maximum results from their work assignments.
    This statement means MOST NEARLY that
    A. supervisors should be aware of the personal problems of their subordinates and make allowances for poor performance because of such problems
    B. standardized work rules are ineffective because of the different capabilities of employees to maintain such work rules
    C. employees' individual needs should be considered by their supervisors to the greatest extent possible, within the practical limitations of the work situation
    D. knowledge of general principles of human behavior is generally of little use to a supervisor in assisting him to supervise his subordinates effectively

23. A supervisor under your jurisdiction reports to you that one of his subordinates has been taking unusually long lunch hours, has been absent from work frequently, and has been doing poorer work than previously.
The BEST procedure for you to follow FIRST is to advise the supervisor to
    A. prefer charges against the employee
    B. arrange for a psychological consultation for the employee
    C. ascertain whether the employee is ill and, if so, arrange a medical examination for him
    D. have a private conversation with the employee to obtain more information about the reasons for his behavior

23.____

24. If the term *executive development* is defined as the continuous, ongoing, on-the-job process of constructing plans to improve individuals in specific positions, both for the purpose of present improvement as well as for any future advancement which is envisaged for the employee, it follows that the emphasis in an executive development program should
    A. provide learning experiences through formal or informal classes, seminars, or conferences, for which the focus is on the function of the position
    B. be oriented to the individual participant and may include a host of planned activities, such as appraisal, coaching, counseling, and job rotation
    C. attempt to create needs, to awaken, enlarge, and stimulate the individual so as to broaden his outlook and potentialities as a human being
    D. insure that the individual is able to plan, organize, direct, and control operations in the bureau, division, or agency

24.____

25. Most psychologists agree that employees have a need for recognition for the work they perform.
Therefore, it can be concluded that
    A. employees should be praised every time they complete a job satisfactorily
    B. praise is a more effective incentive to good performance than is punishment
    C. administrative personnel should be aware that subordinates do not have needs similar to their own
    D. a formalized system of rewards and punishment is better than no system at all, as long as there is a built-in consistency in its administration

25.____

KEY (CORRECT ANSWERS)

1.	C	11.	D
2.	C	12.	A
3.	A	13.	A
4.	C	14.	D
5.	C	15.	D
6.	D	16.	A
7.	D	17.	A
8.	C	18.	A
9.	D	19.	B
10.	A	20.	D

21.	B
22.	C
23.	D
24.	B
25.	B

TEST 2

DIRECTIONS: Each question or incomplete statement is followed by several suggested answers or completions. Select the one that BEST answers the question or completes the statement. *PRINT THE LETTER OF THE CORRECT ANSWER IN THE SPACE AT THE RIGHT.*

1. Studies have shown that the MOST effective kind of safety training program is one in which the
    A. training is conducted by consultants who are expert in the nature of the work performed
    B. lectures are given by the top executives in an agency
    C. employees participate in all phases of the program
    D. supervisors are responsible for the safety training

    1._____

2. Of the following, the MOST effective method of selecting potential top executives would be
    A. situational testing which simulates actual conditions
    B. a written test which covers the knowledge required to perform the job
    C. an oral test which requires candidate to discuss significant aspects of the job
    D. a confidential interview with his former employee

    2._____

3. With regard to staff morale, MOST evidence shows that
    A. employees with positive job attitudes always outproduce those with negative job attitudes
    B. morale always relates to the employee's attitude toward his working conditions and his job
    C. low morale always results in poor job performance
    D. high morale has a direct relationship to effective union leadership

    3._____

4. Of the following groups of factors, the group which has been shown to be related to the incidence of job accidents is
    A. personality characteristics, intelligence, defective vision
    B. experience, fatigue, motor and perceptual speed
    C. coordination, fatigue, intelligence
    D. defective vision, motor and perceptual speed, intelligence

    4._____

5. Executives who have difficulty making decisions when faced with a number of choices USUALLY
    A. have domestic problems which interfere with the decision-making process
    B. can be trained to improve their ability to make decisions
    C. are production-oriented rather than employee-centered
    D. do not know their jobs well enough to act decisively

    5._____

6. Studies of disciplinary dismissals of workers reveal that
   A. the majority of employees were dismissed because of lack of technical competence
   B. the supervisors were unusually demanding of employee competence
   C. most employees were dismissed because of inability to work with their co-workers
   D. the chief executive set unrealistic standards of performance

7. One philosophy of assigning workers to a specific job is that the worker and his job are an integral unit.
   This means MOST NEARLY that the
   A. employee and the job may both require adjustment
   B. employee must meet all the specifications of the job as a prerequisite for employment
   C. employee's morale will be affected by his salary
   D. employee's job satisfaction has a direct effect on his emotional health

8. The statement that the supervisor and the administrator are the *primary personnel men* means MOST NEARLY that
   A. supervisors and administrators are more skilled in personnel techniques than are professional personnel technicians
   B. they are in the best position to implement personnel policies and procedures
   C. employees have more confidence in their supervisors and administrators than in the professional personnel administrator
   D. personnel administration is most effective when it combines both centralized and decentralized approaches

9. Administrators frequently have to interview people in order to obtain information. Although the interview is a legitimate fact-gathering technique, it has limitations which should not be overlooked.
   The one of the following which is an IMPORTANT limitation is that
   A. individuals generally hesitate to give information orally which they would usually answer in writing
   B. the material derived from the interview can usually be obtained at lower cost from existing records
   C. the emotional attitudes of individuals during an interview often affect the accuracy of the information given
   D. the interview is a poor technique for discovering how well clients understand departmental policies

10. Leadership styles have frequently been categorized as authoritarian, laissez-faire, and democratic.
    In general, management's reliance on leadership to produce desired results would be MOST effectively implemented through
    A. the laissez-faire approach when group results are desired
    B. the authoritarian approach in a benevolent manner when quick decisions are required

C. the democratic approach, when quick decisions are unimportant
D. all three approaches, depending upon circumstances

11. As director, you are responsible for enforcing a recently established regulation which has aroused antagonism among many clients.
You should deal with this situation by
    A. explaining to the clients that you are not responsible for making regulations
    B. enforcing the regulation but reporting to your superior the number and kind of complaints against it
    C. carrying out your duty of enforcing the regulation as well as you can without comment
    D. suggesting to your clients that you may overlook violations of the regulation

11._____

12. One of the observations made in a recent psychological study of leadership is that the behavior of a new employee in a leadership position can be predicted more accurately on the basis of the behavior of the previous incumbent in the post than on the behavior of the new employee in his previous job.
The BEST explanation for this observation is that there is a tendency
    A. for a newly appointed executive to avoid making basic changes in operational procedures
    B. to choose similar types of personalities to fill the same type of position
    C. for a given organizational structure and set of duties and responsibilities to produce similar patterns of behavior
    D. for executives to develop more mature patterns of behavior as a result of increased responsibility

12._____

13. A director finds that reports submitted by him to his subordinates tend to emphasize the favorable and minimize the unfavorable aspects of situations.
The MOST valid reason for this is that
    A. subordinates usually hesitate to give their supervisors an honest picture of a situation
    B. the director may not have been sufficiently critical of previous reports submitted by his subordinates
    C. subordinates have a normal tendency to represent themselves and their actions in the best possible light
    D. many subordinates in the field have developed a tendency to understatement in the depiction of unfavorable situations

13._____

14. Effective delegation of authority and responsibility to subordinates is essential for the proper administration of a center. However, the director should retain some activities under his direct control.
Of the following activities, the one for which there is LEAST justification for delegation by the director to a subordinate is one involving
    A. relationships with client groups
    B. physical danger to clients
    C. policies which are unpopular with staff
    D. matters for which there are no established policies

14._____

15. According to the principle of *span of control*, there should be a limited number of subordinates reporting to one supervisor.
    Of the following, the CHIEF disadvantage which may result from the application of this principle is a reduction in the
    A. contact between lower ranking staff members and higher ranking administrative personnel
    B. freedom of action of subordinates
    C. authority and responsibility of subordinates
    D. number of organizational levels through which a matter must pass before action is taken

16. The CHIEF objection to a practice of decentralizing the preparation and distribution of memoranda by bureaus, rather than controlling distribution through central office is that it is LIKELY to result in
    A. overloading bureaus with a multiplicity of communications
    B. limited and specialized rather than broad and general viewpoints in the memoranda
    C. violation of the principle of unit of command
    D. unimportant information being communicated to all bureaus

17. A report has been completed by members of your staff. As director, you have reviewed the report and feel that the information revealed could be damaging to the department. You find yourself in conflict in your multiple role as director, as a professional, and as a citizen.
    The one of the following actions which would be MOST desirable for you to take FIRST would be to
    A. send a copy of the report to your supervisor and request an immediate conference with him
    B. instruct staff to re-check the report and defer issuance of the report until the findings are confirmed
    C. immediately share the report with your supervisors and your advisory committee
    D. file the report until your advisory committee makes a request for it

18. In order for employees to function effectively, they should have a feeling of being treated fairly by management.
    Which of the following general policies is MOST likely to give employees such a feeling?
    A. An employee publication should be mailed directly to the home of each employee.
    B. Employee attitude surveys should be conducted at regular intervals.
    C. Employees should be consulted and kept informed on all matters that affect them.
    D. Employees should be informed when the press publishes statements of policy.

19. In order to give employees greater job satisfaction, some management experts advocate a policy of job enrichment.
The one of the following which would be the BEST example of job enrichment is to
    A. allow an aide to decide which portion of his normal duties and responsibilities he prefers
    B. increase the fringe benefits currently available to paraprofessional employees
    C. add variety to the duties of an employee
    D. permit more flexible working schedules for professional employees

19.____

20. Management of large organizations has often emphasized high salaries and fringe benefits as the most important means of motivating employees.
The one of the following which is NOT an argument used to support this approach is
    A. most people endure work mainly in order to collect the rewards and to have the opportunity to enjoy them
    B. material incentives have proved to be the best means of stimulating creative capacity and the will to work
    C. the majority of employees place little emphasis on work-centered motivation to perform
    D. numerous research studies have shown that pay ranks first on a scale of factors motivating employees in government and industry in the United States

20.____

21. Some organizations provide psychologists or other professionally trained persons with whom employees can consult on a confidential basis regarding personal problems.
Of the following, which is MOST likely to be a benefit management can derive from such a practice?
    A. Increase in the authority of management
    B. Disclosure of the corrupt practices of those handling money
    C. Receipt of new ideas and approaches to organizational problems
    D. Obtaining tighter control on employees' private behavior

21.____

22. Authorities agree that it is generally most desirable for an employee experiencing mental health problems to seek competent professional help without being required or forced to do so by another person.
They view self-referral as a most desirable action PRIMARILY because
    A. it shows that the employee probably is more aware of the problem and more highly motivated to solve his problems
    B. the employee's right to privacy in his personal affairs is maintained
    C. another person cannot be blamed in the event the outcome of the referral is not successful
    D. the employee knows best his problems and will do what is necessary to serve his own best interests

22.____

Questions 23-25.

DIRECTIONS: Questions 23 through 25 consist of three excerpts each. Consider an excerpt correct if all the statements in the excerpt are correct. Mark your answer as follows:
  A. if only excerpts I and II are correct
  B. if only excerpts II and III are correct
  C. if only excerpt I is correct
  D. if only excerpt II is correct

23. I. Many executive decisions are based on assumptions. They may be assumptions supported by sketchy data about future needs for services; assumptions about the attitudes and future behavior of employees, perhaps based on reports of staff members or hearsay evidence; or assumptions about agency values that are as much a reflection of personal desires as of agency goals.
    II. A good pattern of well-conceived plans is only a first step in administration. The administrator must also create an organization to formulate and carry out such plans. Resources must be assembled; supervision of actual operations is necessary; and before the executive's task is completed, he must exercise control.
    III. When a problem is well defined, good alternatives identified, and the likely consequences of each alternative forecast as best we can, one can assume that the final choice of action to be taken would be easy, if not obvious.

23.____

24. I. Principles of motivation are not difficult to establish because human behavior is not complex and is easily understood; individual differences in human beings are substantial; and people are continuously learning and changing.
    II. What gives employees satisfaction or dissatisfaction indicates the nature of the motivation problem and provides positive guidance to the administrator who faces the problem of trying to get people to carry out a set of plans.
    III. The administrator's job of motivation can be described as that of creating a situation in which actions that provide net satisfaction to individual members of the enterprise are at the same time actions that make appropriate contributions toward the objectives of the enterprise.

24.____

25. I. Administrative organization is primarily concerned with legal, technical, or ultimate authority; the operational authority relationships that may be created by organization are of major significance.
    II. Accountability is not removed by delegation. Appraisal of results should be tempered by the extent to which an administrator must rely on subordinates.
    III. In delegations to operating subordinate, authority to plan exceeds authority to do, inasmuch as the executive typically reserves some of the planning for himself.

25.____

KEY (CORRECT ANSWERS)

1.	C	11.	B
2.	A	12.	C
3.	B	13.	C
4.	B	14.	D
5.	B	15.	A
6.	C	16.	A
7.	A	17.	B
8.	B	18.	C
9.	C	19.	C
10.	D	20.	D

21.	C
22.	A
23.	A
24.	B
25.	D

EXAMINATION SECTION
TEST 1

DIRECTIONS: Each question or incomplete statement is followed by several suggested answers or completions. Select the one that BEST answers the question or completes the statement. *PRINT THE LETTER OF THE CORRECT ANSWER IN THE SPACE AT THE RIGHT.*

1. Although some kinds of instructions are best put in written form, a supervisor can give many instructions verbally.
   In which one of the following situations would verbal instructions be MOST suitable?
   A. Furnishing an employee with the details to be checked in doing a certain job
   B. Instructing an employee on the changes necessary to update the office manual used in your unit
   C. Informing a new employee where different kinds of supplies and equipment that he might need are kept
   D. Presenting an assignment to an employee who will be held accountable for following a series of steps

1.____

2. You may be asked to evaluate the organization structure of your unit.
   Which one of the following questions would you NOT expect to take up in an evaluation of this kind?
   A. Is there an employee whose personal problems are interfering with his or her work?
   B. Is there an up-to-date job description for each position in this section?
   C. Are related operations and tasks grouped together and regularly assigned together?
   D. Are responsibilities divided as far as possible, and is this division clearly understood by all employees?

2.____

3. In order to distribute and schedule work fairly and efficiently, a supervisor may wish to make a work distribution study. A simple way of getting the information necessary for such a study is to have everyone for one week keep track of each task doe and the time spent on each.
   Which one of the following situations showing up in such study would MOST clearly call for corrective action?
   A. The newest employee takes longer to do most tasks than do experienced employees.
   B. One difficult operation takes longer to do than most other operations carried out by the section.
   C. A particular employee is very frequently assigned tasks that are not similar and have no relationship to each other.
   D. The most highly skilled employee is often assigned the most difficult jobs.

3.____

4. The authority to carry out a job can be delegated to a subordinate, but the supervisor remains responsible for the work of the section as a whole.
As a supervisor, which of the following rules would be the BEST one for you to follow in view of the above statement?
   A. Avoid assigning important tasks to your subordinates, because you will be blamed if anything goes wrong
   B. Be sure each subordinate understands the specific job he has been assigned, and check at intervals to make sure assignments are done properly
   C. Assign several people to every important job so that responsibility will be spread out as much as possible
   D. Have an experienced subordinate check all work done by other employees so that there will be little chance of anything going wrong

4.____

5. The human tendency to resist change is often reflected in higher rates of turnover, absenteeism, and errors whenever an important change is made in an organization. Although psychologists do not fully understand the reasons why people resist change, they believe that the resistance stems from a threat to the individual's security, that it is a form of fear of the unknown.
In light of this statement, which one of the following approaches would probably be MOST effective in preparing employees for a change in procedure in their unit?
   A. Avoid letting employees know anything about the change until the last possible moment
   B. Sympathize with employees who resent the change and let them know you share their doubts and fears
   C. Promise the employees that if the change turns out to be a poor one, you will allow them to suggest a return to the old system
   D. Make sure that employees know the reasons for the change and are aware of the benefits that are expected from it

5.____

6. Each of the following methods of encouraging employee participation in work planning has been used effectively with different kinds and sizes of employee groups.
Which one of the following methods would be MOST suitable for a group of four technically skilled employees?
   A. Discussions between the supervisor and a representative of the group
   B. A suggestion program with semi-annual awards for outstanding suggestions
   C. A group discussion summoned whenever a major problem remains unsolved for more than a month
   D. Day-to-day exchange of information, opinions, and experience

6.____

7. Of the following, the MOST important reason why a supervisor is given the authority to tell subordinates what work they should do, how they should do it, and when it should be done is that usually
   A. most people will not work unless there is someone with authority standing over them

7.____

B. work is accomplished more effectively if the supervisor plans and coordinates it
C. when division of work is left up to subordinates, there is constant arguing, and very little work is accomplished
D. subordinates are not familiar with the tasks to be performed

8. Fatigue is a factor that affects productivity in all work situations. However, a brief rest period will ordinarily serve to restore a person from fatigue. According to this statement, which one of the following techniques is MOST likely to reduce the impact of fatigue on overall productivity in a unit?
   A. Scheduling several short breaks throughout the day
   B. Allowing employees to go home early
   C. Extending the lunch period an extra half hour
   D. Rotating job assignments every few weeks

8.____

9. After giving a new task to an employee, it is a good idea for a supervisor to ask specific questions to make sure that the employee grasps the essentials of the task and sees how it can be carried out. Questions which ask the employee what he thinks or how he feels about an important aspect of the task are particularly effective.
   Which one of the following questions is NOT the type of question which would be useful in the foregoing situation?
   A. Do you feel there will be any trouble meeting the 4:30 deadline?
   B. How do you feel about the kind of work we do here?
   C. Do you think that combining those two steps will work all right?
   D. Can you think of any additional equipment you may need for this process?

9.____

10. Of the following, the LEAST important reason for having a *continuous* training program is that
    A. employees may forget procedures that they have already learned
    B. employees may develop shortcuts on the job that result in inaccurate work
    C. the job continue to change because of new procedures and equipment
    D. training is one means of measuring effectiveness and productivity on the job

10.____

11. In training a new employee, it is usually advisable to break down the job into meaningful parts and have the new employee master one part before going on to the next.
    Of the following, the BEST reason for using this technique is to
    A. let the new employee know the reason for what he is doing and thus encourage him to remain in the unit
    B. make the employee aware of the importance of the work and encourage him to work harder
    C. show the employee that the work is easy so that he will be encouraged to work faster
    D. make it more likely that the employee will experience success and will be encouraged to continue learning the job

11.____

12. You may occasionally find a serious error in the work of one of your subordinates.
    Of the following, the BEST time to discuss such an error with an employee usually is
    A. immediately after the error is found
    B. after about two weeks, since you will also be able to point out some good things that the employee has accomplished
    C. when you have discovered a pattern of errors on the part of this employee so that he will not be able to dispute your criticism
    D. after the error results in a complaint by your own supervisor

13. For very important announcements to the staff, a supervisor should usually use both written and oral communications. For example, when a new procedure is to be introduced, the supervisor can more easily obtain the group's acceptance by giving his subordinates a rough draft of the new procedure and calling a meeting of all his subordinates.
    The LEAST important benefit of this technique is that it will better enable the supervisor to
    A. explain why the change is necessary
    B. make adjustments in the new procedure to meet valid staff objections
    C. assign someone to carry out the new procedure
    D. answer questions about the new procedure

14. Assume that, while you are interviewing an individual to obtain information, the individual pauses in the middle of an answer.
    The BEST of the following actions for you to take at that time is to
    A. correct any inaccuracies in what he has said
    B. remain silent until he continues
    C. explain your position on the matter being discussed
    D. explain that time is short and that he must complete his story quickly

15. When you are interviewing someone to obtain information, the BEST of the following reasons for you to repeat certain of his exact words is to
    A. assure him that appropriate action will be taken
    B. encourage him to switch to another topic of discussion
    C. assure him that you agree with his point of view
    D. encourage him to elaborate on a point he has made

16. Generally, when writing a letter, the use of precise words and concise sentences is
    A. *good*, because less time will be required to write the letter
    B. *bad*, because it is most likely that the reader will think the letter is unimportant and will not respond favorably
    C. *good*, because it is likely that your desired meaning will be conveyed to the reader
    D. *bad*, because your letter will be too brief to provide adequate information

17. In which of the following cases would it be MOST desirable to have two cards for one individual in a single alphabetic file?
The individual has
   A. a hyphenated surname
   B. two middle names
   C. a first name with an unusual spelling
   D. a compound first name

17._____

18. Of the following, it is MOST appropriate to use a form letter when it is necessary to answer many
   A. requests or inquiries from a single individual
   B. follow-up letters from individuals requesting additional information
   C. request or inquiries about a single subject
   D. complaints from individuals that they have been unable to obtain various types of information

18._____

19. Assume that you are asked to make up a budget for your section for the coming year, and you are told that the most important function of the budget is its "control function."
Of the following, "control" in this context implies MOST NEARLY that
   A. you will probably be asked to justify expenditures in any category when it looks as though these expenditures are departing greatly from the amount budgeted
   B. your section will probably not be allowed to spend more than the budgeted amount in any given category, although it is always permissible to spend less
   C. your section will be required to spend the exact amount budgeted in every category
   D. the budget will be filed in the Office of the Comptroller so that when a year is over the actual expenditures can be compared with the amounts in the budget

19._____

20. In writing a report, the practice of taking up the LEAST important points *first* and the most important points *last* is a
   A. *good* technique, since the final points made in a report will make the greatest impression on the reader
   B. *good* technique, since the material is presented in a more logical manner and will lead directly to the conclusions
   C. *poor* technique, since the reader's time is wasted by having to review irrelevant information before finishing the report
   D. *poor* technique, since it may cause the reader to lose interest in the report and arrive at incorrect conclusions about the report

20._____

21. Typically, when the technique of "supervision by results" is practiced, higher management sets down, either implicitly or explicitly, certain performance standards or goals that the subordinate is expected to meet. So long as these standards are met, management interferes very little.
The MOST likely result of the use of this technique is that it will

21._____

A. lead to ambiguity in terms of goals
B. be successful only to the extent that close direct supervision is practiced
C. make it possible to evaluate both employee and supervisory effectiveness
D. allow for complete dependence on the subordinate's part

22. When making written evaluations and reviews of the performance of subordinates, it is usually ADVISABLE to
    A. avoid informing the employee of the evaluation if it is critical because it may create hard feelings
    B. avoid informing the employee of the evaluation whether critical or favorable because it is tension-producing
    C. to permit the employee to see the evaluation but not to discuss it with him because the supervisor cannot be certain where the discussion might lead
    D. to discuss the evaluation openly with the employee because it helps the employee understand what is expected of him

22._____

23. There are a number of well-known and respected human relations principles that successful supervisors have been using for years in building good relationships with their employees.
    Which of the following does NOT illustrate such a principle?
    A. Give clear and complete instructions
    B. Let each person know how he is getting along
    C. Keep an open-door policy
    D. Make all relationships personal ones

23._____

24. Assume that it is necessary for you to give an unpleasant assignment to one of your subordinates. You expect this employee to raise some objections to this assignment.
    The MOST appropriate of the following actions for you to take FIRST is to issue the assignment
    A. *orally*, with the further statement that you will not listen to any complaints
    B. *in writing*, to forestall any complaints by the employee
    C. *orally*, permitting the employee to express his feelings
    D. *in writing*, with a note that any comments should be submitted in writing

24._____

25. Suppose you have just announced at a staff meeting with your subordinates that a radical reorganization of work will take place next week. Your subordinates at the meeting appear to be excited, tense, and worried.
    Of the following, the BEST action for you to take at that time is to
    A. schedule private conferences with each subordinate to obtain his reaction to the meeting
    B. close the meeting and tell your subordinates to return immediately to their work assignments
    C. give your subordinates some time to ask questions and discuss your announcement
    D. insist that your subordinates do not discuss your announcement among themselves or with other members of the agency

25._____

KEY (CORRECT ANSWERS)

1.	C	11.	D
2.	A	12.	A
3.	C	13.	C
4.	B	14.	B
5.	D	15.	D
6.	D	16.	C
7.	B	17.	A
8.	A	18.	C
9.	B	19.	A
10.	D	20.	D

21.	C
22.	D
23.	D
24.	C
25.	C

TEST 2

DIRECTIONS: Each question or incomplete statement is followed by several suggested answers or completions. Select the one that BEST answers the question or completes the statement. *PRINT THE LETTER OF THE CORRECT ANSWER IN THE SPACE AT THE RIGHT.*

1. Of the following, the BEST way for a supervisor to increase employees' interest in their work is to
    A. allow them to make as many decisions as possible
    B. demonstrate to them that he is as technically competent as they
    C. give each employee a difficult assignment
    D. promptly convey to them instructions from higher management

    1.____

2. The one of the following which is LEAST important in maintaining a high level of productivity on the part of employees is the
    A. provision of optimum physical working conditions for employees
    B. strength of employees' aspirations for promotion
    C. anticipated satisfactions which employees hope to derive from their work
    D. employees' interest in their jobs

    2.____

3. Of the following, the MAJOR advantage of group problem-solving, as compared to individual problem-solving, is that groups will more readily
    A. abide by their own decisions
    B. agree with agency management
    C. devise new policies and procedures
    D. reach conclusions sooner

    3.____

4. The group problem-solving conference is a useful supervisory method for getting people to reach solutions to problems.
    Of the following, the reason that groups usually reach more realistic solutions than do individuals is that
    A. individuals, as a rule, take longer than do groups in reaching decisions and are, therefore, more likely to make an error
    B. bringing people together to let them confer impresses participants with the seriousness of problems
    C. groups are generally more concerned with the future in evaluating organizational problems
    D. the erroneous opinions of group members tend to be corrected by the other members

    4.____

5. A competent supervisor should be able to distinguish between human and technical problems.
    Of the following, the MAJOR difference between such problems is that serious human problems, in comparison to ordinary technical problems
    A. are remedied more quickly
    B. involve a lesser need for diagnosis
    C. are more difficult to define
    D. become known through indications which are usually the actual problem

    5.____

6. Of the following, the BEST justification for a public agency establishing an alcoholism program for its employees is that
   A. alcoholism has traditionally been looked upon with a certain amused tolerance by management and thereby ignored as a serious illness
   B. employees with drinking problems have twice as many on-the-job accidents, especially during the early years of the problem
   C. excessive use of alcohol is associated with personality instability hindering informal social relationships among peers and subordinates
   D. the agency's public reputation will suffer despite an employee's drinking problem being a personal matter of little public concern

7. Assume you are a manager and you find a group of maintenance employees assigned to your project drinking and playing cards for money in an incinerator room after their regular working hours.
   The one of the following actions it would be BEST for you to take is to
   A. suspend all employees immediately if there is no question in your mind as to the validity of the charges
   B. review the personnel records of those involved with the supervisor and make a joint decision on which employees should sustain penalties of loss of annual leave or fines
   C. ask the supervisor to interview each violator and submit written reports to you and thereafter consult with the supervisor about disciplinary actions
   D. deduct three days of annual leave from each employee involved if he pleads guilty in lieu of facing more serious charges

8. Assume that as a manager you must discipline a subordinate, but all of the pertinent facts necessary for a full determination of the appropriate action to take are not yet available. However, you fear that a delay in disciplinary action may damage the morale of other employees.
   The one of the following which is MOST appropriate for you to do in this matter is to
   A. take immediate disciplinary action as if all the pertinent facts were available
   B. wait until all pertinent facts are available before reaching a decision
   C. inform the subordinate that you know he is guilty, issue a stern warning, and then let him wait for your further action
   D. reduce the severity of the discipline appropriate for the violation

9. There are two standard dismissal procedures utilized by most public agencies. The first is the "open back door" policy, in which the decision of a supervisor in discharging an employee for reasons of inefficiency cannot be cancelled by the central personnel agency. The second is the "closed back door" policy, in which the central personnel agency can order the supervisor to restore the discharged employee to his position.
   Of the following, the major DISADVANTAGE of the "closed back door" policy as opposed to the "open back door" policy is that central personnel agencies are
   A. likely to approve the dismissal of employees when there is inadequate justification

B. likely to revoke dismissal actions out of sympathy for employees
  C. less qualified than employing agencies to evaluate the efficiency of employees
  D. easily influenced by political, religious, and racial factors

10. The one of the following for which a formal grievance-handling system is LEAST useful is in
    A. reducing the frequency of employee complaints
    B. diminishing the likelihood of arbitrary action by supervisors
    C. providing an outlet for employee frustrations
    D. bringing employee problems to the attention of higher management

11. The one of the following managers whose leadership style involves the GREATEST delegation of authority to subordinates is the one who presents to subordinates
    A. his ideas and invites questions
    B. his decision and persuades them to accept it
    C. the problem, gets their suggestions, and makes his decision
    D. a tentative decision which is subject to change

12. Which of the following is MOST likely to cause employee productivity standards to be set too high?
    A. Standards of productivity are set by first-line supervisors rather than by higher level managers.
    B. Employees' opinions about productivity standards are sought through written questionnaires.
    C. Initial studies concerning productivity are conducted by staff specialists.
    D. Ideal work conditions assumed in the productivity standards are lacking in actual operations.

13. The one of the following which states the MAIN value of an organization chart for a manager is that such charts show the
    A. lines of formal authority
    B. manner in which duties are performed by each employee
    C. flow of work among employees on the same level
    D. specific responsibilities of each position

14. Which of the following BEST names the usual role of a line unit with regard to the organization's programs?
    A. Seeking publicity   B. Developing
    C. Carrying out   D. Evaluating

15. Critics of promotion *from within* a public agency argue for hiring *from outside* the agency because they believe that promotion from within leads to
    A. resentment and consequent weakened morale on the part of those not promoted
    B. the perpetuation of outdated practices and policies
    C. a more complex hiring procedure than hiring from outside the agency
    D. problems of objectively appraising someone already in the organization

4 (#2)

16. The one of the following management functions which usually can be handled MOST effectively by a committee is the
    A. settlement of interdepartmental disputes
    B. planning of routine work schedules
    C. dissemination of information
    D. assignment of personnel

16._____

17. Assume that you are serving on a committee which is considering proposals in order to recommend a new maintenance policy. After eliminating a number of proposals by unanimous consent, the committee is deadlocked on three proposals.
    The one of the following which is the BEST way for the committee to reach agreement on a proposal they could recommend is to
    A. consider and vote on each proposal separately by secret ballot
    B. examine and discuss the three proposals until the proponents of two of them are persuaded they are wrong
    C. reach a synthesis which incorporates the significant features of each proposals
    D. discuss the three proposals until the proponents of each one concede those aspects of the proposals about which there is disagreement

17._____

18. A commonly used training and development method for professional staff is the case method, which utilizes the description of a situation, real or simulated, to provide a common base for analysis, discussion, and problem-solving.
    Of the following, the MOST appropriate time to use the case method is when professional staff needs
    A. insight into their personality problems
    B. practice in applying management concepts to their own problems
    C. practical experience in the assignment of delegated responsibilities
    D. to know how to function in many different capacities

18._____

19. The incident process is a training and development method in which trainees are given a very brief statement of an event or o a situation presenting a job incident or an employee problem of special significance.
    Of the following, it is MOST appropriate to use the incident process when
    A. trainees need to learn to review and analyze facts before solving a problem
    B. there are a large number of trainees who require the same information
    C. there are too many trainees to carry on effective discussion
    D. trainees are not aware of the effect of their behavior on others

19._____

20. The one of the following types of information about which a clerical employee is usually LEAST concerned during the orientation process is
    A. his specific job duties   B. where he will work
    C. his organization's history   D. who his associates will be

20._____

21. The one of the following which is the MOST important limitation on the degree to which work should be broken down into specialized tasks is the point at which
    A. there ceases to be sufficient work of a specialized nature to occupy employees
    B. training costs equal the half-yearly savings derived from further specialization
    C. supervision of employees performing specialized tasks becomes more technical than supervision of general employees
    D. it becomes more difficult to replace the specialist than to replace the generalist who performs a complex set of functions

22. When a supervisor is asked for his opinion of the suitability for promotion of a subordinate, the supervisor is actually being asked to predict the subordinate's future behavior in a new role.
    Such a prediction is MOST likely to be accurate if the
    A. higher position is similar to the subordinate's current one
    B. higher position requires intangible personal qualities
    C. new position has had little personal association with the subordinate away from the job

23. In one form of the non-directive evaluation interview, the supervisor communicates his evaluation to the employee and then listens to the employee's response without making further suggestions.
    The one of the following which is the PRINCIPAL danger of this method of evaluation is that the employee is MOST likely to
    A. develop an indifferent attitude towards the supervisor
    B. fail to discover ways of improving his performance
    C. become resistant to change in the organization's structure
    D. place the blame for his shortcomings on his co-workers

24. In establishing rules for his subordinates, a superior should be PRIMARILY concerned with
    A. creating sufficient flexibility to allow for exceptions
    B. making employees aware of the reasons for the rules and the penalties for infractions
    C. establishing the strength of his own position in relation to his subordinates
    D. having his subordinates know that such rules will be imposed in a personal manner

25. The practice of conducting staff training sessions on a periodic basis is generally considered
    A. *poor*; it takes employees away from their work assignments
    B. *poor*; all staff training should be done on an individual basis
    C. *good*; it permits the regular introduction of new methods and techniques
    D. *good*; it ensures a high employee productivity rate

KEY (CORRECT ANSWERS)

1. A
2. A
3. A
4. D
5. C

6. B
7. C
8. B
9. C
10. A

11. C
12. D
13. A
14. C
15. B

16. A
17. C
18. B
19. A
20. C

21. A
22. A
23. B
24. B
25. C

INTERPRETING STATISTICAL DATA GRAPHS, CHARTS AND TABLES
TEST 1

DIRECTIONS: Each question or incomplete statement is followed by several suggested answers or completions. Select the one that BEST answers the question or completes the statement. *PRINT THE LETTER OF THE CORRECT ANSWER IN THE SPACE AT THE RIGHT.*

Questions 1-10.

DIRECTIONS: Questions 1 through 10 are to be answered SOLELY on the basis of the following table showing the amounts purchased by various purchasing units during 2018.

Purchasing Unit	First Quarter	Second Quarter	Third Quarter	Fourth Quarter
\multicolumn{5}{c}{DOLLAR VOLUME PURCHASED BY EACH PURCHASING UNIT DURING EACH QUARTER OF 2018 (FIGURES SHOWN REPRESENT THOUSANDS OF DOLLARS)}				
A	578	924	698	312
B	1,426	1,972	1,586	1,704
C	366	494	430	716
D	1,238	1,708	1,884	1,546
E	730	742	818	774
F	948	1,118	1,256	788

1. The total dollar value purchased by all of the purchasing units during 2018 approximated MOST NEARLY

    A. $2,000,000   B. $4,000,000
    C. $20,000,000   D. $40,000,000

    1____

2. During which quarter was the GREATEST total dollar amount of purchases made? _____ quarter.

    A. First   B. Second   C. Third   D. Fourth

    2____

3. Assume that the dollar volume purchased by Unit F during 2018 exceeded the dollar volume purchased by Unit F during 2017 by 50%
Then, the dollar volume purchased by Unit F during 2017 was

    A. $2,055,000   B. $2,550,000
    C. $2,740,000   D. $6,165,000

    3____

4. Which one of the following purchasing units showed the sharpest DECREASE in the amount purchased during the fourth quarter as compared with the third quarter? Unit

    A. A   B. B   C. D   D. E

    4____

99

5. Comparing the dollar volume purchased in the second quarter with the dollar volume purchased in the third quarter, the decrease in the dollar volume during the third quarter was PRIMARILY due to the decrease in the dollar volume purchased by Units _____ _____ and _____.

   A. A; B   B. C; D   C. C; E   D. C; F

6. Of the following, the unit which had the LARGEST number of dollars of increased purchases from any one quarter to the next following quarter was Unit

   A. A   B. B   C. C   D. D

7. Of the following, the unit with the LARGEST dollar volume of purchases during the second half of 2018 was Unit

   A. A   B. B   C. D   D. F

8. Which one of the following MOST closely approximates the percentage which Unit B's total 2018 purchases represents of the total 2018 purchases of all units, including Unit B?

   A. 10%   B. 15%   C. 25%   D. 45%

9. Assume that research showed that each ten thousand dollars ($10,000) of purchases by Unit D during 2018 required an average of thirteen (13) man-hours of buyers' staff time. On that basis, which one of the following MOST closely approximates the number of man-hours of buyers' staff time required by Unit D during 2018?
   _____ man-hours.

   A. 1,800   B. 8,000   C. 68,000   D. 78,000

10. Assume that research showed that each ten thousand dollars ($10,000) of purchases by Unit C during 2018 required an average of ten (10) man-hours of buyers' staff time. This research also showed that during 2018 the average man-hours of buyers' staff time per ten thousand dollars of purchases required by Unit C exceeded by 25% the average man-hours of buyers' staff time per ten thousand dollars of purchases required by Unit E. On that basis, which one of the following MOST closely approximates the number of buyers' staff man-hours required by Unit E during 2018?
    _____ man-hours.

    A. 2,200   B. 2,400   C. 3,000   D. 3,700

KEY (CORRECT ANSWERS)

1. C
2. B
3. C
4. A
5. A

6. B
7. C
8. C
9. B
10. B

TEST 2

Questions 1-5.

DIRECTIONS: Questions 1 through 5 are to be answered SOLELY on the basis of the information below.

DEPARTMENT XYZ SIZE DISTRIBUTION OF PURCHASING ORDERS	
Amount of Order (dollars)	Number of Orders
1 - 9.99	91
10 - 19.99	135
20 - 49.99	320
50 - 99.99	712
100 - 199.99	1,050
200 - 499.99	735
500 - 999.99	305
1,000 - 1,999.99	94
2,000 - 4,999.99	36
5,000 - 9,999.99	18
10,000 - 19,999.99	3
20,000 - 49,000.99	1

1. The number of orders placed was
   A. 2600   B. 3500   C. 4000   D. 4500

2. Of the following graphs, most orders were between
   A. 50-200   B. 100-500   C. 200-2000   D. 10-100

3. The median value is approximately
   A. $100   B. $150   C. $200   D. $1050

4. Fewest orders were placed between
   A. $500-49,000.99   B. $10-49.99   C. $50-99.99   D. $200-499.99

5. The value of all the orders was more than
   A. $900,000
   B. $750,000
   C. $475,000
   D. one cannot tell from the information given

KEY (CORRECT ANSWERS)

1. B
2. B
3. B
4. B
5. C

TEST 3

Questions 1-4.

DIRECTIONS: Questions 1 through 4 are to be answered SOLELY on the basis of the information contained in the chart below.

COMPARATIVE WEIGHTS AND PRICES FOR 4 BRANDS OF PARMESAN CHEESE

PRICES

	SMALL	MEDIUM	LARGE	EXTRA LARGE
Brand W	1.16	$2.52	$5.20	$7.36
Brand X	.72	1.92	3.60	5.40
Brand Y	1.20	2.20	5.72	7.68
Brand Z	.60	1.16	3.36	6.24

WEIGHTS (IN OUNCES)

	SMALL	MEDIUM	LARGE	EXTRA LARGE
Brand W	2	4 1/2	10	16
Brand X	1 1/2	4	9	15
Brand Y	2 1/2	5 1/2	11	16
Brand Z	1	2	6	12

1. Of the following, the brand and size of cheese which costs LEAST per ounce is Brand

   A. W, large
   B. X, extra large
   C. Y, medium
   D. Z, extra large

2. The brand which comes in a small size that costs the SAME per ounce as the extra large size is Brand

   A. W   B. X   C. Y   D. Z

3. Using a combination of the sizes listed in the above chart, the LEAST expensive price for exactly 1 pound, 11 ounces of Brand Z would be

   A. $12.52   B. $14.64   C. $14.80   D. $18.92

4. In the medium size, the brand that is LEAST expensive per ounce is Brand

   A. W   B. X   C. Y   D. Z

KEY (CORRECT ANSWERS)

1. B
2. C
3. B
4. C

TEST 4

Questions 1-4.

DIRECTIONS: Questions 1 through 4 are to be answered SOLELY on the basis of the following graph.

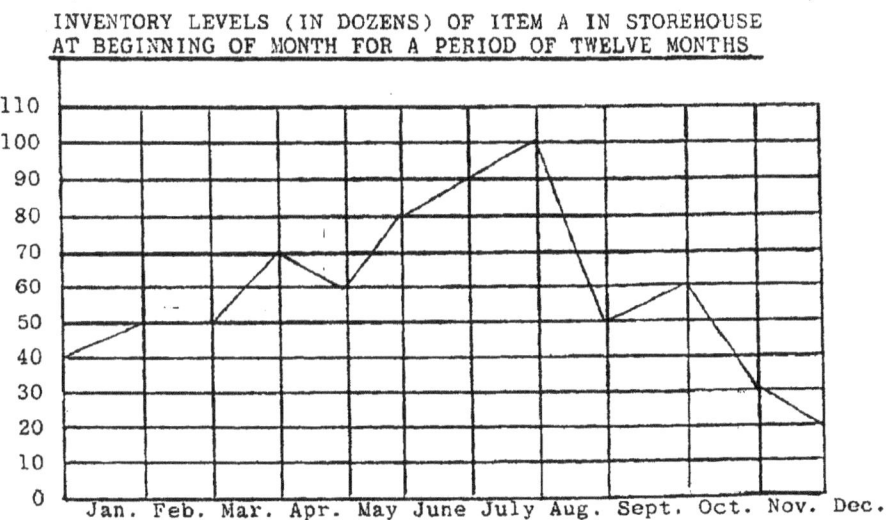

1. The average monthly inventory level during the course of the year was MOST NEARLY _____ dozen.

   A. 45   B. 60   C. 75   D. 90

2. If one dozen items fit in a carton measuring 2 feet by 2 feet by 3 feet, what MINIMUM volume would be required to store the maximum August inventory? _____ cubic feet.

   A. 12   B. 100   C. 700   D. 1,200

3. Assume that deliveries are made to the storehouse on the first working day of each month.
   If 30% of the June inventory was consumed during the month, how many items had to be delivered to reach the July inventory level? _____ items.

   A. 288   B. 408   C. 696   D. 1,080

4. Which three-month period contained the LOWEST average inventory level?

   A. Jan., Feb., March   B. April, May, June
   C. July, Aug., Sept.   D. Oct., Nov., Dec.

KEY (CORRECT ANSWERS)

1. B
2. D
3. B
4. D

TEST 5

Questions 1-6.

DIRECTIONS: Questions 1 through 6 are to be answered SOLELY on the basis of the following table.

REPORT OF SEMI-ANNUAL INVENTORY							
Article		Physical Inventory			Perpetual Inventory		Adjustment	
	Unit	Qty.	Price	Amt.	Qty.	Amt.	Qty.	Amt.
Batteries, flashlight	ea.	63	.08	5.04	60	14.80	+3	+.24
Bolts, flat head with square nuts, 100 in box	box	23	1.47	33.80	9,5	36.75		
Fuse, 15 amp, 4 in box	box	80	.07	5.60	80	5.60		
Fuse, 20 amp, 4 in box	box	77	.07	5.39	80	5.60	3	.21
Tape, friction, 50 ft. to a roll	roll	45	.22	9.90	45	9.90		
Washers, 100 in can 1/8" Beveled	can	35	.32	11.20	35	11.20		
3/8" Beveled	can	41	.33	13.63	45	14.85	4	1.32
Totals				84.47		88.70		

1. In the above report, for which item is there an INCORRECT entry? 1___
   A. 15 amp fuses B. Friction tape
   C. Flashlight batteries D. 1/8" washers

2. In the above report, adjustments were omitted for _____ article(s). 2___
   A. one B. two C. three D. four

3. After all appropriate entries have been made in the adjustment column, the total which must be deducted from the book value of the inventory is 3___
   A. $1.53 B. $1.77 C. $4.23 D. $4.71

4. The quantities shown in Perpetual Inventory exceed those shown in Physical Inventory by a total of 4___
   A. 4 B. 6 C. 10 D. 12

5. The cost of ten washers, 1/8" beveled, is MOST NEARLY 5____
   A. $.003 B. $.032 C. $.320 D. $3.20

6. The cost of 24 fuses is MOST NEARLY 6____
   A. $.28 B. $.42 C. $.80 D. $1.68

KEY (CORRECT ANSWERS)

1. C
2. A
3. C
4. B
5. B
6. B

TEST 6

Questions 1-10.

DIRECTIONS: Questions 1 through 10 are to be answered SOLELY on the basis of Tables I and II below.

TABLE I
Building 5 Storeroom
Report of Dollar Cost of Stores Issued to All Divisions in the Month Of December

Divisions	11 Dept. Reports & Bulletins	12 Food Supplies	13 Motor Vehicle Supplies	14 Office Supplies	15 Printed Stationery & Forms	16 Printing & Reproducing Supplies	17 Small Tools & Implements
A	40		125	85	13	55	45
B	21		231	35	46	32	61
C	68	422		75	37	81	
D	81			93	98	77	91
E	32	168		69	51	43	

TABLE II
Building 5 Storeroom
Summary of Dollar Cost of Stores Issued and Received and Balances, December

1 Supply Code	2 Balance Beginning of Month	3 Receipts from Vendors	4 Receipts from Storehouse A	5 Receipts from Storehouse B	6 Total Receipts	7 Total Issued	8 Balance
11	200	112	83	21	216	242	174
12	472	225	200	46	471	590	119
13	365	400			765	356	409
14	257	75	245	27	347	357	
15	245	89	152	36	277	255	277
16	281	104	190		294	288	287
17	197	32	110	40	182	197	182

1. The average value of small tools and implements received by Division C and E during the month of December

    A. is zero
    B. is approximately 78
    C. is 197
    D. cannot be determined from the information given

1.___

2. The division which received the GREATEST dollar value of stores in the month of December was

   A. A B. B C. C D. D

3. The division which received the GREATEST number of items in all supply categories in December

   A. is A
   B. is B
   C. is D
   D. cannot be determined from the information given

4. In the column *Total Issued,* the entry which is INCORRECT is for

   A. Food Supplies
   B. Motor Vehicle Supplies
   C. Office Supplies
   D. Printed Stationery & Forms

5. In the column *Total Receipts,* the entry which is INCORRECT is for

   A. Department Reports & Bulletins
   B. Motor Vehicle Supplies
   C. Office Supplies
   D. Small Tools & Implements

6. The balance for Supply Code 14 has been omitted. This figure should be

   A. 10 B. 247 C. 367 D. 594

7. The balance has been INCORRECTLY entered for

   A. Department Reports & Bulletins
   B. Food Supplies
   C. Printing & Reproducing Supplies
   D. Small Tools & Implements

8. The dollar value of department reports and bulletins received from vendors in December exceeds that received from the storehouses by

   A. 8   B. 12
   C. 29   D. an indeterminate amount

9. For the classes of items received from Storehouse B during the month of December, the average dollar cost of these classes was MOST NEARLY

   A. 24 B. 34 C. 65 D. 170

10. One space is left blank in Column 4 of Table II.
    Judging only from the above tables, the MOST probable reason for this is that

    A. motor vehicle supplies were obtained from vendors only
    B. number 365 was inadvertently omitted from Column 4
    C. the figures for Columns 4 and 5 were included in Column 3
    D. the motor vehicle supply stock of Storehouse A is below the minimum stock level

KEY (CORRECT ANSWERS)

1. A
2. C
3. D
4. D
5. B
6. B
7. B
8. A
9. B
10. A

TEST 7

Questions 1-5.

DIRECTIONS: Questions 1 through 5 are to be answered SOLELY on the basis of the information given below.

CONTROLLED DRUG A					
Time Period	Purchase Order Number	Quantity Ordered	*Quantity Delivered By Vendor	Quantity Distributed During 2-wk Period	Inventory Balance at end of 2-wk Period
April 23-May 6	110,327	105 oz.	135 oz.	27 oz.	108 oz.
May 7 - May 20	111,437	42 oz.	40 oz.	39 oz.	109 oz.
May 21 - June 3	112,347	37 oz.	27 oz.	32 oz.	104 oz.
June 4 - June 17	112,473	35 oz.	35 oz.	45 oz.	94 oz.
June 18 - July 1	114,029	40 oz.	40 oz.	37 oz.	97 oz.

*Delivery is made on first day of time period.

1. The difference between Quantity Ordered and Quantity Delivered was GREATEST on Purchase Order Number

    A. 110,327   B. 111,437   C. 112,347   D. 112,473

2. The difference between the total number of ounces ordered and the total number of ounces delivered on April 23 through June 18 is _____ ounces.

    A. 17   B. 18   C. 19   D. 20

3. Suppose that average weekly usage was expected to be 26 ounces per week. Your supervisor has asked you to tell him whenever inventory balances get below a four-week level.
   Under these conditions, you should have told your supervisor during the two-week period beginning

    A. April 23, May 21, June 4, June 18
    B. May 21, June 4, June 18
    C. May 21, June 18
    D. June 4, June 18

4. The GREATEST decreases in inventory balances happened between the two-week periods beginning

    A. April 23 and May 7
    B. May 7 and May 21
    C. May 21 and June 4
    D. June 4 and June 18

109

5. Suppose a new program has been started at your hospital and the weekly usage of Drug A is expected to be 52 ounces per week.
   If your supervisor must keep on hand a four-week supply, then the amount that should be delivered for the two-week period beginning on July 2 is _____ ounces. 5____

   A. 52   B. III   C. 208   D. 211

KEY (CORRECT ANSWERS)

1. A
2. C
3. D
4. C
5. B

PHILOSOPHY, PRINCIPLES, PRACTICES, AND TECHNICS
OF
SUPERVISION, ADMINISTRATION, MANAGEMENT, AND ORGANIZATION

TABLE OF CONTENTS

	Page
MEANING OF SUPERVISION	1
THE OLD AND THE NEW SUPERVISION	1
THE EIGHT (8) BASIC PRINCIPLES OF THE NEW SUPERVISION	1
I. Principle of Responsibility	1
II. Principle of Authority	2
III. Principle of Self-Growth	2
IV. Principle of Individual Worth	2
V. Principle of Creative Leadership	2
VI. Principle of Success and Failure	2
VII. Principle of Science	3
VIII. Principle of Cooperation	3
WHAT IS ADMINISTRATION?	3
I. Practices Commonly Classed as "Supervisory"	3
II. Practices Commonly Classed as "Administrative"	3
III. Practices Commonly Classed as Both "Supervisory" and "Administrative"	4
RESPONSIBILITIES OF THE SUPERVISOR	4
COMPETENCIES OF THE SUPERVISOR	4
THE PROFESSIONAL SUPERVISOR-EMPLOYEE RELATIONSHIP	4
MINI-TEXT IN SUPERVISION, ADMINISTRATION, MANAGEMENT, AND ORGANIZATION	5
I. Brief Highlights	5
A. Levels of Management	6
B. What the Supervisor Must Learn	6
C. A Definition of Supervision	6
D. Elements of the Team Concept	6
E. Principles of Organization	6
F. The Four Important Parts of Every Job	7
G. Principles of Delegation	7
H. Principles of Effective Communications	7
I. Principles of Work Improvement	7
J. Areas of Job Improvement	7
K. Seven Key Points in Making Improvements	8

	L.	Corrective Techniques for Job Improvement	8
	M.	A Planning Checklist	8
	N.	Five Characteristics of Good Directions	9
	O.	Types of Directions	9
	P.	Controls	9
	Q.	Orienting the New Employee	9
	R.	Checklist for Orienting New Employees	9
	S.	Principles of Learning	10
	T.	Causes of Poor Performance	10
	U.	Four Major Steps in On-the-Job Instructions	10
	V.	Employees Want Five Things	10
	W.	Some Don'ts in Regard to Praise	11
	X.	How to Gain Your Workers' Confidence	11
	Y.	Sources of Employee Problems	11
	Z.	The Supervisor's Key to Discipline	11
	AA.	Five Important Processes of Management	12
	BB.	When the Supervisor Fails to Plan	12
	CC.	Fourteen General Principles of Management	12
	DD.	Change	12
II.	Brief Topical Summaries		13
	A.	Who/What is the Supervisor?	13
	B.	The Sociology of Work	13
	C.	Principles and Practices of Supervision	14
	D.	Dynamic Leadership	14
	E.	Processes for Solving Problems	15
	F.	Training for Results	15
	G.	Health, Safety, and Accident Prevention	16
	H.	Equal Employment Opportunity	16
	I.	Improving Communications	16
	J.	Self-Development	17
	K.	Teaching and Training	17
		1. The Teaching Process	17
		a. Preparation	17
		b. Presentation	18
		c. Summary	18
		d. Application	18
		e. Evaluation	18
		2. Teaching Methods	18
		a. Lecture	18
		b. Discussion	18
		c. Demonstration	19
		d. Performance	19
		e. Which Method to Use	19

PHILOSOPHY, PRINCIPLES, PRACTICES, AND TECHNICS OF SUPERVISION, ADMINISTRATION, MANAGEMENT, AND ORGANIZATION

MEANING OF SUPERVISION

The extension of the democratic philosophy has been accompanied by an extension in the scope of supervision. Modern leaders and supervisors no longer think of supervision in the narrow sense of being confined chiefly to visiting employees, supplying materials, or rating the staff. They regard supervision as being intimately related to all the concerned agencies of society, they speak of the supervisor's function in terms of "growth," rather than the "improvement" of employees.

This modern concept of supervision may be defined as follows: Supervision is leadership and the development of leadership within groups which are cooperatively engaged in inspection, research, training, guidance, and evaluation.

THE OLD AND THE NEW SUPERVISION

TRADITIONAL
1. Inspection
2. Focused on the employee
3. Visitation
4. Random and haphazard
5. Imposed and authoritarian
6. One person usually

MODERN
1. Study and analysis
2. Focused on aims, materials, methods, supervisors, employees, environment
3. Demonstrations, intervisitation, workshops, directed reading, bulletins, etc.
4. Definitely organized and planned (scientific)
5. Cooperative and democratic
6. Many persons involved (creative)

THE EIGHT (8) BASIC PRINCIPLES OF THE NEW SUPERVISION

I. Principle of Responsibility
   Authority to act and responsibility for acting must be joined.
   A. If you give responsibility, give authority.
   B. Define employee duties clearly.
   C. Protect employees from criticism by others.
   D. Recognize the rights as well as obligations of employees.
   E. Achieve the aims of a democratic society insofar as it is possible within the area of your work.
   F. Establish a situation favorable to training and learning.
   G. Accept ultimate responsibility for everything done in your section, unit, office, division, department.
   H. Good administration and good supervision are inseparable.

II. Principle of Authority
The success of the supervisor is measured by the extent to which the power of authority is not used.
   A. Exercise simplicity and informality in supervision
   B. Use the simplest machinery of supervision
   C. If it is good for the organization as a whole, it is probably justified.
   D. Seldom be arbitrary or authoritative.
   E. Do not base your work on the power of position or of personality.
   F. Permit and encourage the free expression of opinions.

III. Principle of Self-Growth
The success of the supervisor is measured by the extent to which, and the speed with which, he is no longer needed.
   A. Base criticism on principles, not on specifics.
   B. Point out higher activities to employees.
   C. Train for self-thinking by employees to meet new situations.
   D. Stimulate initiative, self-reliance, and individual responsibility
   E. Concentrate on stimulating the growth of employees rather than on removing defects.

IV. Principle of Individual Worth
Respect for the individual is a paramount consideration in supervision.
   A. Be human and sympathetic in dealing with employees.
   B. Don't nag about things to be done.
   C. Recognize the individual differences among employees and seek opportunities to permit best expression of each personality.

V. Principle of Creative Leadership
The best supervision is that which is not apparent to the employee.
   A. Stimulate, don't drive employees to creative action.
   B. Emphasize doing good things.
   C. Encourage employees to do what they do best.
   D. Do not be too greatly concerned with details of subject or method.
   E. Do not be concerned exclusively with immediate problems and activities.
   F. Reveal higher activities and make them both desired and maximally possible.
   G. Determine procedures in the light of each situation but see that these are derived from a sound basic philosophy.
   H. Aid, inspire, and lead so as to liberate the creative spirit latent in all good employees.

VI. Principle of Success and Failure
There are no unsuccessful employees, only unsuccessful supervisors who have failed to give proper leadership.
   A. Adapt suggestions to the capacities, attitudes, and prejudices of employees.
   B. Be gradual, be progressive, be persistent.
   C. Help the employee find the general principle; have the employee apply his own problem to the general principle.
   D. Give adequate appreciation for good work and honest effort.
   E. Anticipate employee difficulties and help to prevent them.
   F. Encourage employees to do the desirable things they will do anyway.
   G. Judge your supervision by the results it secures.

VII. Principle of Science
Successful supervision is scientific, objective, and experimental. It is based on facts, not on prejudices.
- A. Be cumulative in results.
- B. Never divorce your suggestions from the goals of training.
- C. Don't be impatient of results.
- D. Keep all matters on a professional, not a personal, level.
- E. Do not be concerned exclusively with immediate problems and activities.
- F. Use objective means of determining achievement and rating where possible.

VIII. Principle of Cooperation
Supervision is a cooperative enterprise between supervisor and employee.
- A. Begin with conditions as they are.
- B. Ask opinions of all involved when formulating policies.
- C. Organization is as good as its weakest link.
- D. Let employees help to determine policies and department programs.
- E. Be approachable and accessible—physically and mentally.
- F. Develop pleasant social relationships.

WHAT IS ADMINISTRATION

Administration is concerned with providing the environment, the material facilities, and the operational procedures that will promote the maximum growth and development of supervisors and employees. (Organization is an aspect and a concomitant of administration.)

There is no sharp line of demarcation between supervision and administration; these functions are intimately interrelated and, often, overlapping. They are complementary activities.

I. Practices Commonly Classed as "Supervisory"
- A. Conducting employees' conferences
- B. Visiting sections, units, offices, divisions, departments
- C. Arranging for demonstrations
- D. Examining plans
- E. Suggesting professional reading
- F. Interpreting bulletins
- G. Recommending in-service training courses
- H. Encouraging experimentation
- I. Appraising employee morale
- J. Providing for intervisitation

II. Practices Commonly Classified as "Administrative"
- A. Management of the office
- B. Arrangement of schedules for extra duties
- C. Assignment of rooms or areas
- D. Distribution of supplies
- E. Keeping records and reports
- F. Care of audio-visual materials
- G. Keeping inventory records
- H. Checking record cards and books

    I.   Programming special activities
    J.   Checking on the attendance and punctuality of employees

III.   Practices Commonly Classified as Both "Supervisory" and "Administrative"
    A.   Program construction
    B.   Testing or evaluating outcomes
    C.   Personnel accounting
    D.   Ordering instructional materials

RESPONSIBILITIES OF THE SUPERVISOR

A person employed in a supervisory capacity must constantly be able to improve his own efficiency and ability. He represent the employer to the employees and only continuous self-examination can make him a capable supervisor.

Leadership and training are the supervisor's responsibility. An efficient working unit is one in which the employees work with the supervisor. It is his job to bring out the best in his employees. He must always be relaxed, courteous, and calm in his association with his employees. Their feelings are important, and a harsh attitude does not develop the most efficient employees.

COMPETENCES OF THE SUPERVISOR

    I.   Complete knowledge of the duties and responsibilities of his position.
    II.   To be able to organize a job, plan ahead, and carry through.
    III.   To have self-confidence and initiative.
    IV.   To be able to handle the unexpected situation and make quick decisions.
    V.   To be able to properly train subordinates in the positions they are best suited for.
    VI.   To be able to keep good human relations among his subordinates.
    VII.   To be able to keep good human relations between his subordinates and himself and to earn their respect and trust.

THE PROFESSIONAL SUPERVISOR-EMPLOYEE RELATIONSHIP

There are two kinds of efficiency: one kind is only apparent and is produced in organizations through the exercise of mere discipline; this is but a simulation of the second, or true, efficiency which springs from spontaneous cooperation. If you are a manager, no matter how great or small your responsibility, it is your job, in the final analysis, to create and develop this involuntary cooperation among the people whom you supervise. For, no matter how powerful a combination of money, machines, and materials a company may have, this is a dead and sterile thing without a team of willing, thinking, and articulate people to guide it.

The following 21 points are presented as indicative of the exemplary basic relationship that should exist between supervisor and employee:

1. Each person wants to be liked and respected by his fellow employee and wants to be treated with consideration and respect by his superior.
2. The most competent employee will make an error. However, in a unit where good relations exist between the supervisor and his employees, tenseness and fear do not exist. Thus, errors are not hidden or covered up, and the efficiency of a unit is not impaired.

3. Subordinates resent rules, regulations, or orders that are unreasonable or unexplained.
4. Subordinates are quick to resent unfairness, harshness, injustices, and favoritism.
5. An employee will accept responsibility if he knows that he will be complimented for a job well done, and not too harshly chastised for failure; that his supervisor will check the cause of the failure, and, if it was the supervisor's fault, he will assume the blame therefore. If it was the employee's fault, his supervisor will explain the correct method or means of handling the responsibility.
6. An employee wants to receive credit for a suggestion he has made, that is used. If a suggestion cannot be used, the employee is entitled to an explanation. The supervisor should not say "no" and close the subject.
7. Fear and worry slow up a worker's ability. Poor working environment can impair his physical and mental health. A good supervisor avoids forceful methods, threats, and arguments to get a job done.
8. A forceful supervisor is able to train his employees individually and as a team, and is able to motivate them in the proper channels.
9. A mature supervisor is able to properly evaluate his subordinates and to keep them happy and satisfied.
10. A sensitive supervisor will never patronize his subordinates.
11. A worthy supervisor will respect his employees' confidences.
12. Definite and clear-cut responsibilities should be assigned to each executive.
13. Responsibility should always be coupled with corresponding authority.
14. No change should be made in the scope or responsibilities of a position without a definite understanding to that effect on the part of all persons concerned.
15. No executive or employee, occupying a single position in the organization, should be subject to definite orders from more than one source.
16. Orders should never be given to subordinates over the head of a responsible executive. Rather than do this, the officer in question should be supplanted.
17. Criticisms of subordinates should, whoever possible, be made privately, and in no case should a subordinate be criticized in the presence of executives or employees of equal or lower rank.
18. No dispute or difference between executives or employees as to authority or responsibilities should be considered too trivial for prompt and careful adjudication.
19. Promotions, wage changes, and disciplinary action should always be approved by the executive immediately superior to the one directly responsible.
20. No executive or employee should ever be required, or expected, to be at the same time an assistant to, and critic of, another.
21. Any executive whose work is subject to regular inspection should, wherever practicable, be given the assistance and facilities necessary to enable him to maintain an independent check of the quality of his work.

MINI-TEXT IN SUPERVISION, ADMINISTRATION, MANAGEMENT, AND ORGANIZATION

I. Brief Highlights

Listed concisely and sequentially are major headings and important data in the field for quick recall and review.

A. Levels of Management
   Any organization of some size has several levels of management. In terms of a ladder, the levels are:

   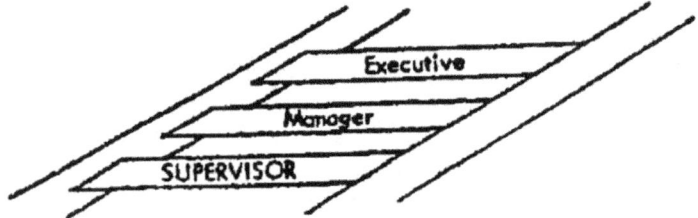

   The first level is very important because it is the beginning point of management leadership.

B. What the Supervisor Must Learn
   A supervisor must learn to:
   1. Deal with people and their differences
   2. Get the job done through people
   3. Recognize the problems when they exist
   4. Overcome obstacles to good performance
   5. Evaluate the performance of people
   6. Check his own performance in terms of accomplishment

C. A Definition of Supervisor
   The term supervisor means any individual having authority, in the interests of the employer, to hire, transfer, suspend, lay-off, recall, promote, discharge, assign, reward, or discipline other employees or responsibility to direct them, or to adjust their grievances, or effectively to recommend such action, if, in connection with the foregoing, exercise of such authority is not of a merely routine or clerical nature but requires the use of independent judgment.

D. Elements of the Team Concept
   What is involved in teamwork? The component parts are:
   1. Members
   2. A leader
   3. Goals
   4. Plans
   5. Cooperation
   6. Spirit

E. Principles of Organization
   1. A team member must know what his job is.
   2. Be sure that the nature and scope of a job are understood.
   3. Authority and responsibility should be carefully spelled out.
   4. A supervisor should be permitted to make the maximum number of decisions affecting his employees.
   5. Employees should report to only one supervisor.
   6. A supervisor should direct only as many employees as he can handle effectively.
   7. An organization plan should be flexible.

8. Inspection and performance of work should be separate.
9. Organizational problems should receive immediate attention.
10. Assign work in line with ability and experience.

F. The Four Important Parts of Every Job
1. Inherent in every job is the *accountability* for results.
2. A second set of factors in every job is *responsibilities*.
3. Along with duties and responsibilities one must have the *authority* to act within certain limits without obtaining permission to proceed.
4. No job exists in a vacuum. The supervisor is surrounded by key *relationships*.

G. Principles of Delegation
Where work is delegated for the first time, the supervisor should think in terms of these questions:
1. Who is best qualified to do this?
2. Can an employee improve his abilities by doing this?
3. How long should an employee spend on this?
4. Are there any special problems for which he will need guidance?
5. How broad a delegation can I make?

H. Principles of Effective Communications
1. Determine the media.
2. To whom directed?
3. Identification and source authority.
4. Is communication understood?

I. Principles of Work Improvement
1. Most people usually do only the work which is assigned to them.
2. Workers are likely to fit assigned work into the time available to perform it.
3. A good workload usually stimulates output.
4. People usually do their best work when they know that results will be reviewed or inspected.
5. Employees usually feel that someone else is responsible for conditions of work, workplace layout, job methods, type of tools/equipment, and other such factors.
6. Employees are usually defensive about their job security.
7. Employees have natural resistance to change.
8. Employees can support or destroy a supervisor.
9. A supervisor usually earns the respect of his people through his personal example of diligence and efficiency.

J. Areas of Job Improvement
The areas of job improvement are quite numerous, but the most common ones which a supervisor can identify and utilize are:
1. Departmental layout
2. Flow of work
3. Workplace layout
4. Utilization of manpower
5. Work methods
6. Materials handling

7. Utilization
8. Motion economy

K. Seven Key Points in Making Improvements
1. Select the job to be improved
2. Study how it is being done now
3. Question the present method
4. Determine actions to be taken
5. Chart proposed method
6. Get approval and apply
7. Solicit worker participation

l. Corrective Techniques of Job Improvement
Specific Problems
1. Size of workload
2. Inability to meet schedules
3. Strain and fatigue
4. Improper use of men and skills
5. Waste, poor quality, unsafe conditions
6. Bottleneck conditions that hinder output
7. Poor utilization of equipment and machine
8. Efficiency and productivity of labor

General Improvement
1. Departmental layout
2. Flow of work
3. Work plan layout
4. Utilization of manpower
5. Work methods
6. Materials handling
7. Utilization of equipment
8. Motion economy

Corrective Techniques
1. Study with scale model
2. Flow chart study
3. Motion analysis
4. Comparison of units produced to standard allowance
5. Methods analysis
6. Flow chart and equipment study
7. Down time vs. running time
8. Motion analysis

M. A Planning Checklist
1. Objectives
2. Controls
3. Delegations
4. Communications
5. Resources
6. Manpower

7. Equipment
8. Supplies and materials
9. Utilization of time
10. Safety
11. Money
12. Work
13. Timing of improvements

N. Five Characteristics of Good Directions
In order to get results, directions must be:
1. Possible of accomplishment
2. Agreeable with worker interests
3. Related to mission
4. Planned and complete
5. Unmistakably clear

O. Types of Directions
1. Demands or direct orders
2. Requests
3. Suggestion or implication
4. volunteering

P. Controls
A typical listing of the overall areas in which the supervisor should establish controls might be:
1. Manpower
2. Materials
3. Quality of work
4. Quantity of work
5. Time
6. Space
7. Money
8. Methods

Q. Orienting the New Employee
1. Prepare for him
2. Welcome the new employee
3. Orientation for the job
4. Follow-up

R. Checklist for Orienting New Employees   Yes   No
1. Do you appreciate the feelings of new employees when they first report for work? ___ ___
2. Are you aware of the fact that the new employee must make a big adjustment to his job? ___ ___
3. Have you given him good reasons for liking the job and the organization? ___ ___
4. Have you prepared for his first day on the job? ___ ___
5. Did you welcome him cordially and make him feel needed? ___ ___

	Yes	No

6. Did you establish rapport with him so that he feels free to talk and discuss matters with you?
7. Did you explain his job to him and his relationship to you?
8. Does he know that his work will be evaluated periodically on a basis that is fair and objective?
9. Did you introduce him to his fellow workers in such a way that they are likely to accept him?
10. Does he know what employee benefits he will receive?
11. Does he understand the importance of being on the job and what to do if he must leave his duty station?
12. Has he been impressed with the importance of accident prevention and safe practice?
13. Does he generally know his way around the department?
14. Is he under the guidance of a sponsor who will teach the right way of doing things?
15. Do you plan to follow-up so that he will continue to adjust successfully to his job?

S. Principles of Learning
1. Motivation
2. Demonstration or explanation
3. Practice

T. Causes of Poor Performance
1. Improper training for job
2. Wrong tools
3. Inadequate directions
4. Lack of supervisory follow-up
5. Poor communications
6. Lack of standards of performance
7. Wrong work habits
8. Low morale
9. Other

U. Four Major Steps in On-The-Job Instruction
1. Prepare the worker
2. Present the operation
3. Tryout performance
4. Follow-up

V. Employees Want Five Things
1. Security
2. Opportunity
3. Recognition
4. Inclusion
5. Expression

W. Some Don'ts in Regard to Praise
1. Don't praise a person for something he hasn't done.
2. Don't praise a person unless you can be sincere.
3. Don't be sparing in praise just because your superior withholds it from you.
4. Don't let too much time elapse between good performance and recognition of it

X. How to Gain Your Workers' Confidence
Methods of developing confidence include such things as:
1. Knowing the interests, habits, hobbies of employees
2. Admitting your own inadequacies
3. Sharing and telling of confidence in others
4. Supporting people when they are in trouble
5. Delegating matters that can be well handled
6. Being frank and straightforward about problems and working conditions
7. Encouraging others to bring their problems to you
8. Taking action on problems which impede worker progress

Y. Sources of Employee Problems
On-the-job causes might be such things as:
1. A feeling that favoritism is exercised in assignments
2. Assignment of overtime
3. An undue amount of supervision
4. Changing methods or systems
5. Stealing of ideas or trade secrets
6. Lack of interest in job
7. Threat of reduction in force
8. Ignorance or lack of communications
9. Poor equipment
10. Lack of knowing how supervisor feels toward employee
11. Shift assignments

Off-the-job problems might have to do with:
1. Health
2. Finances
3. Housing
4. Family

Z. The Supervisor's Key to Discipline
There are several key points about discipline which the supervisor should keep in mind:
1. Job discipline is one of the disciplines of life and is directed by the supervisor.
2. It is more important to correct an employee fault than to fix blame for it.
3. Employee performance is affected by problems both on the job and off.
4. Sudden or abrupt changes in behavior can be indications of important employee problems.
5. Problems should be dealt with as soon as possible after they are identified.
6. The attitude of the supervisor may have more to do with solving problems than the techniques of problem solving.
7. Correction of employee behavior should be resorted to only after the supervisor is sure that training or counseling will not be helpful.

8. Be sure to document your disciplinary actions.
9. Make sure that you are disciplining on the basis of facts rather than personal feelings.
10. Take each disciplinary step in order, being careful not to make snap judgments, or decisions based on impatience.

AA. Five Important Processes of Management
1. Planning
2. Organizing
3. Scheduling
4. Controlling
5. Motivating

BB. When the Supervisor Fails to Plan
1. Supervisor creates impression of not knowing his job
2. May lead to excessive overtime
3. Job runs itself—supervisor lacks control
4. Deadlines and appointments missed
5. Parts of the work go undone
6. Work interrupted by emergencies
7. Sets a bad example
8. Uneven workload creates peaks and valleys
9. Too much time on minor details at expense of more important tasks

CC. Fourteen General Principles of Management
1. Division of work
2. Authority and responsibility
3. Discipline
4. Unity of command
5. Unity of direction
6. Subordination of individual interest to general interest
7. Remuneration of personnel
8. Centralization
9. Scalar chain
10. Order
11. Equity
12. Stability of tenure of personnel
13. Initiative
14. Esprit de corps

DD. Change

Bringing about change is perhaps attempted more often, and yet less well understood, than anything else the supervisor does. How do people generally react to change? (People tend to resist change that is imposed upon them by other individuals or circumstances.

Change is characteristic of every situation. It is a part of every real endeavor where the efforts of people are concerned.

1. Why do people resist change?
   People may resist change because of:
   a. Fear of the unknown
   b. Implied criticism
   c. Unpleasant experiences in the past
   d. Fear of loss of status
   e. Threat to the ego
   f. Fear of loss of economic stability

2. How can we best overcome the resistance to change?
   In initiating change, take these steps:
   a. Get ready to sell
   b. Identify sources of help
   c. Anticipate objections
   d. Sell benefits
   e. Listen in depth
   f. Follow up

II. Brief Topical Summaries

   A. Who/What is the Supervisor?
      1. The supervisor is often called the "highest level employee and the lowest level manager."
      2. A supervisor is a member of both management and the work group. He acts as a bridge between the two.
      3. Most problems in supervision are in the area of human relations, or people problems.
      4. Employees expect: Respect, opportunity to learn and to advance, and a sense of belonging, and so forth.
      5. Supervisors are responsible for directing people and organizing work. Planning is of paramount importance.
      6. A position description is a set of duties and responsibilities inherent to a given position.
      7. It is important to keep the position description up-to-date and to provide each employee with his own copy.

   B. The Sociology of Work
      1. People are alike in many ways; however, each individual is unique.
      2. The supervisor is challenged in getting to know employee differences. Acquiring skills in evaluating individuals is an asset.
      3. Maintaining meaningful working relationships in the organization is of great importance.
      4. The supervisor has an obligation to help individuals to develop to their fullest potential.
      5. Job rotation on a planned basis helps to build versatility and to maintain interest and enthusiasm in work groups.
      6. Cross training (job rotation) provides backup skills.

7. The supervisor can help reduce tension by maintaining a sense of humor, providing guidance to employees, and by making reasonable and timely decisions. Employees respond favorably to working under reasonably predictable circumstances.
8. Change is characteristic of all managerial behavior. The supervisor must adjust to changes in procedures, new methods, technological changes, and to a number of new and sometimes challenging situations.
9. To overcome the natural tendency for people to resist change, the supervisor should become more skillful in initiating change.

C. Principles and Practices of Supervision
1. Employees should be required to answer to only one superior.
2. A supervisor can effectively direct only a limited number of employees, depending upon the complexity, variety, and proximity of the jobs involved.
3. The organizational chart presents the organization in graphic form. It reflects lines of authority and responsibility as well as interrelationships of units within the organization.
4. Distribution of work can be improved through an analysis using the "Work Distribution Chart."
5. The "Work Distribution Chart" reflects the division of work within a unit in understandable form.
6. When related tasks are given to an employee, he has a better chance of increasing his skills through training.
7. The individual who is given the responsibility for tasks must also be given the appropriate authority to insure adequate results.
8. The supervisor should delegate repetitive, routine work. Preparation of recurring reports, maintaining leave and attendance records are some examples.
9. Good discipline is essential to good task performance. Discipline is reflected in the actions of employees on the job in the absence of supervision.
10. Disciplinary action may have to be taken when the positive aspects of discipline have failed. Reprimand, warning, and suspension are examples of disciplinary action.
11. If a situation calls for a reprimand, be sure it is deserved and remember it is to be done in private.

D. Dynamic Leadership
1. A style is a personal method or manner of exerting influence.
2. Authoritarian leaders often see themselves as the source of power and authority.
3. The democratic leader often perceives the group as the source of authority and power.
4. Supervisors tend to do better when using the pattern of leadership that is most natural for them.
5. Social scientists suggest that the effective supervisor use the leadership style that best fits the problem or circumstances involved.
6. All four styles—telling, selling, consulting, joining—have their place. Using one does not preclude using the other at another time.

7. The theory X point of view assumes that the average person dislikes work, will avoid it whenever possible, and must be coerced to achieve organizational objectives.
8. The theory Y point of view assumes that the average person considers work to be a natural as play, and, when the individual is committed, he requires little supervision or direction to accomplish desired objectives.
9. The leader's basic assumptions concerning human behavior and human nature affect his actions, decisions, and other managerial practices.
10. Dissatisfaction among employees is often present, but difficult to isolate. The supervisor should seek to weaken dissatisfaction by keeping promises, being sincere and considerate, keeping employees informed, and so forth.
11. Constructive suggestions should be encouraged during the natural progress of the work.

E. Processes for Solving Problems
1. People find their daily tasks more meaningful and satisfying when they can improve them.
2. The causes of problems, or the key factors, are often hidden in the background. Ability to solve problems often involves the ability to isolate them from their backgrounds. There is some substance to the cliché that some persons "can't see the forest for the trees."
3. New procedures are often developed from old ones. Problems should be broken down into manageable parts. New ideas can be adapted from old one.
4. People think differently in problem-solving situations. Using a logical, patterned approach is often useful. One approach found to be useful includes these steps:
   a. Define the problem
   b. Establish objectives
   c. Get the facts
   d. Weigh and decide
   e. Take action
   f. Evaluate action

F. Training for Results
1. Participants respond best when they feel training is important to them.
2. The supervisor has responsibility for the training and development of those who report to him.
3. When training is delegated to others, great care must be exercised to insure the trainer has knowledge, aptitude, and interest for his work as a trainer.
4. Training (learning) of some type goes on continually. The most successful supervisor makes certain the learning contributes in a productive manner to operational goals.
5. New employees are particularly susceptible to training. Older employees facing new job situations require specific training, as well as having need for development and growth opportunities.
6. Training needs require continuous monitoring.
7. The training officer of an agency is a professional with a responsibility to assist supervisors in solving training problems.

8. Many of the self-development steps important to the supervisor's own growth are equally important to the development of peers and subordinates. Knowledge of these is important when the supervisor consults with others on development and growth opportunities.

G. Health, Safety, and Accident Prevention
1. Management-minded supervisors take appropriate measures to assist employees in maintaining health and in assuring safe practices in the work environment.
2. Effective safety training and practices help to avoid injury and accidents.
3. Safety should be a management goal. All infractions of safety which are observed should be corrected without exception.
4. Employees' safety attitude, training and instruction, provision of safe tools and equipment, supervision, and leadership are considered highly important factors which contribute to safety and which can be influenced directly by supervisors.
5. When accidents do occur, they should be investigated promptly for very important reasons, including the fact that information which is gained can be used to prevent accidents in the future.

H. Equal Employment Opportunity
1. The supervisor should endeavor to treat all employees fairly, without regard to religion, race, sex, or national origin.
2. Groups tend to reflect the attitude of the leader. Prejudice can be detected even in very subtle form. Supervisors must strive to create a feeling of mutual respect and confidence in every employee.
3. Complete utilization of all human resources is a national goal. Equitable consideration should be accorded women in the work force, minority-group members, the physically and mentally handicapped, and the older employee. The important question is: "Who can do the job?"
4. Training opportunities, recognition for performance, overtime assignments, promotional opportunities, and all other personnel actions are to be handled on an equitable basis.

I. Improving Communications
1. Communications is achieving understanding between the sender and the receiver of a message. It also means sharing information—the creation of understanding.
2. Communication is basic to all human activity. Words are means of conveying meanings; however, real meanings are in people.
3. There are very practical differences in the effectiveness of one-way, impersonal, and two-way communications. Words spoken face-to-face are better understood. Telephone conversations are effective, but lack the rapport of person-to-person exchanges. The whole person communicates.
4. Cooperation and communication in an organization go hand in hand. When there is a mutual respect between people, spelling out rules and procedures for communicating is unnecessary.
5. There are several barriers to effective communications. These include failure to listen with respect and understanding, lack of skill in feedback, and misinterpreting the meanings of words used by the speaker. It is also common

practice to listen to what we want to hear, and tune out things we do not want to hear.
6. Communication is management's chief problem. The supervisor should accept the challenge to communicate more effectively and to improve interagency and intra-agency communications.
7. The supervisor may often plan for and conduct meetings. The planning phase is critical and may determine the success or the failure of a meeting.
8. Speaking before groups usually requires extra effort. Stage fright may never disappear completely, but it can be controlled.

J. Self-Development
1. Every employee is responsible for his own self-development.
2. Toastmaster and toastmistress clubs offer opportunities to improve skills in oral communications.
3. Planning for one's own self-development is of vital importance. Supervisors know their own strengths and limitations better than anyone else.
4. Many opportunities are open to aid the supervisor in his developmental efforts, including job assignments; training opportunities, both governmental and non-governmental—to include universities and professional conferences and seminars.
5. Programmed instruction offers a means of studying at one's own rate.
6. Where difficulties may arise from a supervisor's being away from his work for training, he may participate in televised home study or correspondence courses to meet his self-development needs.

K. Teaching and Training
1. The Teaching Process
Teaching is encouraging and guiding the learning activities of students toward established goals. In most cases this process consists of five steps: preparation, presentation, summarization, evaluation, and application.

   a. Preparation
   Preparation is two-fold in nature; that of the supervisor and the employee. Preparation by the supervisor is absolutely essential to success. He must know what, when, where, how, and whom he will teach. Some of the factors that should be considered are:
   1) The objectives
   2) The materials needed
   3) The methods to be used
   4) Employee participation
   5) Employee interest
   6) Training aids
   7) Evaluation
   8) Summarization

   Employee preparation consists in preparing the employee to receive the material. Probably the most important single factor in the preparation of the employee is arousing and maintaining his interest. He must know the objectives of the training, why he is there, how the material can be used, and its importance to him.

b. Presentation
In presentation, have a carefully designed plan and follow it. The plan should be accurate and complete, yet flexible enough to meet situations as they arise. The method of presentation will be determined by the particular situation and objectives.

c. Summary
A summary should be made at the end of every training unit and program. In addition, there may be internal summaries depending on the nature of the material being taught. The important thing is that the trainee must always be able to understand how each part of the new material relates to the whole.

d. Application
The supervisor must arrange work so the employee will be given a chance to apply new knowledge or skills while the material is still clear in his mind and interest is high. The trainee does not really know whether he has learned the material until he has been given a chance to apply it. If the material is not applied, it loses most of its value.

e. Evaluation
The purpose of all training is to promote learning. To determine whether the training has been a success or failure, the supervisor must evaluate this learning.
In the broadest sense, evaluation includes all the devices, methods, skills, and techniques used by the supervisor to keep himself and the employees informed as to their progress toward the objectives they are pursuing. The extent to which the employee has mastered the knowledge, skills, and abilities, or changed his attitudes, as determined by the program objectives, is the extent to which instruction has succeeded or failed.
Evaluation should not be confined to the end of the lesson, day, or program but should be used continuously. We shall note later the way this relates to the rest of the teaching process.

2. Teaching Methods
A teaching method is a pattern of identifiable student and instructor activity used in presenting training material.
All supervisors are faced with the problem of deciding which method should be used at a given time.

a. Lecture
The lecture is direct oral presentation of material by the supervisor. The present trend is to place less emphasis on the trainer's activity and more on that of the trainee.

b. Discussion
Teaching by discussion or conference involves using questions and other techniques to arouse interest and focus attention upon certain areas, and by doing so creating a learning situation. This can be one of the most

valuable methods because it gives the employees an opportunity to express their ideas and pool their knowledge.

    c. Demonstration
The demonstration is used to teach how something works or how to do something. It can be used to show a principle or what the results of a series of actions will be. A well-staged demonstration is particularly effective because it shows proper methods of performance in a realistic manner.

    d. Performance
Performance is one of the most fundamental of all learning techniques or teaching methods. The trainee may be able to tell how a specific operation should be performed but he cannot be sure he knows how to perform the operation until he has done so.
As with all methods, there are certain advantages and disadvantages to each method.

    e. Which Method to Use
Moreover, there are other methods and techniques of teaching. It is difficult to use any method without other methods entering into it. In any learning situation, a combination of methods is usually more effective than any one method alone.

Finally, evaluation must be integrated into the other aspects of the teaching-learning process.

It must be used in the motivation of the trainees; it must be used to assist in developing understanding during the training; and it must be related to employee application of the results of training.

This is distinctly the role of the supervisor.

Food Preparation-Handling and Storage

1. FOOD PREPARATION

    Begin with clean, fresh food. Handle food only when necessary.

    Don't dip fingers into food or use a stirring spoon to taste.

    Use oysters, clams and other frozen foods, fluid milk products and frozen milk desserts from approved sources.

    Never lean or sit on work surfaces.

    Foods should never be prepared in yards, alleys, stairs or hallways.

    Keep food that is on display covered so it can't be touched or coughed on by customers or contaminated by flies and other bugs.

    Always follow the recipe. Cook custards and cream sauces well. Chill them at once.

    Wash thoroughly with brush and clean water all vegetables and fruits which are to be served raw.

    As a food safeguard, boil leftover vegetables, gravies, soups, and other liquid foods before serving.

    Make sure that all mixing, grinding and chopping machines are thoroughly cleaned after each use. In order to properly clean one of these machines, one should know how to take it apart and assemble it.

    Work only in a well-lighted area that is well-ventilated.

2. FOOD STORAGE AND HANDLING

    Food should be stored well off the floor, away from walls or dripping pipes.

    Keep all food, bulk or otherwise, covered and safe from contamination.

    Check food daily and throw away any spoiled or dirty food.

    Store cleaning, disinfection, insect and rodent-killing powders and liquids away from foods, PLAINLY MARKED.

    Keep foods in refrigerator at temperature of 45° F or below.

    Check the temperature regularly with a good thermometer.

    Keep all cooling compartments closed except when you're using them.

    Store food in a refrigerator in such a way that inside air can circulate freely.

    Always refrigerate meats, creamed foods and custard desserts.

    Keep all refrigerated foods covered, and use up stored leftovers quickly.

    When dishes and utensils are sparkling clean, keep them that way by proper storage. Keep all cups and glasses inverted.

    Cakes, doughnuts and fruit pies may be kept inside a covered display area.

    The only goods that should be left on the counter uncovered are those which are wrapped and do not contain anything which could spoil at room temperature.

    Don't set dirty dishes, pots, cartons or boxes on food tables.

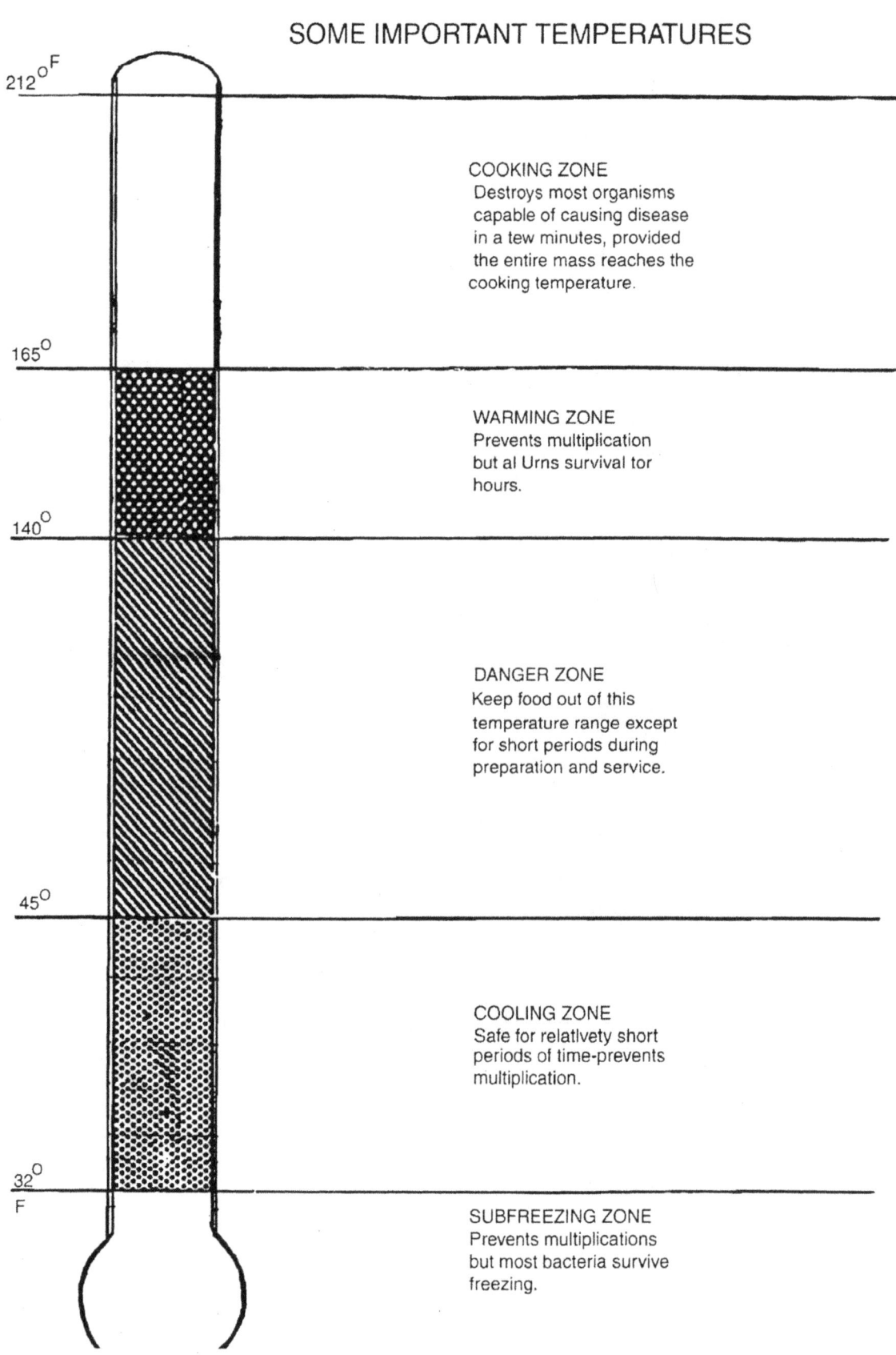

TEMPERATURE RANGE FOR SAFE STORAGE OF FOODS

Zone I Sub-freezing temperatures 0° F to - 15° F (-18° to -9.4° C)

- A. Frozen meat, fish, and vegetables
- B. Frozen fruits
- C. Ice Cream
- D. Homemade frozen deserts

Zone II High Humidity (85%) and Moderate Air Circulation 34° to 37° F (1.1° to 2.7 °C)

- A. Fresh meat, chicken, and fish
- B. Sliced smoked ham and bacon
- C. Sliced cold cuts of meat
- D. Leftover canned and cooked meat

Zone III 38° to 40° F (3.3° to 4.4° C)

- A. Fresh milk, cream, and buttermilk
- B. Cottage cheese and butter (both covered)
- C. Fresh orange and tomato juice (covered)
- D. Bottled beverage (for chilling)

Zone IV 40° to 43° F (4.4° to 6.1° C) Moderate Humidity

- A. Berries, pears, and peaches
- B. Ripe grapefruit and oranges
- C. Ripe tomatoes (short time only)
- D. Fresh eggs
- E. Margarine
- F. Custards and puddings (day or two only)
- G. Prepared salads (for chilling)

Zone V 40° to 45° F (4.4° to 7.2° C) High Humidity

- A. Cherries and cranberries
- B. Lettuce and celery
- C. Spinach, kale, and other greens
- D. Beets, carrots, parsnips, and turnips
- E. Peas and lima beans
- F. Cucumbers and eggplant (short time only)

Zone VI 55° to 60° F (12.7° to 15.1° C) Fairly High Humidity and Moderate Circulation. (Good Fruit Cellar or Storage Cellar Well Ventilated).

- A. Apples, cabbage, potatoes, pumpkin, squash, unripened tomatoes, and maple syrup (in tight container)

Zone VII   Normal Room Temperature. Dry Storage
    A. Ready prepared cereals
    B. Crackers
    C. Bottled beverages

Zone VIII   Normal Room Temperature Storage

    A. Peanut Butter and honey
    B. Salad oils and vegetable shortenings
    C. Catsup and pickles
    D. Jelly and preserves
    E. Dried fruits and bananas (short time)
    F. Flour
    G. Dried peas and beans
    H. Sugar and salt

MICROBIOLOGY OF FOODS: BACTERIA

In order to understand the reasons behind food sanitation practices, it is necessary to know a few facts about the microorganisms which cause food spoilage and foodborne disease.

Bacteria, commonly called germs, are extremely small, plant-like organisms which must be viewed through a microscope in order to be seen. If 25,000,000 bacteria were placed in a line, that line would be only one inch long; one million could fit on the head of a pin. Like any living thing, bacteria require food, moisture, and the proper temperature for growth. Most of them need air, but some can thrive only in the absence of air (these are called anaerobic) and some can grow with or without air (facultative). Bacteria are found everywhere on the earth, in the air, and in the water. Soil abounds with bacteria which grow on dead organic matter.

SHAPES OF BACTERIA

One method of classifying bacteria is by their shape. All bacteria can be assigned to one of the following categories.

A. Cocci (plural of coccus) are round or spherical in shape. While they are able to live alone, they often exist in groups. Single chains are called streptococci. Those which form a grape-like cluster are called staphylococci, while those that form pairs are called diplococci. Some bacteria are named after the portion of the human anatomy they infect; for example, pneumococci infect the lungs, enterococci infect the intestines, and meningococci infect the meninges (protective sheath around the brain). Some of the common diseases caused by the cocci group are pneumonia, septic sore throat, scarlet fever, and meningitis.

B. Bacilli (plural of bacillus) are rod-shaped. Some of these also congregate in the single chain form, and are called streptobacilli. Some common diseases caused by bacilli are typhoid fever, tuberculosis, and anthrax.

C. Spirilla (plural of spirillum) are spiral or comma-shaped. Diseases caused by spirilla include cholera and syphilis.

SPORES

Some bacilli are able to protect themselves under adverse conditions by forming a protective shell or wall around themselves; in this form they are in the non-vegetative stage and are called spores. These bacterial spores can be likened to the seeds of a plant which are also resistant to adverse conditions. During the spore stage, bacteria do not reproduce or multiply. As soon as these spores find themselves under proper conditions of warmth, moisture, food and possibly air requirements. they resume their normal (vegetative) stage, and resume their growth. Since spores are designed to withstand rigorous conditions, they are difficult to destroy by the normal methods. Much higher killing temperatures and longer time periods are required. Fortunately, there are only a relatively few pathogenic or disease-causing bacilli which are spore formers. Tetanus, anthrax, and botulism are diseases caused by spore formers.

BACTERIAL REPRODUCTION

Bacteria reproduce by splitting in two, this is called binary fission. For this reason, their numbers are always doubling: one bacterium generates two; each of these generates two, resulting in a new total of four: etc. The time it takes for bacteria to double (generation time) is roughly fifteen to thirty minutes under good conditions.

TYPES OF BACTERIA ACCORDING TO THEIR EFFECT ON MAN
Types of bacteria, classified according to their effect on us, are:

    A. Harmful or disease-producing
    B. Undesirable
    C. Beneficial
    D. Benign

    A. Harmful or disease-producing bacteria are known as pathogenic bacteria or pathogens. They cause various diseases of man, animals, and plants.

    B. Undesirable bacteria, which cause decomposition of foods, are often referred to as putrefying bacteria. Bacteria that act on sugars in food, resulting in souring, are called saccharolytic bacteria.

    C. Beneficial bacteria are used in the production of various foods, including cultured milk, yogurt, cheese, and sauerkraut.

The large intestine, or colon, contains millions of bacteria which are normal inhabitants of the intestinal tract, and we call this type *"coliform"* bacteria. It can be seen, therefore, that where coliform bacteria are found in food or water, they are an indication of fecal contamination. The coliforms themselves are not pathogenic, but where fecal contamination occurs, it is probable that other pathogenic organisms from the intestine may be present. The presence of coliform bacteria is often used as an index of good or bad sanitary practices.

Bacteria are essential in the operation of certain sewage disposal plants, known as *"activated sludge plants"*. In these plants the bacteria digest the organic sewage and either liquefy the solid matter which is in colloid form, or change it so that it settles out.

The greatest number of bacteria are found in the soil where they thrive on dead organic matter. They are constantly decomposing it, so that eventually it is changed into an inorganic form. This essential process of nature makes it possible for plants to absorb inorganic nutriment. Other types of bacteria *"fix"* nitrogen from the air, forming nitrates in the soil, generally on the roots of legumes.

    D. Benign bacteria, as far as we know at the present time, are neither helpful nor harmful to man. Of the hundreds of thousands of strains of bacteria, most fall into this category.

It must be realized that may bacteria are essential in the balance of nature, and the destruction of all bacteria in the world would be catastrophic. Our main objective in public health protection, in which food handling plays a vital role, is the control and destruction of the pathogenic bacteria and those that cause food spoilage.

CONDITIONS FOR GROWTH

    A. Food - Bacterial require food for growth. Food must be absorbed in liquid form through the cell wall of the organism. Generally bacteria prefer neutral foods (ph 6-8) but some can thrive on highly acid or alkaline media.

    B. Moisture - Moisture (water) is an essential requirement. If moisture is not present, bacteria will not multiply and eventually may die. Processes which depend on removing available water, i.e., water in liquid form, from bacteria are used to preserve foods. Such methods include dehydration, freezing, and preserving in salt or sugar.

    C. Temperature - In general, bacteria prefer a warm temperature and grow best between 90-100° F. (Optimum temperature) The temperature of the body, 98.6° F, is excellent for bacterial growth; when bacteria are cultured in the laboratory, they are kept at this temperature. However, different types of bacteria prefer different temperatures, and are as follows:

    <u>Mesophilic</u>: Grow best at temperatures between 50-110° F. Most bacteria are in this group.

Thermophilic: Love heat. These grow best at temperatures between 110-150° F. or mo.re

Psvchrophilic: Love cold. These grow best at temperatures below 50° F.

Where heat is employed to destroy pathogenic bacteria, the food processor often must contend with thermophilic or thermoduric bacteria, which may withstand the pasteurizing or sterilizing processes. These bacteria are not pathogenic, but may be putrefactive.

D. Air - With respect to air atmospheric oxygen, we find that some bacteria can grow only where air is present; these are called aerobes. Some bacteria can grow only in a medium where air is absent, and these are called anaerobes. They can thrive in a sealed can, jar, or bottle of food. Those bacteria which prefer to live where air is present but may grow without air are termed facultative aerobes, and those which prefer to grow in the absence of air but may grow where air is present are called facultative anaerobes.

LOCOMOTION

Bacteria cannot crawl, fly, or move about. A few types do have thread-like appendages called flagella, with which they can propel themselves to a very limited extent. Therefore, they must be carried from place to place by some vehicle or through some channel. The channels of transmission include: air, water, food, hands, coughing, sneezing, insects, rodents, dirty equipment, unsafe plumbing connections, and unclean utensils. Hands are one of the most dangerous vehicles. There is no doubt that better care of food handlers' hands would aid greatly in cutting down the transmission of disease.

DESTRUCTION BY HEAT

The most reliable and time-tested method of destroying bacteria is heat. This method is effective only when both time and temperature factors are applied. In other words, not only do we have to reach the desired temperature to kill bacteria, but we must allow sufficient time to permit the heat to kill the more sturdy members. The lower the temperature (to certain limits, of course) the longer the time required to kill bacteria. Conversely, the higher the temperature, the less time is necessary. An example of this principle involves the two accepted methods for pasteurizing milk. In the *"holding"* method, milk is held at a temperature of 145° F for thirty minutes. In the more recently developed *"flash"* or *"high temperature-short time"* method, milk is held at 161° F for fifteen seconds.

In sterilizing foods for canning, the type of food and size of the containers must be taken into consideration in determining the proper time and temperature. The smaller the container, the faster the heat will be conducted through the food.

It is important to note once more that in order to destroy spore-forming bacilli completely, very high temperatures, often higher than 212° F are required for long time periods.

DESTRUCTION BY CHEMICALS

Bacteria can be destroyed by chemical agents. Those which kill all bacteria are called germicides or bactericides. Examples are phenol (carbolic acid), formaldehyde, iodine, chlorine, and others, such as the group of chemicals known as quarternary compounds. The effectiveness of the chemical bactericide depends on the concentration and the method with which it is used. If it is used to kill pathogenic organisms only, it is called a disinfectant. If a mild concentration is used on wounds to inhibit the growth of disease organisms, it is called an antiseptic. Some chemicals have been used in foods to inhibit the growth of spoilage bacteria, and these are called preservatives. Examples of these are sulphur dioxide, benzoate of soda, salt, sugar, and vinegar.

OTHER METHODS OF DESTRUCTION

When exposed to air and sunlight, bacteria are destroyed due to the combined effects of lack of moisture and food and exposure to the natural ultraviolet rays of the sun. Ultraviolet lamps are used for bactericidal purposes but their field is limited. Aeration is not used commercially as the sole means of sterilizing a product.

REFRIGERATION

Refrigeration of foods in refrigerators (32-45° F) does not kill bacteria. However, these temperatures do inhibit the growth of bacteria, both putrefactive and pathogenic, so that foods under proper refrigeration remain wholesome and free from disease for some time.

MICROBIOLOGY OF FOODS: BACTERIA AND OTHER MICROORGANISMS

Extremely low freezing temperatures for prolonged periods may result in the death of some bacteria, while others may survive. However, refrigeration or freezing should never be considered as a means of destroying bacteria; these methods merely retard bacterial growth.

VIRUSES

Viruses are minute organic forms which seem to be intermediate between living cells and organic compounds. They are smaller than bacteria, and are sometimes called filterable viruses because they are so small that they can pass through the tiny pores of a porcelain filter which retain bacteria. They cannot be seen through a microscope (magnification of 1500 x) but can be seen through an electron microscope (magnification of 1,000,000 x). Viruses cause poliomyelitis, smallpox, measles, mumps, encephalitis, influenza, and the common cold. Viruses, like bacteria are presumed to exist everywhere.

YEASTS

Yeasts are one-celled organisms which are larger than bacteria. They, too, are found everywhere, and require food, moisture, warmth, and air for proper growth. Unlike some bacteria which live without air, yeasts must have air in order to grow. They need sugar, but have the ability to change starch into sugar. When yeasts act on sugar, the formation of alcohol and carbon dioxide results. In the baking industry, yeast is used to *"raise dough"* through the production of carbon dioxide. The alcohol is driven off by the heat of the oven. In wine production, the carbon dioxide gas bubbles off, leaving the alcohol. The amount of alcohol produced by yeasts is limited to 18%, because yeasts are killed at this concentration of alcohol.

Yeasts reproduce by budding, which is similar to binary fission. Generally, the methods described for the destruction of bacteria will kill yeasts as well.

Yeasts are not generally considered to be pathogenic or harmful although a few of them do cause skin infections. Wild yeasts or those that get into a food by accident rather than by design of the food processor cause food spoilage and decomposition of starch and sugar, and therefore are undesirable.

MOLDS

Molds are multicellular (many-celled) microscopic plants which become visible to the naked eye when growing in sufficient quantity. Mold colonies have definite colors (white, black, green, etc.) They are larger than bacteria or yeasts. Some molds are pathogenic, causing such diseases as athletes' foot, ringworm, and other skin diseases. However, moldy foods usually do not cause illness. In fact, molds are encouraged to grow in certain cheeses to produce a characteristic flavor.

The structure of the mold consists of a root-like structure called the mycelium, a stem (ariel filament) called the hypha, and the spore sac, called the sporangium. All molds reproduce by means of spores. Molds are the lowest form of life that have these specialized reproductive cells.

Molds require moisture and air for growth and can grow on almost any organic matter, which does not necessarily have to be food. Molds do not require warmth, and grow very well in refrigerators. Neither do molds require much moisture, although the more moisture present, the better they multiply.

Methods of destruction for molds are similar to those required for bacteria. Heat, chemicals, and ultraviolet rays destroy mold spores as well as the molds. Refrigeration does not necessarily retard their growth.

Certain chemicals act as mold inhibitors. Calcium propionate (Mycoban) is one used in making bread. This chemical when used in the dough, retards the germination of mold spores, and bread so treated will remain mold-free for about five days.

One of the most beneficial molds is the Penicillium mold from which penicillin, an antibiotic, is extracted. The discovery, by Dr. Alexander Fleming, of the mold's antibiotic properties open up a whold field of research, and other antibiotic products from molds have been discovered.

CLASSIFICATION OF FOODBORNE DISEASE

Several terms are used to describe illness in which the causative agent is obtained by ingestion of food; the expression *"food poisoning"* is commonly employed to describe any of these. However, such usage is inaccurate and confusing.

Foodborne diseases caused by bacteria are divided into two classes. The first is called food intoxication (this is the real food poisoning) and designates illnesses due to toxins (poisons) secreted by bacteria growing in large numbers on the food prior to ingestion. In the second type of bacterial disease, called food infection, the symptoms are caused by the activity of large numbers of bacterial cells, having grown to some extent in the contaminated food, within the gastrointestinal system of the victim.

Other microbial contaminants of food, such as viruses, rickettsiae, and protozoa, can cause disease, as can other parasites. Chemical poisonings are characterized by a relatively sudden onset of symptoms, often in minutes. In addition, certain plants and animals contain chemical poisons, some of which produce illness within a short period after ingestion.

I. Food Intoxications
    A. Botulism
        1. Toxins are produced by growth of Clostridium botulinum in foods under anaerobic conditions. There are six major types of toxins: A, B, C, D, E and F. Types A, B, and E affect man. Antitoxins exist, although few hospitals routinely stock them.
        2. Symptoms: Toxin affects the central nervous system, producing difficulty in swallowing, double vision, and difficulty in speech and respiration, followed by death from paralysis of muscles of respiration.
        3. Onset of symtoms: 2 hours to 8 days, average 1 to 2 days.
        4. Inactivation of toxins: 15 minutes at 212° F.
        5. Foods usually involved: home-canned, low-acid vegetables. On rare occasions, commercially packed tuna, smoked fish, mushrooms, and vichysoisse.
    B. Staphylococcus Food Poisoning
        1. Toxin produced by coagulase positive Staphylococcus aureus.
        2. Symptoms: Nausea, vomiting, diarrhea, acute prostration, and abdominal cramps.
        3. Onset of symptoms: 1 to 6 hours, average 2-3 hours.
        4. Inactivation of toxin: Not inactivated by normal cooking times and temperatures.
        5. Foods usually involved: Ham, poultry, cream-filled bakery goods, protein salads.

II. Bacterial Food Infections
    A. Salmonellosis
        1. Salmonella typhimurium, Salmonella enteritidis, and others.
        2. Symptoms: Abdominal pain, diarrhea, chills, fever, frequent vomiting, and prostration.
        3. Onset of symptoms: 7 to 12 hours; average 12 to 24 hours.
        4. Inactivation: 165° F for period of cooking or heating.
        5. Foods usually involved: poultry, poultry products, inadequately cooked egg products, meats, and other foods.

B. Bacillary dysentery (Shigellosis)
   1. Various species of Shigella (Shigella dysenteriae, Shigella sonnei, and others.)
   2. Symptoms: Diarrhea, bloody stools, fever.
   3. Onset of symptoms: 1 to 7 days; average 2-3 days.
   4. Inactivation: 165° for period of cooking.
   5. Foods usually involved: Moist prepared foods and dairy products contaminated with excreta from carrier.
C. Streptococcal Infections (Scarlet fever or septic sore throat)
   1. Certain strains of beta-hemolytic streptococci
   2. Symptoms: Fever, sore throat.
   3. Onset of symptoms: 1 to 7 days; average 3 days.
   4. Inactivation: 165° F for period of cooking.
   5. Foods usually involved: Food contaminated with nasal or oral discharges from a case or carrier; raw milk from infected cows.
D. Enterococci (Fecal Streptococci)
   1. Various strains of Streptococcus fecalis.
   2. Symptoms: Nausea, sometimes vomiting and diarrhea.
   3. Onset of symptoms: 2 to 18 hours
   4. Inactivation: 165° F for period of cooking.
   5. Foods usually involved: Prepared food products contaminated with excreta.
E. Clostridium Perfringens
   1. Growth of Clostridium perfringens in food under anaerobic conditions.
   2. Symptoms: Acute abdominal pain and diarrhea, nausea, and rarely, vomiting.
   3. Onset of symptoms: 8 to 22 hours; average 8-12 hours.
   4. Inactivation: Variable, usually not inactivated by cooking temperatures.
   5. Foods usually involved: Poultry and meat products.

III. Viral Infections
   A. Infectious Hepatitis
      1. Virus of infectious hepatitis
      2. Symptoms: Fever, lack of appetite, malaise, fatigue, headache, nausea, chills, vomiting, jaundice may be present.
      3. Onset of symptoms: 14 to 35 days, average 25 days.
      4. Inactivation: not known.
      5. Foods usually involved: Shellfish (oyster, clams, mussels) taken from polluted waters and eaten raw; foods contaminated with excreta from an infected person.

IV. Parasitic Infections
   A. Trichinosis
      1. Trichinella spiralis.
      2. Symptoms: Nausea, vomiting, diarrhea (during digestion of trichinae); muscular pains, fever labored breathing, swelling of eyelids. Occassionally fatal.

3. Onset of symptoms: 2 to 28 days; average 9 days.
4. Inactivation: All parts of meat must reach 150° F to destroy cysts.
5. Foods usually involved: Raw or insufficiently cooked pork and pork products. Whale, seal, bear, and walrus meat have also been implicated.

B. Tapeworm (Taeniasis)
1. Taenia saginata (beef tapeworm); Taenia solium (pork tapeworm).
2. Symptoms: Beef tapeworm: abdominal pain, hungry feeling, vague discomfort. Pork tapeworm: varies from mild chronic digestive disorder to severe malaise.
3. Onset of symptoms: Several weeks.
4. Inactivation: All parts of the meat must reach 150° F.
5. Foods usually involved: Raw or insufficiently cooked beef or pork containing live larvae.

C. Fish Tapeworm Disease (Diphyllobothriasis)
1. Diphyllobothrium latum.
2. Symptoms: Anemia in heavy infections.
3. Onset of symptoms: 3 to 6 weeks.
4. Inactivation: All parts of fish meat must reach 150° F.
5. Foods usually involved: Raw or insufficiently cooked fish containing live larvae.

D. Amebic Dysentery
1. Entamoeba histolytica
2. Symptoms: Chronic diarrhea of varying severity or diarrhea alternating with constipation; occasionally fatal.
3. Onset of symptoms: 5 days to several months; average 3 to 4 weeks.
4. Inactivation: Cysts on vegetables destroyed by heating 30 minutes in water at 122° F.
5. Foods usually involved: Moist food contaminated with excreta from a carrier; contaminated water.

V. Poisonous Plants
A. Mushroom poisoning
1. Symptoms caused by phalloidine and other alkaloids of certain species of mushrooms.
2. Symptoms: Salivation: abdominal pain, intense thirst, nausea, vomiting, water stools, excessive perspiration, flow of tears; often fatal.
3. Onset of symptoms: 15 minutes to 15 hours.
4. Inactivation: Not inactivated by cooking.
5. Foods usually involved: Wild mushrooms, such as Amanita phalloides and Amanita muscaria, which are mistaken for edible mushrooms.

VI. Dangerous Chemicals
A. Antimony

1. Occurrence: Chipped grey enamelware in contact with acid foods and beverages.
2. Symptoms: Nausea, violent vomiting.
3. Onset of symptoms: 15 to 30 minutes.
4. Duration: Several hours.

B. Cadmium
1. Occurence: Cadmium used as plating, e.g., ice cube trays, dissolved in food or beverages.
2. Symptoms: Propulsive vomiting, nausea.
3. Onset of symptoms: 15 to 30 minutes.
4. Duration: Several hours.

C. Cyanide
1. Occurrence: Foods contaminated with silver polish containing cyanide.
2. Symptoms: Cyanosis (bluish discoloration of skin) mental confusion, glassy eyes, blue lips, often fatal.
3. Onset of symptoms: Almost instantaneous.

D. Lead
1. Occurrence: Food containers, solder containing more that 5% lead used on food equipment.
2. Symptoms: Blue line on gums, cramps in stomach, bowels, and legs, constipation, loss of appetite, headache, irritability.

E. Copper
1. Occurrence: Foods contaminated by copper salts (verdigris) on unclean copper utensils; beverages containing copper salts due to action of carbonation (carbon dioxide and water) on copper tubing.
2. Symptoms: Vomiting, abdominal pain, diarrhea.
3. Onset of symptoms: Usually immediate.

F. Zinc
1. Occurrence (rare): Acid foods cooked in galvanized (zinc-plated) utensils.
2. Symptoms: Dizziness, nausea, vomiting, tightness of throat.
3. Onset of symptoms: a few minutes to two hours.

G. Nitrites
1. Occurrence: Contamination of foods by nitrates, or nitrites used as a preservative in excess of 200 parts per million.
2. Symptoms: Cyanosis, shock, lowered blood pressure, methemoglobinemia (hemoglobin in blood combines with nitrites instead of oxygen producing internal asphyxiation.)
3. Onset of symptoms: 15 to 30 minutes.

H. Pesticides
1. Occurence: Foods accidentally contaminated with pesticides.

VII. Dangerous Animals
A. Shellfish
1. Occurrence: Shellfish grown in polluted waters, if eaten raw, can cause typhoid fever, cholera, and infectious hepatitis.

DISEASE PREVENTION IN RESTAURANTS

WHAT ARE THE MOST FAVORABLE CONDITIONS FOR THE GROWTH OF DISEASE GERMS?

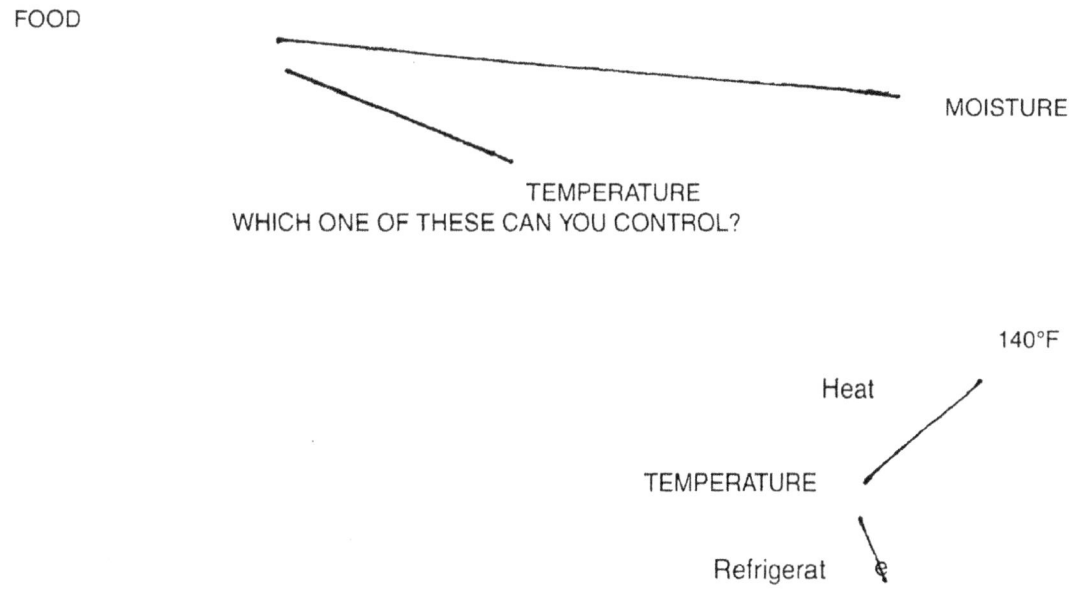

FOOD

MOISTURE

TEMPERATURE
WHICH ONE OF THESE CAN YOU CONTROL?

140°F
Heat

TEMPERATURE

Refrigerat
45°F

YOU CAN SPREAD DISEASE BY:

Carelessness
    Not washing hands before touching food, dishes, or utensils. Leaving food unprotected from dust, sneezes, rodents and insects. Using dirty equipment.
    Leaving food stand at room temperature.

Working when sick or with open sores
    Through food you infect.
    By direct contact with customers and fellow workers.
    By contaminating dishes and utensils.

YOU CAN GET DISEASE BY:
    Infection from a sick customer or fellow worker.
    Careless handling of soiled dishes.
    Eating infected food.
    Infection from rats, mice and insects.

FOOD PROTECTION

To Prevent Bacterial Food Poisoning and Infection
    Keep harmful bacteria out if possible.
    Keep them from growing if they do get in.
    How? By watching time and temperature, as well as cleanliness.

TIME
    Don't let food ready to serve stand longer than one hour at room temperature.

TEMPERATURE
>   Keep cold foods refrigerated at 45° F or lower until they are served.
>
>   Keep hot foods hot, above 140° F, until they are served.
>   WATCH THESE FOODS ESPECIALLY-BACTERIA LOVE THEM!
>   Cream filled or custard filled pastries, cakes and puddings.
>   Any dish made with cream sauce.
>   Meats, poultry and fish.
>   Dressing for poultry or meat.
>   Sandwiches, sandwich filling.

To Prevent Chemical Food Poisoning
>   Be sure all poisons are clearly labeled.
>   Never store poisons in food preparation areas.
>   Don't use insect sprays over or near food.
>   Don't keep any acid food or drink in a galvanized container.

SAFE STORAGE METHODS
>   Clean storage rooms, used for no other purpose.
>   All food stored at least six inches above floor.
>   Clean, neat refrigerator.
>   Food refrigerated in shallow containers, always covered.
>   Refrigerator shelves free of shelf-coverings.

SEVEN EASY RULES FOR SAFE FOOD
1. KEEP COLD FOODS COLD-HOT FOODS HOT. Don't let foods stand at room temperature.
2. KEEP HANDS CLEAN and touch food with hands as little as possible.
3. Don't let anyone with a skin infection or a cold handle food.
4. Keep kitchen, dining rooms and storage rooms free from rats, mice and insects.
5. Protect food from sneezes, customer handling, and dust.
6. Be sure poisons are well labeled and kept away from food preparation areas.
7. Wash dishes, glasses, silver and utensils by methods recommended by your health department.

FOOD PURCHASING GUIDE

TABLE OF CONTENTS

	Page
Introduction	1
Explanation of Terms Used	1
Quantities to purchase for 25 and 100 portions	4
Table 1: Meat	4
Table 2: Combination foods containing meat	9
Table 3: Poultry	11
Table 4: Combination foods containing poultry	13
Table 5: Fish and shellfish	14
Table 6: Eggs	17
Table 7: Nuts	18
Table 8: Dairy products	19
Table 9: Vegetables—fresh	21
Table 10: Vegetables—canned	24
Table 11: Vegetables—frozen	27
Table 12: Vegetables—dried	29
Table 13: Fruits—fresh	30
Table 14: Fruits—canned	33
Table 15: Fruits—frozen	35
Table 16: Fruits—dried	37
Table 17: Flour, cereals and mixes	38
Table 18: Bakery foods	41
Table 19: Fats and oils	42
Table 20: Sugars and sweets	43
Table 21: Beverages	44
Other useful information for estimating food quantities	45
Table 22: Conversion factors for computing the number of purchase units needed for portions of various sizes	45
Table 23: Cost per portion for food priced from 10 cents to $2 per purchase unit	45
Table 24: Beef—approximate percentages edible	46
Table 25: Lamb—approximate percentages edible	46
Table 26: Pork—approximate percentages edible	46
Table 27: Vegetables and fruits—approximate amounts	47
Table 28: Common can and jar sizes	49
Ounce equivalents in decimal parts of pound	49
Approximate scoop equivalents	49
Common food-measure equivalents	49

FOOD PURCHASING GUIDE FOR GROUP FEEDING

INTRODUCTION

This food purchasing guide contains information useful in estimating the number of purchase units of foods to buy to serve a specific number of portions.

Foods have been listed by major groups in tables 1 through 21. Within each group the individual foods are arranged alphabetically. For each purchase unit specified, these data are given: Weight of the unit of purchase, yield from weight "as purchased" to weight "as served," size and description of portion, number of portions from each purchase unit, and the approximate number of purchase units needed for 25 and 100 portions. Table 22 presents an easy method for computing the number of purchase units needed for portions of sizes other than those given in tables 1 through 21. Table 23 gives an easy method for finding the cost of a portion of food.

The yields of edible meat from the carcass of wholesale cuts of beef, lamb, and pork given in tables 24 to 26 are useful to institutions that raise their own meat animals or purchase meat by the carcass or wholesale cuts. The yields of canned and frozen products from fresh vegetables and fruits given in table 27 are useful to institutions that produce and preserve their own vegetables and fruits.

Table 28 gives the common can and jar sizes, and on page 48 equivalents used frequently by food planners are given.

EXPLANATION OF TERMS USED

Food as purchased. Foods are described in the forms as purchasedfresh, frozen, canned, dried. Further descriptive information that would affect the yield is also given, such as: for meatsbone in, bone out; for carrotswith tops, without tops; and for potatoesto be pared, ready-to-cook.

Unit of purchase. Sizes of cans, packages, or other containers and weights of units in common use in the wholesale and retail markets are given. Usually, data for the 1-pound unit are given; from these the yield of any weight purchase unit can be determined.

Weight per unit. Weights given for purchase units refer to weights as purchased on the market. Legal weights for contents of such units as bushels, lugs, crates, and boxes may vary in different States. The lowest of these weights is used to insure that the specified portions can be obtained. Weights for canned goods are the same as those given as net weight on the label.

Yield as served. Yield as served refers to the weight of food "as served" as a percentage of weight "as purchased." Absence of information in this column means a weight yield was not used to determine the number of portions per purchase unit.

The same item "as purchased" may have more than one yield, depending on the way it is served.

For example, 1 pound of fresh carrots without tops will yield 0.75 pound cooked and 0.82 pound grated raw.

The yield does not always refer to a serving that is all edible. For example, because pork chops are usually served with bone, the yield given is the percentage of the "as purchased" weight represented by the cooked chop with the bone in. On the other hand, the yield of the chuck roast, usually served without bone, is, the percentage of the chuck "as purchased" that is, cooked and served without the bone. For meats, the yield of cooked lean is given in an additional column.

The amount of ready-to-serve food obtained from a given amount of food "as purchased" may vary widely, depending on the size, grade, and general condition of the food, discards in preparation, and the method and time of cooking. For yields given in this Handbook, it is assumed that the food used is in good condition (free of rot, insect infestation, bruising), that only usual amounts are discarded in preparation, and that usual cooking methods and time of cooking for the food specified are used.

For yields given, discard of inedible material such as bones, pits, and shells, except where otherwise specified, is assumed. Also assumed as discard are some foods that could be eaten but are usually discarded, such as potato parings and outer leaves of vegetables.

The yields presented in these tables were obtained from Agriculture Handbook No. 102, "Food Yields Summarized by Different Stages of Preparation," and unpublished data from the Agricultural Research Service of the U.S. Department of Agriculture and from the Fish and Wildlife Service of the U.S. Department of the Interior. Yields for commercially prepared meat combinations (table 2) are based on minimum meat requirements for meat food products packed for interstate shipment under Federal inspection. Contents of cooked poultry meat in poultry products are based on regulations governing the inspection of poultry and poultry products, effective January 1, 1965.

Size and description of portion. Weight or volume of portion commonly used is given. This portion for most foods refers to the amount served. For foods often used in combination with other foods, such as canned milk, nonfat dry milk, eggs, nuts, flour, and uncooked cereals, a portion refers to a measure commonly called for in institution recipes.

For meat, poultry, and fish, data for two sizes of portions are given. The larger portion may be appropriate for an adult serving; the smaller may be sufficient for a child's meal or a luncheon menu. The size of meat portions is given (1) in ounces of cooked meat as served including fat and, in some cases, bone; and (2) in ounces of conked lean only.

For vegetables and fruits, the portion size is generally the weight of 1/2 cup rounded to the nearest ounce. It is assumed that canned, cooked fresh, and cooked dried fruits are served with sirup, and that heated canned vegetables and cooked fresh and frozen vegetables are served drained. It is assumed that solid-pack fruits are served without liquid.

Institutions that use a different portion size than those given may adjust the amount to purchase by the method given in table 22.

Portions per purchase unit. In obtaining the portions per purchase unit or the yield of a purchase unit in portions, average quantities of refuse and usual weight losses in cooking are assumed. The number of portions may vary from that shown if the condition of the food purchased is poor or unusual waste occurs in preparation and cooking.

To obtain the number of units to purchase, the number of portions per purchase unit can be divided into the number of persons to be served. This may be the most practical method of computing the amount to purchase if the institution does not serve 25 or 100 persons or easy multiples of these numbers of persons.

For example, if 1 pound of meat will serve 2.57 portions of the size desired, the food manager of an institution serving 580 persons may divide 580 by 2.57 to get the amount of meat needed 226 pounds. It is because of such use of these figures, and not because the figures represent this degree of accuracy, that they have been carried to the nearest one-hundredth of a portion. Had the portions per pound of meat been rounded to the nearest number of portions per pound (3), the food manager would purchase only 193 pounds of meat33 pounds short of the best estimate of his needs.

The number of portions per purchase unit can be used with the cost of the purchase unit and table 23 in obtaining the cost for one portion.

Approximate purchase units for 25 and 100 portions. These columns represent 25 and 100 divided by the number of portions per purchase unit in the preceding column. The resulting number of purchase units is always carried to the next even one-quarter (1/4) unit. Thus, the number of purchase units specified is always sufficient if the yield and portion size are as shown in the table. If the purchase units serve many portions, such as a bushel of apples or a No. 10 can of vegetables, this 1/4 purchase unit may be very significant. If the purchase unit serves few portions as in the case of a pound of meat, the 1/4 purchase unit is relatively unimportant.

QUANTITIES TO PURCHASE FOR 25 AND 100 PORTIONS

Table 1.—MEAT

Meat as purchased	Unit of purchase	Yield, cooked: As served	Yield, cooked: Lean only	Description of portion as served	Size of portion: As served	Size of portion: Lean only	Portions per purchase unit	Approximate purchase units for—: 25 portions	Approximate purchase units for—: 100 portions
BEEF, FRESH OR FROZEN									
		Percent	*Percent*		*Ounces*	*Ounces*	*Number*	*Number*	*Number*
Brisket:									
Corned, bone out	Pound	60	41	Simmered	4	2.8	2.40	10½	41¾
					3	2.1	3.20	8	31¼
Fresh:									
Bone in	do	52	36	Simmered, bone out	4	2.8	2.08	12¼	48¼
					3	2.1	2.77	9¼	36¼
Bone out	do	67	46	Simmered	4	2.8	2.68	9½	37½
					3	2.1	3.57	7¼	28¼
Ground beef:									
Lean	do	75	75	Broiled	3	3.0	4.00	6¼	25
					2	2.0	6.00	4¼	16¾
Regular	do	72	72	Pan-fried	3	3.0	3.84	6¾	26¼
					2	2.0	5.76	4½	17½
Heart	do	39	39		2	2.0	3.12	8¼	32¼
Kidney	do	39	39		2	2.0	3.12	8¼	32¼
Liver	do	69	69	Braised	3	3.0	3.68	7	27¼
					2	2.0	5.52	4¾	18¼
Oxtails	do	29	29		(1)	(1)	(1)	(1)	(1)
Roasts:									
Chuck:									
Bone in	do	52	42	Roasted, moist heat, bone out	4	3.2	2.08	12¼	48¼
					3	2.4	2.77	9¼	36¼
Bone out	do	67	54	Roasted, moist heat	4	3.2	2.68	9½	37½
					3	2.4	3.57	7¼	28¼
7-Rib (shortribs removed):									
Bone in	do	65	42	Roasted, dry heat, bone out	4	2.6	2.60	9¾	38½
					3	1.9	3.47	7¼	29
Bone out	do	73	47	Roasted, dry heat	4	2.6	2.92	8¾	34¼
					3	1.9	3.89	6½	25¾
Round:									
Bone in	do	69	56	Roasted, dry heat, medium, bone out	4	3.3	2.76	9¼	36¼
					3	2.5	3.68	7	27¼
Bone out	do	73	60	Roasted, dry heat, medium	4	3.3	2.92	8¾	34¼
					3	2.5	3.89	6½	25¾
Rump:									
Bone in	do	58	43	Roasted, dry heat, bone out	4	3.0	2.32	11	43¼
					3	2.2	3.09	8¼	32½
Bone out	do	73	55	Roasted, dry heat	4	3.0	2.92	8¾	34¼
					3	2.2	3.89	6½	25¾
Shortribs	do	67	32	Braised, bone in	6	2.9	1.79	14	56
					4	1.9	2.68	9½	37½

See footnotes at end of table.

TABLE 1.—MEAT—Continued

Meat as purchased	Unit of purchase	Yield, cooked		Description of portion as served	Size of portion		Portions per purchase unit	Approximate purchase units for—	
		As served	Lean only		As served	Lean only		25 portions	100 portions
		Percent	Percent		Ounces	Ounces	Number	Number	Number
BEEF, FRESH OR FROZEN—Continued									
Steaks:									
Club:									
Bone in	Pound	73	33	Broiled, bone in	6	2.7	1.95	13	51½
					4	1.8	2.92	8¾	34¼
Bone out	do	73	42	Broiled	4	2.3	2.92	8¾	34¼
					3	1.7	3.89	6½	25¾
Flank	do	67	67	Braised	3	3.0	3.57	7¼	28¼
					2	2.0	5.36	4¾	18¾
Hip:									
Bone in	do	73	32	Broiled, bone in	6	2.6	1.95	13	51½
					4	1.8	2.92	8¾	34¼
Bone out	do	73	40	Broiled	4	2.2	2.92	8¾	34¼
					3	1.6	3.89	6½	25¾
Minute, cubed	do	75	75	Pan-fried	3	3.0	4.00	6½	25
					2	2.0	6.00	4¼	16¾
Porterhouse:									
Bone in	do	73	36	Broiled, bone in	8	4.0	1.46	17¼	68½
					6	3.0	1.95	13	51½
					4	2.0	2.92	8¾	34¼
					3	1.7	3.89	6½	25¾
Bone out	do	73	42	Broiled	4	2.3	2.92	8¾	34¼
Round:									
Bone in	do	73	56	Broiled, bone in	4	3.1	2.92	8¾	34¼
					3	2.3	3.89	6½	25¾
Bone out	do	73	60	Broiled	4	3.3	2.92	8¾	34¼
					3	2.5	3.89	6½	25¾
Sirloin (wedge and round):									
Bone in	do	73	44	Broiled, bone in	6	3.6	1.95	13	51½
					4	2.4	2.92	8¾	34¼
Bone out	do	73	48	Broiled	4	2.6	2.92	8¾	34¼
					3	2.0	3.89	6½	25¾
T-bone:									
Bone in	do	73	34	Broiled, bone in	8	3.8	1.46	17¼	68½
					6	2.8	1.95	13	51½
					4	1.9	2.92	8¾	34¼
Bone out	do	73	41	Broiled	4	2.2	2.92	8¾	34¼
					3	1.7	3.89	6½	25¾
Stew meat (chuck), bone out	do	67	54	Cooked, moist heat	3	2.4	3.57	7¼	28¼
					2	1.6	5.36	4¾	18¾
Tongue:									
Fresh	do	59	59	do	3	3.0	3.15	8	31¾
					2	2.0	4.72	5½	21¼
Smoked	do	51	51	do	3	3.0	2.72	9¼	37
					2	2.0	4.08	6¼	24¾

BEEF, CANNED[3]									
Beef, corned	do	100	100	Heated	3	3.0	5.33	4¾	19
					2	2.0	8.00	3¼	12⅓
	6-pound can	100	100	do	3	3.0	32.00	1	3¼
BEEF, DRIED									
Beef, chipped	Pound	125	125	Cooked, moist heat	3	3.0	6.67	3¾	15
					2	2.0	10.00	2½	10
LAMB, FRESH OR FROZEN									
Chops:									
Loin	do	76	41	Broiled, bone in	5.0	2.7	2.43	10½	41¼
Rib	do	76	34	do	5.0	2.2	2.43	10½	41¼
Shoulder	do	70	41	do	5.0	2.9	2.24	11¼	44¾
Ground lamb	do	68	68	Broiled patties	3.0	3.0	3.63	7	27¾
					2.0	2.0	5.44	4¾	18⅓
Roasts:									
Leg:									
Bone in	do	54	45	Roasted, bone out	4.0	3.3	2.16	11¾	46½
					3.0	2.5	2.88	8¾	34¾
Bone out	do	70	58	Roasted	4.0	3.3	2.80	9	35¾
					3.0	2.5	3.73	6¾	27
Shoulder:									
Bone in	do	55	41	Roasted, bone out	4.0	3.0	2.20	11½	45½
					3.0	2.2	2.93	8¾	34¼
Bone out	do	70	52	Roasted	4.0	3.0	2.80	9	35¾
					3.0	2.2	3.73	6¾	27
Stew meat,[3] bone out	do	66		Simmered	3.0		3.52	7¼	28½
					2.0		5.28	4¾	19
PORK, CURED (MILD)									
Bacon (24 slices per pound)	do	32		Fried or broiled	2 slices		12.00	2¼	8½
Canadian bacon	do	63	63	Broiled, sliced	2	2.0	5.04	5	20
					1	1.0	10.08	2½	10
Ham:									
Bone in	do	67	54	Roasted, slices and pieces	4	2.9	2.68	9½	37½
					3	2.2	3.57	7¼	28¼
	do	56	44	Roasted, slices	4	2.4	2.24	11¼	44¾
					3	1.8	2.99	8½	33½
Bone out	do	77	72	Roasted, slices and pieces	4	2.9	3.08	8¼	32½
					3	2.2	4.11	6¼	24½
	do	64	60	Roasted, slices	4	2.4	2.56	10	39¼
					3	1.8	3.41	7½	29½
Ground	do	77	77	Patties	3	3.0	4.11	6¼	24½
					2	2.0	6.16	4¼	16¼
Shoulder, Boston butt:									
Bone in	do	67	52	Roasted, bone out	4	3.1	2.68	9½	37½
					3	2.3	3.57	7¼	28¼
Bone out	do	74	58	Roasted	4	3.1	2.96	8½	34
					3	2.3	3.95	6½	25½
Shoulder, picnic:									
Bone in	do	56	41	Roasted, bone out	4	3.9	2.24	11¼	44¾
					3	2.2	2.99	8⅓	33⅓
Bone out	do	74	53	Roasted	4	3.9	2.96	8½	34
					3	2.2	3.95	6½	25½

See footnotes at end of table.

Table 1.—MEAT—Continued

Meat as purchased	Unit of purchase	Yield, cooked: As served	Yield, cooked: Lean only	Description of portion as served	Size of portion: As served	Size of portion: Lean only	Portions per purchase unit	Approximate purchase units for—: 25 portions	Approximate purchase units for—: 100 portions
		Percent	*Percent*		*Ounces*	*Ounces*	*Number*	*Number*	*Number*
PORK, FRESH									
Chops:									
Loin	Pound	69	42	Broiled, bone in	5	3.0	2.21	11½	45¼
					3	1.8	3.68	7	27¼
Rib	do	70	37	do	5	2.6	2.24	11¼	44¾
					3	1.6	3.73	6¾	27
Cutlet, tenderloin	do	75	75	Broiled	3	3.0	4.00	6¼	25
					2	2.0	6.00	4¼	16¾
Ground pork	do	57	57	do	3	3.0	3.04	8¼	33
					2	2.0	4.56	5½	22
Liver	do	60	60	Pan- or oven-fried	3	3.0	3.20	8	31¼
					2	2.0	4.80	5¼	21
Roasts:									
Ham:									
Bone in	do	54	40	Roasted, bone out	4	3.0	2.16	11¾	46½
					3	2.2	2.88	8¾	34¾
Bone out	do	68	50	Roasted	4	3.0	2.72	9¼	37
					3	2.2	3.63	7	27¾
Loin:									
Bone in	do	68	37	Roasted, bone in	5	2.8	2.18	11½	46
					4	2.2	2.72	9¼	37
	do	47	37	Roasted, bone out	4	3.2	1.88	13½	53¼
					3	2.4	2.51	10	40
Bone out	do	68	54	Roasted	4	3.2	2.72	9¼	37
					3	2.4	3.63	7	27¾
Shoulder, Boston butt:									
Bone in	do	62	49	Roasted, bone out	4	3.2	2.48	10¼	40½
					3	2.4	3.31	7¾	30¼
Bone out	do	68	54	Roasted	4	3.2	2.72	9¼	37
					3	2.4	3.63	7	27¾
Shoulder, picnic:									
Bone in	do	47	35	Simmered, bone out	4	3.0	1.88	13½	53¼
					3	2.2	2.51	10	40
Bone out	do	64	47	Simmered	4	3.0	2.56	10	39¼
					3	2.2	3.41	7½	29½
Sausage:									
Brown and serve	do	81	81	Heated	3	3.0	4.32	6	23¼
					2	2.0	6.48	4	15½
Bulk or link	do	48	48	Oven-fried	3	3.0	2.56	10	39¼
					2	2.0	3.84	6¾	26¼
Spareribs	do	66	26	Braised, bone in	6	[4] 2.3	1.76	14¼	57
					4	[4] 1.6	2.64	9½	38
PORK, CANNED [5]									
Ham, chopped	do	100	100	Sliced	3	3.0	5.33	4¾	19
					2	2.0	8.00	3¼	12½

Ham, smoked	do	77	75	Slices and pieces	3	2.9	4.11	6¼	24½
					2	1.9	6.16	4¼	16¼
	do	73	71	Slices	3	2.9	3.89	6½	25¾
					2	1.9	5.84	4½	17¼
Pork luncheon meat (with natural juices).	do	89	89	Unheated	3	3.0	4.75	5½	21¼
					2	2.0	7.12	3¾	14¼
SAUSAGES									
Frankfurters:									
8 per pound	do	98		2 frankfurters			4.00	6¼	25
				1 frankfurter			8.00	3¼	12½
10 per pound	do	98		2 frankfurters			5.00	5	20
				1 frankfurter			10.00	2½	10
Luncheon meats (all meat varieties).	do	100	100		3	3.0	5.33	4¾	19
					2	2.0	8.00	3¼	12½
Vienna sausage (all meat)	Pound (drained weight).	100	100	About 4 sausages	2	2.0	8.00	3¼	12½
				About 2 sausages	1	1.0	16.00	1¾	6¼
VEAL, FRESH OR FROZEN									
Chops:									
Loin	Pound	78	47	Broiled, bone in	5	3.0	2.50	10	40
					3	1.8	4.16	6	24¼
Rib	do	69	38	do	5	2.8	2.21	11½	45¾
					3	1.6	3.68	7	27¼
Shoulder	do	66	40	do	5	3.0	2.11	12	47½
					3	1.8	3.52	7¼	28½
Cutlet, bone out	do	75	75	Broiled	4	3.0	3.00	8½	33½
					3	2.2	4.00	6¼	25
Ground	do	64	64	Oven- or pan-fried	3	3.0	3.41	7½	29½
					2	2.0	5.12	5	19¾
Heart	do	35	35	Braised	2	2.0	2.80	9	35¾
Liver, calf	do	58	58	Fried or braised	3	3.0	3.09	8¼	32½
					2	2.0	4.64	5½	21¾
Roasts:									
Chuck (shoulder):									
Bone in	do	46	40	Braised, bone out	4	3.4	1.84	13¾	54½
					3	2.6	2.45	10¼	41
Bone out	do	66	56	Braised	4	3.4	2.64	9½	38
					3	2.6	3.52	7¼	28½
Leg:									
Bone in	do	44	36	Roasted, bone out	4	3.3	1.76	14¼	57
					3	2.5	2.35	10¾	42¾
Bone out	do	66	54	Roasted	4	3.3	2.64	9½	38
					3	2.5	3.52	7¼	28½
Plate (breast):									
Bone in	do	45	33	Stewed, bone out	4	2.9	1.80	14	55¾
					3	2.2	2.40	10½	41¾
Bone out	do	66	48	Stewed	4	2.9	2.64	9½	38
					3	2.2	3.52	7¼	28½
Stew meat	do	66	48	do	4	2.9	2.64	9½	38
					3	2.2	3.52	7¼	28½

[1] Size of portion and number of portions per purchase unit are determined by use.
[2] For combination foods including beef, see p. 8.
[3] Breast, flank.
[4] Fat and lean.
[5] For combination foods including pork, see p. 8.

TABLE 2.—COMBINATION FOODS CONTAINING MEAT

Meat combinations, canned or frozen, as purchased	Unit of purchase	Weight per unit [1]	Cooked meat	Size of portion	Meat in portion	Portions per purchase unit	Approximate purchase units for— 25 portions	100 portions
		Pounds	*Percent*	*Ounces*	*Ounces*	*Number*	*Number*	*Number*
Beans with frankfurters in sauce	Pound	1.00	20	8	1.6	2.00	12½	50
	No. 3 cylinder	3.12	20	8	1.6	6.24	4¼	16¼
	No. 10 can	6.75	20	8	1.6	13.50	2	7½
Beans with ham in sauce	Pound	1.00	12	8	1.0	2.00	12½	50
	No. 3 cylinder	3.19	12	8	1.0	6.38	4	15¾
Beans with meat in chili sauce	Pound	1.00	8	8	.6	2.00	12½	50
	No. 10 can	6.50	8	8	.6	13.00	2	7¾
Beef goulash:								
Canned	Pound	1.00	18	8	1.4	2.00	12½	50
	No. 3 cylinder	3.12	18	8	1.4	6.24	4¼	16¼
Frozen	Carton	5.00	18	8	1.4	10.00	2½	10
	do	6.75	18	9	1.6	12.00	2¼	8½
	do	8.25	18	11	2.0	12.00	2¼	8½
Beef stew	Pound	1.00	18	8	1.4	2.00	12½	50
	No. 3 cylinder	3.12	18	8	1.4	6.24	4¼	16¼
	No. 10 can	6.62	18	8	1.4	13.24	2	7¾
Beef with barbecue sauce	Pound	1.00	50	6	3.0	2.67	9½	37½
	No. 3 cylinder	3.25	50	6	3.0	8.67	3	11¾
	No. 10 can	6.50	50	6	3.0	17.33	1½	6
Beef with gravy	Pound	1.00	50	6	3.0	2.67	9½	37½
	No. 3 cylinder	3.00	50	6	3.0	8.00	3¼	12¾
	No. 10 can	6.50	50	6	3.0	17.33	1½	6
Brunswick stew	Pound	1.00	18	8	1.4	2.00	12½	50
	No. 10 can	6.62	18	8	1.4	13.24	2	7¾
Chili con carne	Pound	1.00	28	8	2.2	2.00	12½	50
	No. 3 cylinder	3.19	28	8	2.2	6.38	4	15¾
	No. 10 can	6.75	28	8	2.2	13.50	2	7½
Chili con carne with beans	Pound	1.00	18	8	1.4	2.00	12½	50
	No. 3 cylinder	3.19	18	8	1.4	6.38	4	15¾
	No. 10 can	6.75	18	8	1.4	13.50	2	7½
Chili mac	Pound	1.00	18	8	1.4	2.00	12½	50
	No. 3 cylinder	3.19	18	8	1.4	6.38	4	15¾
	No. 10 can	6.50	18	8	1.4	13.00	2	7¾

Chop suey or chow mein vegetables with meat:								
Canned	Pound	1.00	8	8	.6	2.00	12½	50
	No. 3 cylinder	3.06	8	8	.6	6.12	4¼	16½
Frozen	Carton	5.00	8	8	.6	10.00	2½	10
Hash, corn beef, roast beef, beef	Pound	1.00	35	7	2.4	2.29	11¼	44¼
	No. 3 cylinder	3.19	35	7	2.4	7.29	3½	14
	No. 10 can	6.50	35	7	2.4	14.86	1¾	7
Lamb stew	Pound	1.00	18	8	1.4	2.00	12½	50
	No. 3 cylinder	3.19	18	8	1.4	6.38	4	15¾
	No. 10 can	6.62	18	8	1.4	13.24	2	7¾
Macaroni and beef in tomato sauce	Pound	1.00	8	8	.6	2.00	12½	50
	No. 10 can	6.50	8	8	.6	13.00	2	7¾
Meatballs with gravy:								
Canned	Pound	1.00 (10 count)	38	6	2.3 (4 count)	2.67	9½	37½
	No. 10 can	6.50 (70 count)	38	6	2.3 (4 count)	17.33	1½	6
Frozen	Carton	8.00 (160 count)	38	6	2.3 (7½ count)	21.33	1¼	5
	do	10.00 (100 count)	38	6	2.3 (4 count)	26.67	1	4
Pork with barbecue sauce:								
Canned	Pound	1.00	50	6	3.0	2.67	9½	37½
	No. 3 cylinder	3.19	50	6	3.0	8.51	3	12
	No. 10 can	6.62	50	6	3.0	17.65	1½	5¾
In waxed tub (perishable)	4-pound tub	4.00	50	6	3.0	10.67	2½	9½
	5-pound tub	5.00	50	6	3.0	13.33	2	7¾
Pork with gravy	Pound	1.00	50	6	3.0	2.67	9½	37½
	No. 3 cylinder	3.12	50	6	3.0	8.32	3¼	12¼
	No. 10 can	6.50	50	6	3.0	17.33	1½	6
Ravioli with meat in sauce	Pound	1.00	7	8	.6	2.00	12½	50
	No. 3 cylinder	3.19	7	8	.6	6.38	4	15¾
		3.62	7	8	.6	7.24	3½	14
Spaghetti with meatballs and sauce	Pound	1.00	8	8	.6	2.00	12½	50
	No. 3 cylinder	3.19	8	8	.6	6.38	4	15¾
	No. 10 can	6.62	8	8	.6	13.24	2	7¾
Tamales, frozen	Pound	1.00 (4 tamales)	18	8 (2 tamales)	1.4	2.00	12½	50
	Carton	6.00 (24 tamales)	18	8 (2 tamales)	1.4	12.00	2¼	8½
	do	18.00	18	8	1.4	36.00	(2)	3
Tamales with gravy or sauce (Packed in sizes from 1½ oz. to 6 oz. per tamale).	Pound	1.00	14	8	1.1	2.00	12½	50
	No. 10 can	6.50	14	8	1.1	13.00	2	7¾

[1] Net weights of containers are not standardized and may vary depending on establishment preparing the product.
[2] Number of purchase units needed is less than one.

TABLE 3.—POULTRY

Poultry as purchased	Unit of purchase	Yield, as served	Description of portion as served	Size of portion: As served	Size of portion: Edible portion [1]	Portions per purchase unit	Approximate purchase units for— 25 portions	Approximate purchase units for— 100 portions
CHICKEN, FRESH OR FROZEN		*Percent*		*Ounces*	*Ounces*	*Number*	*Number*	*Number*
Live:								
Roasters	Pound	30	Boned, excludes neck and giblets.	3.0	3.0	1.60	15¾	62½
				2.0	2.0	2.40	10½	41¾
Stewers	do	34	Boned, includes neck and giblets.	3.0	3.0	1.81	14	55¼
				2.0	2.0	2.72	9¼	37
Ready-to-cook:								
Broilers	1½-pound bird	70	½ bird	8.3	5.4	2.00	12½	50
Fryers	Pound [2]	43	Boned	3.0	3.0	2.29	11	43¾
				2.0	2.0	3.44	7½	29¼
	2½-pound bird	65	¼ bird	5.8	3.9	4.00	6¼	25
			⅙ bird	3.9	2.6	6.00	4¼	16¾
			⅛ bird	2.9	1.9	8.00	3¼	12½
Parts (from 2½-pound bird):								
Breast half	Pound	67	With bone	3.2	2.6	3.35	7½	30
Drumstick	do	72	do	2.1	1.4	5.49	4¾	18¼
Thigh	do	68	do	2.2	1.6	4.95	5¼	20¼
Drumstick and thigh	do	70	do	4.3	3.1	2.60	9¾	38½
Wing	do	64	do	1.6	0.8	6.40	4	15¾
Back	do	49	do	2.5	1.3	3.14	8	32
Rib	do	65	do	2.5	1.3	4.16	6¼	24¼
Giblets:								
Gizzards	do	26		2	2	2.08	12¼	48¼
Hearts	do	38		2	2	3.04	8¼	33
Livers	do	65		2	2	5.20	5	19¼
Roasters	do	42	Boned, excludes neck and giblets.	3	3	2.24	11¼	44¾
				2	2	3.36	7½	30
Stewers	do	47	Boned, includes neck and giblets.	3	3	2.51	10	40
				2	2	3.76	6¾	26¾
CHICKEN, CANNED								
Boned	do	90	Meat	3	3	4.80	5¼	21
				2	2	7.20	3½	14
	Can (35 ounces)	90	do	3	3	10.50	2½	9¾
				2	2	15.75	1¾	6½
Boned, solid pack	Pound	95	do	3	3	5.07	5	19¾
				2	2	7.60	3½	13¼

Boned, with broth	do	80	do	3	3	4. 27	6	23½
				2	2	6. 40	4	15¾
Whole	do	32	do	3	3	1. 71	14¾	58½
				2	2	2. 56	10	39¼
TURKEY, FRESH OR FROZEN								
Live	do	36	Excludes neck and giblets	3	3	1. 92	13¼	52¼
				2	2	2. 88	8¾	34¾
Ready-to-cook: Roasters	do	47	do	3	3	2. 51	10	40
				2	2	3. 76	6¾	26¾
Parts: Breasts, whole	do	60		3	3	3. 20	8	31¼
				2	2	4. 80	5¼	21
Legs (thigh and drumstick)	do	48		3	3	2. 56	10	39¼
				2	2	3. 84	6¾	26¼
Giblets: Gizzards	do	34		2	2	2. 72	9¼	37
Hearts	do	38		2	2	3. 04	8¼	33
Livers	do	67		2	2	5. 36	4¾	18¾
TURKEY, FROZEN ONLY								
Stuffed, whole	do	33	Boned meat	3	3	1. 76	14¼	57
				2	2	2. 64	9½	38
Rolls, precooked	do	92	Meat	3	3	4. 91	5¼	20½
				2	2	7. 36	3½	13¾
Rolls, ready-to-cook	do	61	do	3	3	3. 25	7¾	31
				2	2	4. 88	5¼	20½
TURKEY, CANNED								
Boned	do	90	do	3	3	4. 80	5¼	21
				2	2	7. 20	3½	14
	Can (35 ounces)	90	do	3	3	10. 50	2½	9¾
				2	2	15. 75	1¾	6½
Boned, solid pack	Pound	95	do	3	3	5. 07	5	19¾
				2	2	7. 60	3½	13¼
Boned, with broth	do	80	do	3	3	4. 27	6	23½
				2	2	6. 40	4	15¾
OTHER POULTRY, FRESH OR FROZEN								
Duck, ready-to-cook	do	38	Boned, excludes neck and giblets.	3	3	2. 03	12½	49½
				2	2	3. 04	8¼	33
Goose, ready-to-cook	do	39	do	3	3	2. 08	12¼	48¼
				2	2	3. 12	8¼	32¼

[1] Includes edible skin.

[2] Based on 2½-pound bird as purchased; neck and giblets not served.

TABLE 4.—COMBINATION FOODS CONTAINING POULTRY

Poultry combinations, canned or frozen, as purchased	Unit of purchase [1]	Weight per unit	Cooked meat	Size of portion	Meat in portion	Portions per purchase unit	Approximate purchase units for—	
							25 portions	100 portions
		Pounds	Percent	Ounces	Ounces	Number	Number	Number
Chicken a la king	Pound	1.00	20	8	1.60	2.00	12½	50
Chickenburgers	do	1.00	100	3	3.00	5.33	4¾	19
Chicken cacciatore	do	1.00	20	8	1.60	2.00	12½	50
Chicken chop suey	do	1.00	4	8	.32	2.00	12½	50
Chicken chow mein	do	1.00	4	8	.32	2.00	12½	50
Chicken fricassee	do	1.00	20	8	1.60	2.00	12½	50
Chicken noodles or dumplings	do	1.00	15	8	1.20	2.00	12½	50
Chicken potpie	do	1.00	14	8	1.12	2.00	12½	50
Chicken stew	do	1.00	12	8	.96	2.00	12½	50
Chicken tamales	do	1.00	6	8	.48	2.00	12½	50
Creamed chicken	do	1.00	20	8	1.60	2.00	12½	50
Creamed turkey	do	1.00	20	8	1.60	2.00	12½	50
Minced chicken barbecue	do	1.00	40	3	1.20	5.33	4¾	19
Noodles or dumplings with chicken	do	1.00	6	8	.48	2.00	12½	50
Sliced chicken with gravy	do	1.00	35	6	2.10	2.67	9⅜	37½
Sliced turkey with gravy	do	1.00	35	6	2.10	2.67	9⅜	37½
Turkey a la king	do	1.00	20	8	1.60	2.00	12½	50
Turkey fricassee	do	1.00	20	8	1.60	2.00	12½	50
Turkey potpie	do	1.00	14	8	1.12	2.00	12½	50

[1] There is no standardization of can or carton sizes for canned and frozen poultry products. Information given for a pound may be related to the weight of the contents of the can or carton.

Table 5.—FISH AND SHELLFISH

Fish and shellfish as purchased	Unit of purchase	Weight per unit	Yield, as served	Portion as served	Portions per purchase unit	Approximate purchase units for— 25 portions	Approximate purchase units for— 100 portions
FISH, CANNED		*Pounds*	*Percent*		*Number*	*Number*	*Number*
Gefilte fish	16-ounce can (9¼ ounces drained).	1.00	58	3 ounces drained	3.08	8¼	32½
				2 ounces drained	4.62	5½	21¾
	32-ounce can (20½ ounces drained).	2.00	64	3 ounces drained	6.83	3¾	14¾
				2 ounces drained	10.25	2½	10
	51-ounce can (39 ounces drained).	3.19	76	3 ounces drained	13.00	2	7¾
				2 ounces drained	19.50	1⅓	5¼
Mackerel	15-ounce can (12½ ounces drained).	.94	83	3 ounces drained	4.17	6	24
				2 ounces drained	6.25	4	16
Salmon	3¾-ounce can (2¼ ounces drained).	.23	60	2¼ ounces drained	1.00	25	100
	16-ounce can (13 ounces drained).	1.00	81	3 ounces drained	4.33	6	23¼
				2 ounces drained	6.50	4	15½
	64-ounce can (50 ounces drained).	4.00	78	3 ounces drained	16.67	1½	6
				2 ounces drained	25.00	1	4
Sardines:							
Maine	3¾- to 4-ounce can (3¾ ounces drained).	.23 to .25	100	3 ounces drained	1.25	20	80
				2 ounces drained	1.87	13½	53½
	12-ounce can (10¼ ounces drained).	.75	90	3 ounces drained	3.58	7	28
				2 ounces drained	5.38	4¾	18¾
Pacific:							
In brine	15-ounce can (11½ ounces drained).	.94	77	3 ounces drained	3.83	6¾	26¼
				2 ounces drained	5.75	4½	17½
In mustard or tomato sauce	15-ounce can	.94	100	3 ounces	5.00	5	20
				2 ounces	7.50	3⅓	13⅓
Tuna	3½- to 4-ounce can (3¼ ounces drained).	.22 to .25	93	3¼ ounces drained	1.00	25	100
	6- to 7-ounce can (6 ounces drained).	.38 to .44	100	3 ounces drained	2.00	12½	50
				2 ounces drained	3.00	8⅓	33⅓
	60- to 66½-ounce can (58 ounces drained).	3.75 to 4.16	97	3 ounces drained	19.33	1⅓	5¼
				2 ounces drained	29.00	(1)	3½
FISH, DRIED							
Salt cod	Pound	1.00	72	3 ounces	3.84	6¾	26¼
				2 ounces	5.76	4½	17½
FISH, FRESH OR FROZEN							
Fillets	do	1.00	64	3 ounces	3.41	7⅓	29⅓
				2 ounces	5.12	5	19½
Steaks (backbone in)	do	1.00	[2] 58	3 ounces	3.09	8¼	32½
				2 ounces	4.64	5½	21¾
Dressed (scaled and eviscerated, usually head, tail, and fins removed).	do	1.00	[2] 45	3 ounces	2.40	10½	41¾
				2 ounces	3.60	7	28
Drawn (entrails removed)	do	1.00	[2] 32	3 ounces	1.71	14¾	58½
				2 ounces	2.56	10	39¼
Whole, or round (as caught)	do	1.00	[2] 27	3 ounces	1.44	17½	69½
				2 ounces	2.16	11¾	46½

See footnotes at end of table.

Table 5.—FISH AND SHELLFISH—Continued

Fish and shellfish as purchased	Unit of purchase	Weight per unit	Yield, as served	Portion as served	Portions per purchase unit	Approximate purchase units for— 25 portions	Approximate purchase units for— 100 portions
FISH, FROZEN							
Portions:							
Breaded, fried or raw:		*Pounds*	*Percent*		*Number*	*Number*	*Number*
5⅓-ounce	Pound	1.00	95	1 portion	3.00	8½	33½
4-ounce	do	1.00	95	do	4.00	6¼	25
3-ounce	do	1.00	95	do	5.33	4¾	18¾
2-ounce	do	1.00	95	do	8.00	3¼	12½
Unbreaded:							
4-ounce	do	1.00	69	do	4.00	6¼	25
3-ounce	do	1.00	69	do	5.33	4¾	18¾
2-ounce	do	1.00	68	do	8.00	3¼	12½
Sticks, breaded, fried or raw, 1-ounce	do	1.00	85	4 sticks	4.00	6¼	25
				3 sticks	5.33	4¾	18¾
				2 sticks	8.00	3¼	12½
SHELLFISH, CANNED							
Clam chowder	8-ounce can, ready-to-serve.	.50	100	8 ounces	1.00	25	100
	10½-ounce can, condensed.	.66	200	do	2.62	9¾	38¼
	15-ounce can, condensed	.94	200	do	3.75	6¾	26¾
	50- to 51-ounce can, condensed.	3.12 to 3.19	200	do	12.50	2	8
Clam juice	8-fluid-ounce can		100	3 fluid ounces	2.67	9½	37½
	12-fluid-ounce can		100	do	4.00	6¼	25
Clams, minced	7½-ounce can	.47	100	3 ounces	2.50	10	40
				2 ounces	3.75	6¾	26¾
	51-ounce can	3.19	100	3 ounces	17.00	1½	6
				2 ounces	25.50	1	4
Crabmeat	6½-ounce can (5½ ounces drained).	.41	85	3 ounces drained	1.83	13¾	54¾
				2 ounces drained	2.75	9¼	36½
Oysters, whole	5-ounce can (5 ounces drained).	.31	100	3 ounces drained	1.67	15	60
				2 ounces drained	2.50	10	40
Oyster stew	10½-ounce can, ready-to-serve.	.66	100	8 ounces	1.31	19¼	76½
Shrimp	4½-ounce can (4½ ounces drained).	.28	100	3 ounces drained	1.50	16¾	66¾
				2 ounces drained	2.25	11¼	44½
SHELLFISH, FRESH, LIVE IN SHELL							
Clams:							
Hard	Dozen		[2] 14	6 clams on half shell	2.00	12½	50
Soft	do		[2] 29	12 clams in the shell	1.00	25	100
Crabs:							
Blue	Pound	1.00	14	3 ounces cooked	.75	33½	133½
				2 ounces cooked	1.12	22½	89½
Dungeness	do	1.00	24	3 ounces cooked	1.28	19¾	78¼
				2 ounces cooked	1.92	13¼	52¼

Oysters	Dozen		[2] 12	6 oysters on half shell	2. 00	12½	50
SHELLFISH, FRESH OR FROZEN							
Clams, shucked	Pound	1. 00	48	3 ounces meat	2. 56	10	39¼
				2 ounces meat	3. 82	6¾	26
Crabs, cooked in shell:							
Blue	do	1. 00	14	3 ounces meat	. 75	33⅓	133⅓
				2 ounces meat	1. 12	22½	89½
Dungeness	do	1. 00	24	3 ounces meat	1. 28	19¾	78¼
				2 ounces meat	1. 92	13¼	52¼
Crabmeat	do	1. 00	97	3 ounces	5. 17	5	19½
				2 ounces	7. 76	3¼	13
Lobster, cooked in shell	do	1. 00	[2] 25	1 lobster	1. 00	25	100
				½ lobster	2. 00	12½	50
Lobster meat	do	1. 00	91	3 ounces	4. 85	5¼	20¾
				2 ounces	7. 28	3½	13¾
Oysters, shucked	do	1. 00	40	3 ounces	2. 13	11¾	47
				2 ounces	3. 20	8	31¼
Scallops, shucked	do	1. 00	63	3 ounces	3. 36	7½	30
				2 ounces	5. 04	5	20
Shrimp:							
Cooked, peeled, cleaned	do	1. 00	100	3 ounces	5. 33	4¾	19
				2 ounces	8. 00	3¼	12½
Raw, in shell	do	1. 00	50	3 ounces meat	2. 67	9½	37½
				2 ounces meat	4. 00	6¼	25
Raw, peeled	do	1. 00	62	3 ounces meat	3. 30	7¾	30½
				2 ounces meat	4. 96	5¼	20¼
SHELLFISH, FROZEN							
Clams, breaded:							
Fried	do	1. 00	85	3 ounces	4. 53	5¾	22¼
				2 ounces	6. 80	3¾	14¾
Raw	do	1. 00	83	3 ounces	4. 43	5¾	22¾
				2 ounces	6. 64	4	15¼
Crabcakes, fried	do	1. 00	95	3 ounces	5. 07	5	19¾
				2 ounces	7. 60	3½	13¼
Lobster, spiny tails:							
8 ounce	do	1. 00	[2] 51	1 tail	2. 00	12½	50
6 ounce	do	1. 00	[2] 51	do	2. 67	9½	37½
4 ounce	do	1. 00	[2] 51	do	4. 00	6¼	25
Oysters, breaded, raw	do	1. 00	88	3 ounces	4. 69	5½	21½
				2 ounces	7. 04	3¾	14¼
Scallops, breaded:							
Fried	do	1. 00	93	3 ounces	4. 96	5¼	20¼
				2 ounces	7. 44	3½	13½
Raw	do	1. 00	81	3 ounces	4. 32	6	23¼
				2 ounces	6. 48	4	15½
Shrimp, breaded:							
Fried	do	1. 00	88	3 ounces	4. 69	5½	21½
				2 ounces	7. 04	3¾	14¼
Raw	do	1. 00	85	3 ounces	4. 53	5¾	22¼
				2 ounces	6. 80	3¾	14¾

[1] Number of purchase units needed is less than one.

[2] Yield, edible portion.

TABLE 6.—EGGS

Eggs, in shell, frozen, and dried, as purchased	Unit of purchase	Weight per unit	Portion as served or used	Portions per purchase unit	Approximate purchase units for—	
					25 portions	100 portions
In shell:		*Pounds*		*Number*	*Number*	*Number*
Large	Dozen	1.50	1 egg	12.00	2⅛	8½
	Case	45.00	do	360.00	(¹)	(¹)
Medium	Dozen	1.31	do	12.00	2¼	8½
	Case	39.50	do	360.00	(¹)	(¹)
Small	Dozen	1.12	do	12.00	2¼	8½
	Case	34.00	do	360.00	(¹)	(¹)
Frozen:						
Whole eggs	Pound	1.00	1 egg (3 tablespoons thawed)	10.00	(²)	(²)
	Can	10.00	12 eggs (2¼ cups thawed)	83	(²)	(²)
		30.00	1 egg	100.00	(²)	(²)
	do		do	300.00	(²)	(²)
Egg yolks	Pound	1.00	1 yolk (1½ tablespoons thawed)	26.00	(²)	(²)
			12 yolks (1 cup thawed)	2.16	(²)	(²)
Egg whites	do	1.00	1 white (2 tablespoons thawed)	16.00	(²)	(²)
			12 whites (1½ cups thawed)	1.33	(²)	(²)
Dried:						
Whole eggs	do	1.00	1 large egg (½ ounce or 2½ tablespoons dried + 2½ tablespoons water)	32.00	(²)	(²)
			12 large eggs (6 ounces or 2 cups dried + 2 cups water)	2.67	(²)	(²)
	13-ounce package	.81	1 large egg	26.00	(²)	(²)
	No. 10 can	3.00	do	96.00	(²)	(²)
	Package	25.00	do	800.00	(²)	(²)
	do	50.00	do	1,600.00	(²)	(²)
Egg yolks	Pound	1.00	1 large yolk (2 tablespoons dried + 2 teaspoons water)	54.00	(²)	(²)
			12 large yolks (1½ cups dried + ½ cup water)	4.50	(²)	(²)
	Package	3.00	1 large yolk	162.00	(²)	(²)
Egg white, spray-dried	Pound	1.00	1 large white (2 teaspoons dried + 2 tablespoons water)	100.00	(²)	(²)
			12 large whites (½ cup dried + 1½ cups water)	8.33	(²)	(²)
	Package	3.00	1 large white	300.00	(²)	(²)

¹ Number of purchase units needed is less than one. ² Number of purchase units needed is determined by use.

FOOD PURCHASING GUIDE

TABLE 7.—NUTS

Nuts in shell and peanut butter as purchased	Unit of purchase	Weight per unit	Yield, as served	Portion as used	Portions per purchase unit	Approximate purchase units for—	
						25 portions	100 portions
		Pounds	*Percent*		*Number*	*Number*	*Number*
Almonds:							
Nonpareil (softshell)	Pound	1.00	60	1 cup (0.31 pound)	1.94	(¹)	(¹)
Peerless (hardshell)	do	1.00	35	do	1.13	(¹)	(¹)
Brazil nuts	do	1.00	48	do	1.55	(¹)	(¹)
Cashew nuts	do	1.00	22	1 cup (0.30 pound)	.73	(¹)	(¹)
Chestnuts	do	1.00	84	8 large nuts (0.11 pound)	7.64	(¹)	(¹)
Coconut:							
Dried	do	1.00	100	1 cup (0.14 pound)	7.14	(¹)	(¹)
Fresh, in shell	do	1.00	52	1 cup (0.21 pound)	2.48	(¹)	(¹)
Filberts	do	1.00	39	1 cup (0.30 pound)	1.50	(¹)	(¹)
Peanuts, roasted	do	1.00	68	1 cup (0.32 pound)	2.12	(¹)	(¹)
Peanut butter	do	1.00	100	2 tablespoons (0.07 pound)	14.29	1¾	7
	No. 10 can	6.75	100	do	96.43	(²)	1¼
Pecans	Pound	1.00	52	1 cup halves (0.24 pound)	2.17	(²)	(¹)
Walnuts:							
Black	do	1.00	22	1 cup (0.28 pound)	.79	(¹)	(¹)
English	do	1.00	45	1 cup (0.22 pound)	2.05	(¹)	(¹)

¹ Number of purchase units needed is determined by use. ² Number of purchase units needed is less than one.

TABLE 8.—DAIRY PRODUCTS

Dairy products as purchased	Unit of purchase	Weight per unit	Yield, as served	Portion as served or used	Portions per purchase unit	Approximate purchase units for— 25 portions	100 portions
		Pounds	*Percent*		*Number*	*Number*	*Number*
Cheese:							
Cheddar	Pound	1. 00	100	4 ounces, grated, 1 cup	4. 00	6¼	25
	do	1. 00	100	2 ounces	8. 00	3¼	12½
	do	1. 00	100	1 ounce	16. 00	1¾	6¼
	Longhorn	11 to 13	100	2 ounces	88–104	(1)	1¼
	Daisies	20 to 25	100	do	160–200	(1)	(1)
	Flats	32 to 37	100	do	256–296	(1)	(1)
	Cheddars	70 to 78	100	do	560–624	(1)	(1)
	Block	20	100	do	160. 00	(1)	(1)
	do	40	100	do	320. 00	(1)	(1)
Cottage, small or large curd, with pineapple or chive.	Pound	1. 00	100	4 ounces	4. 00	6¼	25
				2 ounces	8. 00	3¼	12½
	32-ounce carton	2. 00	100	4 ounces	8. 00	3¼	12½
	Tin	30. 00	100	do	120. 00	(1)	(1)
Cream	8-ounce package	. 50	100	1 ounce	8. 00	3¼	12½
	12-ounce package	. 75	100	do	12. 00	2¼	8½
	16-ounce package	1. 00	100	do	16. 00	1¾	6¼
Processed, cheese food	Pound	1. 00	100	2 ounces	8. 00	3¼	12½
				1 ounce, 1 slice	16. 00	1¾	6¼
	Package	2. 00	100	2 ounces	16. 00	1¾	6¼
	do	5. 00	100	do	40. 00	(1)	2½
Cream:							
Half and half	Pint	1. 07	100	1⅓ tablespoons	21. 33	1¼	4¾
	Quart	2. 14	100	do	42. 67	(1)	2½
Light	Pint	1. 06	100	do	21. 33	1¼	4¾
	Quart	2. 13	100	do	42. 67	(1)	2½
Sour	½ pint	. 53	100	1 tablespoon	16. 00	1¾	6¼
	¾ pint	. 80	100	do	24. 00	1¼	4¼
Whipping (volume doubles when whipped).	Pint	1. 05	100	1¼ tablespoons	25. 60	1	4
	Quart	2. 10	100	do	51. 20	(1)	2

20

FOOD PURCHASING GUIDE

Food	Purchase unit			Size of serving	Servings per purchase unit	Purchase units for 25 servings	Purchase units for 100 servings
Ice cream:							
Brick	Quart	1.25	100	1 slice (½ cup)	8.00	3¼	12½
Bulk	Gallon	4.50	100	No. 12 scoop (sundae)	22-26	1	4
				No. 16 scoop	31-35		3
				No. 20 scoop (a la mode)	38-42		2½
				No. 24 scoop	47-51		2
Cups	3-ounce	.19	100	1 cup	1.00	25	100
	5-ounce	.31	100	1 cup	1.00	25	100
Sherbet	Gallon	6.00	100	No. 12 scoop	25.00	1	4
				No. 16 scoop	35.00		3
				No. 20 scoop	42.00		2½
				No. 24 scoop	50.00		2
Milk:							
Fluid [1]	Quart	2.15	100	1 cup	4.00	6¼	25
	Gallon	8.60	100	do	16.00	1½	6¼
	5-gallon	43.00	100	do	80.00		1¼
Condensed	14-ounce can	.88	100	do	1.24	[3]	[3]
	15-ounce can	.94	100	do	1.33	[3]	[3]
Evaporated	14½-ounce can	.91	100	1 cup as is	1.67	[3]	[3]
	14½-ounce can	.91	200	1 cup reconstituted	3.33	[3]	[3]
	No. 10 can	8.00	100	1 cup as is	14.00	[3]	[3]
	No. 10 can	8.00	200	1 cup reconstituted	28.00	[3]	[3]
Dry:			(measure)				
Nonfat:							
Instant	Pound (about 6½ cups)	1.00	100	1 cup as is	6.50	[3]	[3]
		1.00	267	1 cup reconstituted	17.06	[3]	[3]
Regular (USDA)	Pound (about 3¼ cups)	1.00	100 (measure)	1 cup as is	3.25	[3]	[3]
		1.00	533	1 cup reconstituted	17.06	[3]	[3]
Whole	Pound (about 3½ cups)	1.00	100 (measure)	1 cup as is	3.50	[3]	[3]
		1.00	400	1 cup reconstituted	14.22	[3]	[3]

[1] Number of purchase units needed is less than one.
[2] Skim milk and buttermilk weigh slightly more than whole fluid milk.
[3] Number of purchase units needed is determined by use.

TABLE 9.—VEGETABLES—FRESH

Fresh vegetables as purchased	Unit of purchase	Weight per unit [1]	Yield, as served	Portion as served	Portions per purchase unit	Approximate purchase units for— 25 portions	100 portions
		Pounds	*Percent*		*Number*	*Number*	*Number*
Asparagus	Pound	1.00		4 medium spears, cooked	3.38	7½	29¾
	do	1.00	49	3 ounces cut spears, cooked	2.61	9¾	38½
	Crate	28.00	49	do	73.17	(2)	1½
Beans, lima, green:							
In pod	Pound	1.00	40	3 ounces cooked	2.13	11¾	47
	Bushel	32.00	40	do	68.27	(2)	1½
Shelled	Pound	1.00	102	do	5.44	4¾	18½
Beans, snap, green or wax	do	1.00	84	do	4.48	5¾	22½
	Bushel	30.00	84	do	134.40	(2)	(2)
Beet greens, untrimmed	Pound	1.00	44	do	2.35	10¾	42¾
	Bushel	20.00	44	do	46.93	(2)	2¼
Beets:							
With tops	Pound	1.00	43	3 ounces sliced or diced, cooked	2.29	11	43¾
Without tops	do	1.00	76	do	4.05	6¼	24¾
	Burlap bag	50.00	76	do	202.67	(2)	(2)
Blackeye peas, shelled	Pound	1.00	93	3 ounces cooked	4.96	5¼	20¼
Broccoli	do	1.00		2 medium spears, cooked	4.57	5½	22
	do	1.00	62	3 ounces cut spears, cooked	3.31	7¾	30¼
	Crate	40.00	62	do	132.27	(2)	(2)
Brussels sprouts	Pound	1.00	77	3 ounces cooked	4.11	6¼	24½
Cabbage	Bulk	1.00	79	2 ounces coleslaw	6.32	4	16
	do	1.00	75	3 ounces sliced, cooked	4.00	6¼	25
	do	1.00	80	3-ounce wedge, cooked	4.27	6	23½
	Crate or sack	50.00	80	do	213.33	(2)	(2)
Cabbage, Chinese	Pound	1.00	88	2 ounces raw	7.04	3¾	14¼
Carrots, without tops	do	1.00	82	2 ounces shredded or grated, strips or diced, raw.	6.56	4	15¼
	do	1.00	75	3 ounces sliced or diced, cooked	4.00	6¼	25
	Bushel	50.00	75	do	200.00	(2)	(2)
Cauliflower	Pound	1.00	45	2 ounces sliced, raw	3.60	7	28
	do	1.00	44	3 ounces cooked	2.35	10¾	42¾
	Crate	37.00	44	do	86.83	(2)	1¼
	Crate, large	50.00	44	do	117.33	(2)	(2)
Celery	Pound	1.00	70	3 ounces chopped, cooked	3.73	6¾	27
	do	1.00	75	3 ounces sliced, raw	4.00	6¼	25
	do	1.00	75	2 ounces strips, raw	6.00	4¼	16¾
	Crate	60.00	75	3 ounces chopped, raw	240.00	(2)	(2)
Celery hearts (24 pack)	Crate or box	30.00	95	2 ounces strips, raw	228.00	(2)	(2)
Chard, untrimmed	Pound	1.00	56	3 ounces	2.99	8½	33½
Collards	do	1.00	81	3 ounces cooked	4.32	6	23¼
	Bushel	20.00	81	do	86.40	(2)	1¼
Corn, in husks	Dozen	8.00	37	3 ounces cooked kernels	15.79	1¾	6½
	do	8.00		1 ear, cooked	12.00	2¼	8½
	5-dozen crate or bag.	40.00		do	60.00	(2)	1¾

Cucumber	Pound	1.00	73	3 ounces sliced, peeled, raw	3.89	6¼	25¾
	do	1.00	95	3 ounces sliced, unpeeled, raw	5.07	5	19¾
	Bushel	48.00	95	do	243.20	[2]	[2]
Eggplant	Pound	1.00	75	4 ounces cooked	3.00	8½	33½
	Bushel	33.00	75	do	100.00	[2]	1
Endive, escarole, chicory	Pound	1.00	75	1 ounce raw	12.00	2¼	8½
	Bushel	25.00	75	do	300.00	[2]	[2]
Kale, untrimmed	Pound	1.00	81	3 ounces cooked	4.32	6	23¼
	Bushel	18.00	81	do	77.76	[2]	1½
Kohlrabi	Pound	1.00	50	do	2.67	9½	37½
Lettuce:							
Head	do	1.00	74	2 ounces raw	5.92	4¼	17
Iceberg	Carton	2 doz. heads		⅛ head, raw	144.00	4¼ heads	17 heads
Romaine	Pound	1.00	64	1 ounce raw	10.24	2½	10
Mushrooms	do	1.00	67	1 ounce sliced, cooked	10.72	2½	9½
	Basket	3.00	67	3 ounces sliced, cooked	10.72	2½	9½
	do	9.00	67	do	32.16	[2]	3¼
Mustard greens	Pound	1.00	59	3 ounces cooked	3.15	8	31¾
	Bushel	20.00	59	do	62.93	[2]	1¼
Okra	Pound	1.00	96	do	5.12	5	19¾
	Bushel	30.00	96	do	153.60	[2]	[2]
Onions:							
Green, partly topped	Pound	1.00	60	3 ounces raw	3.20	8	31¼
	Wirebound crate	50.00	60	do	160.00	[2]	[2]
Mature	Pound	1.00	89	1 ounce chopped or grated, raw	14.24	2	7¼
	do	1.00	76	3 ounces small whole or pieces, cooked.	4.05	6¼	24¾
	Sack	50.00	76	do	202.67	[2]	[2]
Parsley	Pound	1.00		½ cup	16.00	[2]	[2]
	Crate	19.00		do	304.00	[2]	[2]
Parsnips	Pound	1.00	84	3 ounces cooked	4.48	5¾	22½
	Bushel	50.00	84	do	224.00	[2]	[2]
Peas, green:							
In pod	Pound	1.00	36	do	1.92	13¼	52¼
	Basket	15.00	36	do	28.80	[2]	3½
	Bushel	28.00	36	do	53.76	[2]	2
Shelled	Pound	1.00	96	do	5.12	5	19¾
Peppers, green	do	1.00	82	1 ounce diced or strips, raw	13.12	2	7¾
	Bushel	25.00	82	do	328.00	[2]	[2]
	Carton	30.00	82	do	393.60	[2]	[2]
	Pound	1.00	75	2 ounces strips, cooked	6.00	4¼	16¾
Potatoes:							
To be pared by hand	do	1.00		1 medium, boiled	3.00	8½	33½
	do	1.00	54	2 ounces french fried	4.32	6	23¼
	do	1.00	80	3 ounces cubed and diced, cooked	4.27	6	23½
	do	1.00	95	4 ounces mashed	3.80	6¾	26½
To be pared by machine	do	1.00		1 medium, boiled	3.00	8½	33½
	do	1.00	52	2 ounces french fried	4.16	6¼	24¼
	do	1.00	76	3 ounces cubed and diced, cooked	4.05	6¼	24¾
	do	1.00	90	4 ounces mashed	3.60	7	28
Ready-to-cook	do	1.00		1 medium, boiled	3.00	8½	33½
	do	1.00	68	2 ounces french fried	5.44	4¾	18½
	do	1.00	119	4 ounces mashed	4.76	5¼	21½
To be cooked in jacket	do	1.00		1 medium, baked in jacket	3.00	8½	33½
	do	1.00		1 medium, boiled	3.00	8½	33½
	do	1.00	87	3 ounces cubed and diced	4.64	5½	21¾
	do	1.00	104	4 ounces mashed	4.16	6¼	24¼

See footnotes at end of table.

TABLE 9.—VEGETABLES—FRESH—Continued

Fresh vegetables as purchased	Unit of purchase	Weight per unit [1]	Yield, as served	Portion as served	Portions per purchase unit	Approximate purchase units for— 25 portions	100 portions
		Pounds	*Percent*		*Number*	*Number*	*Number*
Pumpkin	Pound	1.00	63	4 ounces mashed, cooked	2.52	10	39¼
Radishes:							
With tops	do	1.00	63	1 ounce sliced, raw	10.08	2½	10
	do	1.00		4 small	11.34	2¼	9
Without tops	do	1.00	90	1 ounce sliced, raw	14.40	1¾	7
Rutabagas	do	1.00	79	3 ounces cubed, cooked	4.21	6	24
	do	1.00	77	4 ounces mashed	3.08	8¼	32½
	Bushel	56.00	77	do	172.48	(2)	(2)
Spinach:							
Partly trimmed	Pound	1.00	92	1 ounce raw for salad	14.72	1¾	7
Untrimmed	do	1.00	72	do	11.52	2¼	8¾
	do	1.00	67	3 ounces cooked	3.57	7¼	28¼
	Bushel	20.00	67	do	71.47	(2)	1½
Squash, summer	Pound	1.00	83	3 ounces diced or sliced, cooked	4.43	5¾	22¾
	Bushel	35.00	83	do	154.93	(2)	(2)
	Pound	1.00	83	4 ounces mashed	3.32	7¾	30¼
Squash, winter:							
Acorn	do	1.00		½ medium, baked	2.00	12½	50
Hubbard	do	1.00	58	4 ounces cubed, cooked	2.32	11	43¼
	do	1.00	57	4 ounces mashed	2.28	11	44
Sweetpotatoes	do	1.00		1 medium, cooked in jacket	2.00	12½	50
	do	1.00	83	3 ounces sliced	4.43	5¾	22¾
	do	1.00	81	4 ounces mashed	3.24	7¾	31
	Bushel	50.00		1 medium, cooked in jacket	100.00	(2)	1
Tomatoes (medium)	Pound	1.00	91	2 slices	7.50	3½	13½
	do	1.00		1 wedge	12.00	2¼	8½
	Lug	32.00		do	384.00	(2)	(2)
	Bushel	53.00		do	636.00	(2)	(2)
Turnip greens, untrimmed	Pound	1.00	48	3 ounces cooked	2.56	10	39¼
	Bushel	20.00	48	do	51.20	(2)	(2)
Turnips, without tops	Pound	1.00	74	3 ounces cubed, cooked	3.95	6½	25½
	do	1.00	73	4 ounces mashed	2.92	8¾	34¼
	Bushel	50.00	73	do	146.00	(2)	(2)
Watercress	Bunch	1.00	92	½ cup	27.77	(3)	(3)

[1] Legal weights for contents of bushels, lugs, crates, and boxes vary among States.

[2] Number of purchase units needed is less than one.

[3] Number of purchase units needed is determined by use.

TABLE 10.—VEGETABLES—CANNED

Canned vegetables as purchased	Unit of purchase	Weight per unit	Yield, as served	Portion as served	Portions per purchase unit	Approximate purchase units for— 25 portions	Approximate purchase units for— 100 portions
		Pounds	*Percent*		*Number*	*Number*	*Number*
Asparagus:							
Cuts and tips	No. 300 can	0.88	61	3 ounces	2.80	8¾	35
	No. 10 can	6.31	60	do	20.10	1¼	5
Spears	No. 300 can	.91		6 medium	2.57	9¾	39
	No. 10 can	6.44		do	18.53	1½	5½
Beans, lima, green	No. 303 can	1.00	69	3 ounces	3.08	7	27¼
	No. 10 can	6.56	69	do	24.14	1¼	4¼
Beans, snap, green or wax	No. 303 can	.97	59	do	3.05	8¼	33
	No. 2½ can	1.75	59	do	5.51	4¾	18¼
	No. 10 can	6.31	62	do	20.87	1¼	5
Beans, dry—kidney, lima, or navy	No. 303 can	1.00	80	6 ounces	2.13	11¾	47
	No. 10 can	6.75	80	do	14.40	1¾	6¾
Bean sprouts	do	6.62	52	3 ounces	18.37	1½	5½
Beets:							
Diced	No. 303 can	1.00	66	do	3.52	7¼	28½
	No. 10 can	6.50	69	do	23.92	1¼	4¼
Sliced	No. 303 can	1.00	61	do	3.25	7¾	31
	No. 10 can	6.50	65	do	22.53	1¼	4½
Whole baby beets	No. 303 can	1.00	62	do	3.31	7¾	30¼
	No. 10 can	6.50	66	do	22.88	1¼	4½
Carrots:							
Diced	No. 303 can	1.00	62	do	3.31	7¾	30¼
	No. 10 can	6.50	69	do	23.92	1¼	4¼
Sliced	No. 303 can	1.00	62	do	3.31	7¾	30¼
	No. 10 can	6.50	66	do	22.88	1¼	4½
Chop suey vegetables	do	6.38	100	do	34.00	(1)	3
Collards	No. 303 can	.94	72	4 ounces	2.71	9¼	37
	No. 2½ can	1.69	70	do	4.73	5½	21¼
	No. 10 can	6.12	61	do	14.93	1¾	6¾
Corn:							
Cream style	No. 303 can	1.00	100	do	4.00	6¼	25
	No. 10 can	6.62	100	do	26.48	1	4
Whole kernel	No. 303 can	1.00	66	3 ounces	3.52	7¼	28½
	No. 10 can	6.62	66	do	23.30	1¼	4½
Kale	No. 303 can	.94	72	4 ounces	2.71	9¼	37
	No. 2½ can	1.69	70	do	4.73	5½	21¼
	No. 10 can	6.12	61	do	14.93	1¾	6¾
Mushrooms	No. 8 Z	.78	64	3 ounces	2.66	9½	37¾
	No. 10 can	6.44	66	do	22.67	1¼	4½
Mustard greens	No. 303 can	.94	72	4 ounces	2.71	9¼	37
	No. 2½ can	1.69	70	do	4.73	5½	21¼
	No. 10 can	6.12	61	do	14.93	1¾	6¾
Okra	No. 303 can	.97	68	3 ounces	3.51	7¼	28½
	No. 10 can	6.19	61	do	20.14	1¼	5
Okra and tomatoes	No. 303 can	.94	100	do	5.01	5	20
	No. 10 can	6.31	100	do	33.65	(1)	3

See footnotes at end of table.

TABLE 10.—VEGETABLES—CANNED—Continued

Canned vegetables as purchased	Unit of purchase	Weight per unit	Yield, as served	Portion as served	Portions per purchase unit	Approximate purchase units for— 25 portions	Approximate purchase units for— 100 portions
Olives, large:							
Ripe:		*Pounds*	*Percent*		*Number*	*Number*	*Number*
Pitted	No. 1 tall	[2] 0.47		2 olives	21.33	1¼	4¾
Whole	do	[2] .56		do	25.60	1	4
	No. 10	[2] 4.12		do	187.69	(1)	(1)
Green, whole	Gallon	[2] 5.50		do	250.25	(1)	(1)
Onions, small, whole	No. 303 can	1.00	56	3 ounces	2.99	8½	33½
	No. 10 can	6.31	59	do	19.86	1½	5¼
Peas, green	No. 303 can	1.00	64	do	3.41	7½	29½
	No. 10 can	6.56	64	do	22.39	1¼	4½
Peas and carrots	No. 303 can	1.00	69	do	3.68	7	27¼
	No. 10 can	6.56	69	do	24.14	1¼	4¼
Pickles:							
Dill or sour:							
Sliced or cut	Quart jar	[2] 1.38	100	1 ounce	22.00	1¼	4¾
	No. 10 jar	[2] 4.50	100	do	72.00	(1)	1½
	Gallon jar	[2] 5.62	100	do	90.00	(1)	1¼
Whole	No. 2½ jar	[2] 1.19	100	do	19.00	1½	5½
	Quart jar	[2] 1.31	100	do	21.00	1¼	5
Sweet:							
Sliced or cut	do	[2] 1.50	100	do	24.00	1¼	4¼
	No. 10 jar	[2] 4.88	100	do	78.00	(1)	1½
	Gallon jar	[2] 5.94	100	do	95.00	(1)	1¼
Whole	No. 2½ jar	[2] 1.28	100	do	20.50	1¼	5
	Quart jar	[2] 1.38	100	do	22.00	1¼	4¾
Pickle relish:							
Sour	Quart	[2] 1.61	100	do	25.75	1	4
	No. 10 jar	[2] 5.73	100	do	91.75	(1)	1¼
	Gallon jar	[2] 7.16	100	do	114.50	(1)	(1)
Sweet	Quart	[2] 1.75	100	do	28.00	1	3¾
	No. 10 jar	[2] 6.25	100	do	100.00	(1)	1
	Gallon jar	[2] 7.81	100	do	125.00	(1)	(1)
Pimientos, chopped	No. 2½ can	1.75	73	½ cup	4.80	(3)	(3)
	No. 10 can	6.81	68	do	17.39	(3)	(3)
Potatoes, small whole	No. 2 can	1.25		2–3	4.00	6¼	25
	No. 10 can	6.38		2–3	25.00	1	4
Pumpkin, mashed	No. 300 can	.91	100	4 ounces	3.64	7	27½
	No. 2½ can	1.81	100	do	7.24	3½	14
	No. 10 can	6.62	100	do	26.50	1	4
Sauerkraut	No. 303 can	1.00	82	3 ounces	4.37	5¾	23
	No. 2½ can	1.69	85	do	7.66	3½	13¼
	No. 10 can	6.19	81	do	26.74	1	3¾

Soups:							
Condensed	No. 1 picnic	.66 to .75	200	1 cup diluted	2.50	10	40
	No. 3 cylinder	3.12	200	do	11.50	2¼	8¾
Ready-to-serve	12-fluid-ounce can		100	1 cup	1.50	16¾	66¾
	25-fluid-ounce can (No. 2½)		100	do	3.12	8¼	32¼
Spinach	No. 303 can	.94	72	4 ounces	2.71	9¼	37
	No. 2½ can	1.69	70	do	4.73	5½	21¼
	No. 10 can	6.12	61	do	14.93	1¾	6¾
Squash, summer	No. 303 can	1.00	69	do	2.75	9¼	36½
	No. 10 can	6.62	69	do	17.50	1½	5¾
Squash, winter	No. 300 can	.91	100	do	3.64	7	27½
	No. 2½ can	1.81	100	do	7.24	3½	14
	No. 10 can	6.62	100	do	26.48	1	4
Succotash	No. 303 can	1.00	65	3 ounces	3.47	7¼	29
	No. 10 can	6.75	65	do	23.40	1¼	4½
Sweetpotatoes	No. 3 vacuum or squat	1.44	65	4 ounces	3.74	6¾	26¾
	No. 2½ can, with sirup	1.81	66	do	4.78	5¼	21
	No. 10 can, with sirup	6.38	71	do	18.00	1½	5¾
Tomatoes	No. 303 can	1.00	100	do	4.00	6¼	25
	No. 2½ can	1.75	100	do	7.00	3¾	14½
	No. 10 can	6.38	100	do	25.52	1	4
Tomato products:							
Catsup	14-ounce bottle	.88	100	1 ounce	14.00	2	7¼
	No. 10 can	6.94	100	do	111.00	(1)	1
Chili sauce	12-ounce jar	.75	100	1 tablespoon	20.27	1¼	5
	No. 10 can	6.56	100	do	177.30	(1)	(1)
Juice, concentrate [4]	6-fluid-ounce can	.43	400	4 fluid ounces	6.00	4¼	16¾
Turnip greens	No. 303 can	.94	72	4 ounces	2.71	9¼	37
	No. 2½ can	1.69	70	do	4.73	5½	21¼
	No. 10 can	6.12	61	do	14.93	1¾	6¾
Vegetable juices	23-fluid-ounce can	1.54	100	4 fluid ounces	5.75	4½	17½
	46-fluid-ounce can	3.07	100	do	11.50	2¼	8¾
	96-fluid-ounce can	6.41	100	do	24.00	1¼	4¼
Vegetables, mixed	No. 303 can	1.00	68	3 ounces	3.63	7	27¾
	No. 10 can	6.50	68	do	23.57	1¼	4¼

[1] Number of purchase units needed is less than one.
[2] Drained weight.
[3] Number of purchase units needed is determined by use.
[4] See vegetable juices for canned tomato juice.

Table 11.—VEGETABLES—FROZEN

Frozen vegetables as purchased	Unit of purchase	Weight per unit	Yield, as served	Portion as served	Portions per purchase unit	Approximate purchase units for— 25 portions	100 portions
		Pounds	*Percent*		*Number*	*Number*	*Number*
Asparagus:							
Spears	Pound	1.00		4 medium, cooked	3.38	7½	29¾
	Package	2.50		do	8.44	3	12
Cuts and tips	Pound	1.00	80	3 ounces cooked	4.27	6	23½
	Package	2.50	80	do	10.67	2½	9½
Beans, butter (lima)	Pound	1.00	100	do	5.33	4¾	19
	Package	2.50	100	do	13.33	2	7½
	do	3.00	100	do	16.00	1¾	6¼
Beans, lima, green	Pound	1.00	100	do	5.33	4¾	19
	Package	2.50	100	do	13.33	2	7½
Beans, snap, green or wax	Pound	1.00	91	do	4.85	5¼	20¾
	Package	2.50	91	do	12.13	2¼	8¼
Blackeye peas	Pound	1.00	111	do	5.92	4¼	17
	Package	2.50	111	do	14.80	1¾	7
	do	3.00	111	do	17.76	1½	5¾
Broccoli:							
Spears	Pound	1.00		2 medium	4.57	5½	22
	Package	2.50		do	11.43	2¼	8¾
Cut or chopped	Pound	1.00	85	3 ounces cooked	4.53	5¾	22¼
	Package	2.50	85	do	11.33	2¼	9
Brussel sprouts	Pound	1.00	96	do	5.12	5	19¾
	Package	2.50	96	do	12.80	2	8
Carrots, sliced or diced	Pound	1.00	96	do	5.12	5	19¾
	Package	2.50	96	do	12.80	2	8
Cauliflower	Pound	1.00	90	do	4.80	5¼	21
	Package	2.50	90	do	12.00	2¼	8½
Collards	Pound	1.00	89	do	4.75	5½	21¼
	Package	2.50	89	do	11.87	2¼	8½
Corn:							
On cob	Pound (about three 5-inch ears).	1.00		1 ear, cooked	3.00	8½	33⅓
Whole kernel	Pound	1.00	97	3 ounces cooked	5.17	5	19½
	Package	2.50	97	do	12.93	2	7¾
Kale	Pound	1.00	77	do	4.11	6¼	24½
	Package	2.50	77	do	10.27	2½	9¾
	do	3.00	77	do	12.32	2¼	8¼

Mustard greens, leaf or chopped	Pound	1.00	80	do	4.27	6	23½
	Package	2.50	80	do	10.67	2½	9½
	do	3.00	80	do	12.80	2	8
Okra, whole	Pound	1.00	82	do	4.37	5¾	23
	Package	2.50	82	do	10.93	2½	9¼
	do	3.00	82	do	13.12	2	7¾
Peas, green	Pound	1.00	96	do	5.12	5	19¾
	Package	2.50	96	do	12.80	2	8
	do	3.00	96	do	15.36	1¼	6¾
Peas and carrots	Pound	1.00	98	do	5.23	5	19¼
	Package	2.50	98	do	13.07	2	7¾
Peppers, green:							
Whole	do	1.00		½ pepper, cooked	12.00	2¼	8½
	do	2.50		do	30.00	(1)	3½
Diced or sliced	Pound	1.00	97	1 ounce cooked	15.52	1¾	6½
	Package	2.50	97	do	38.80	(1)	2¾
Potatoes:							
French fried	do	1.00		10 pieces	8.00	3¼	12½
	do	5.00		do	40.00	(1)	2½
Small whole	Container	5.00		3 cooked	16.67	1½	6
Spinach	Pound	1.00	80	3 ounces cooked	4.27	6	23½
	Package	2.50	80	do	10.67	2½	9½
	do	3.00	80	do	12.80	2	8
Squash, summer, sliced	Pound	1.00	87	do	4.64	5½	21¾
	Package	2.50	87	do	11.60	2¼	8¾
	do	3.00	87	do	13.92	2	7¼
Squash, winter, mashed	Pound	1.00	92	4 ounces cooked	3.68	7	27¼
	Package	2.50	92	do	9.20	2¾	11
Sweetpotatoes:							
Whole	Pound	1.00		1 whole, cooked	2.63	9¾	38¼
	do	1.00	98	4 ounces cooked	3.92	6½	25¾
Sliced	Package	2.50	98	do	9.80	2¾	10¼
	do	3.00	98	do	11.76	2¼	8¾
Succotash	Pound	1.00	106	3 ounces cooked	5.65	4½	17¾
	Package	2.50	106	do	14.13	2	7¼
Turnip greens, leaf or chopped	Pound	1.00	80	do	4.27	6	23½
	Package	2.50	80	do	10.67	2½	9½
	do	3.00	80	do	12.80	2	8
Turnip greens with turnips	Pound	1.00	89	do	4.75	5½	21¼
	Package	3.00	89	do	14.24	2	7¼
Vegetables, mixed	Pound	1.00	95	do	5.07	5	19¾
	Package	2.50	95	do	12.67	2	8

[1] Number of purchase units needed is less than one.

TABLE 12.—VEGETABLES—DRIED

Vegetables, dried, regular and low-moisture, as purchased	Unit of purchase	Weight per unit	Yield, as served	Portion as served	Portions per purchase unit	Approximate purchase units for—	
						25 portions	100 portions
REGULAR		*Pounds*	*Percent*		*Number*	*Number*	*Number*
Beans (includes white beans, lima beans, kidney beans, blackeye beans or peas).	Pound	1.00	232	3 ounces cooked	12.37	2¾	8¾
Peas (includes any type, whole peas, split peas, or lentils).	----do----	1.00	223	----do----	11.89	(¹)	8¾
	Bushel	60.00	223	----do----	713.60		
LOW-MOISTURE							
Onions, sliced	Pound	1.00	417	----do----	22.24	1¼	4½
Potatoes, white:							
Flakes	----do----	1.00	521	4 ounces cooked	20.84	1¼	5
	Package	2.50	521	----do----	52.10	(¹)	2
Granules	Pound	1.00	506	----do----	20.24	1¼	5
	Package	2.50	506	----do----	50.60	(¹)	2
Sweetpotatoes, flakes	Pound	1.00	294	----do----	11.76	2¼	8¾

¹ Number of purchase units needed is less than one.

TABLE 13.—FRUITS—FRESH

Fresh fruits as purchased	Unit of purchase	Weight per unit [1]	Yield, as served	Portion as served	Portions per purchase unit	Approximate purchase units for—	
						25 portions	100 portions
		Pounds	*Percent*		*Number*	*Number*	*Number*
Apples	Pound	1.00		1 medium, baked or raw	3.00	8½	33½
	Bushel	40.00		do	120.00	(2)	(2)
	Pound	1.00	76	2 ounces raw, chopped or diced	6.08	4¼	16½
	do	1.00	87	4 ounces applesauce	3.48	7¼	28¾
	do	1.00	63	4 ounces cooked, sliced or diced	2.52	10	39¾
	do	1.00		⅙ 9-inch pie (2.12 pounds of apples per pie).	2.83	9	35¼
	do	1.00		⅛ 9-inch pie	3.77	6¾	26¾
Apricots	do	1.00		2 medium	6.00	4¼	16¾
	Lug	24.00		do	144.00	(2)	(2)
Avocados	Pound	1.00	75	2 ounces sliced, diced, or wedges	6.00	4¼	16¾
	Lug	12.00	75	do	72.00	(2)	1½
	Box (⅝ bushel)	36.00	75	do	216.00	(2)	(2)
Bananas	Pound	1.00		1 medium	3.00	8½	33½
	Box	25.00		do	75.00	(2)	1½
	Pound	1.00	68	2 ounces sliced for fruit cup	5.44	4¾	18½
	do	1.00	68	3 ounces sliced for dessert	3.63	7	27¾
	do	1.00	68	4 ounces mashed	2.72	9¼	37
Blackberries	Quart	1.42	95	1 ounce salad garnish	21.53	1¼	4¾
	do	1.42	95	3 ounces	7.18	3½	14
	Crate (24 quarts)	34.00	95	do	172.22	(2)	(2)
	Quart	1.42		⅙ 9-inch pie (0.92 quart per pie)	6.54	4	15½
	do	1.42		⅛ 9-inch pie	8.70	3	11½
Blueberries	do	1.97	92	1 ounce salad garnish	28.98	(2)	3½
	do	1.97	92	3 ounces	9.66	2¾	10½
	Crate (24 quarts)	47.25	92	do	231.84	(2)	(2)
	Quart	1.97		⅙ 9-inch pie (0.59 quart per pie)	10.20	2½	10
	do	1.97		⅛ 9-inch pie	13.51	2	7½
Cantaloup	Pound	1.00	50	3 ounces sliced or diced	2.67	9½	37½
	1 (No. 36 size)	2.50		½ medium	2.00	12½	50
	Crate (No. 36)	80.00		do	64.00	(2)	1¾
Cherries	Pound	1.00	89	3 ounces pitted, raw	4.75	5½	21¼
	Lug	16.00	89	do	75.95	(2)	1½
	Pound	1.00		⅙ 9-inch pie (1.60 pounds per pie)	3.75	6¾	26¾
	do	1.00		⅛ 9-inch pie	5.00	5	20
Cranberries	do	1.00	96	1 ounce raw, chopped, for relish	15.36	1¾	6¾
	do	1.00	182	2 ounces sauce, strained	14.56	1¾	7
	do	1.00	239	2 ounces cooked, whole	19.12	1½	5¼
	Box	25.00	239	do	478.00	(2)	(2)
Figs	Pound	1.00		3 medium	4.00	6¼	25
	Box	6.00		do	24.00	1¼	4¼

See footnotes at end of table.

TABLE 13.—FRUITS—FRESH—Continued

Fresh fruits as purchased	Unit of purchase	Weight per unit [1]	Yield, as served	Portion as served	Portions per purchase unit	Approximate purchase units for— 25 portions	100 portions
		Pounds	*Percent*		*Number*	*Number*	*Number*
Grapefruit	Pound	1.00	44	4 fluid ounces juice	1.61	15¾	62¼
	Dozen (No. 64 size)	15.00	44	do	24.22	1¼	4¼
	Pound	1.00	47	4 ounces segments	1.88	13½	53¼
	Dozen	15.00	47	do	28.20	(2)	3¾
	do	15.00		½ medium	24.00	1¼	4¼
Grapefruit segments	½-gallon jar	4.22	100	4 ounces	16.88	1½	6
Grapes:							
With seeds	Pound	1.00	89	4 ounces, seeds removed	3.56	7¼	28¼
Seedless	do	1.00	94	4 ounces	3.76	6¾	26¾
	Lug	24.00	94	do	90.24	(2)	1¼
Honeydew melon	Pound	1.00	60	3 ounces sliced or diced	3.20	8	31¼
	1 melon	4.00		Wedge, ⅛ melon	8.00	3¼	12½
	do	4.00	60	3 ounces sliced or diced	12.80	2	8
Lemons	1 lemon (medium)	.23		1 slice	8.00	3¼	12½
	do	.23		1 wedge	6.00	4¼	16¾
	Pound (about 4 lemons)	1.00	43	2 fluid ounces juice	3.16	8	31¾
	Carton	36.00	43	do	113.76	(2)	(2)
Limes	1 lime (medium)	.15		Wedge, ¼ lime	4.00	6¼	25
	Pound	1.00	48	2 fluid ounces juice	3.52	7¼	28½
	Box (⅘ bushel)	40.00	48	do	140.80	(2)	(2)
Mangoes	Pound	1.00	67	3 ounces sliced or diced	3.57	7¼	28¼
	Lug	24.00	67	do	85.76	(2)	1¼
Oranges	Pound	1.00	50	4 fluid ounces juice	1.83	13¾	54¾
	do	1.00	56	4 ounces sections (no membrane)	2.24	11¼	44¾
	do	1.00	70	4 ounces sections (with membrane)	2.80	9	35¾
California	Carton	38.00	70	do	106.40	(2)	(2)
Florida	Box	85.00	50	4 fluid ounces juice	155.55	(2)	(2)
Medium No. 176	Pound	1.00		1 whole	2.00	12½	50
	Dozen	6.00	50	4 fluid ounces juice	11.01	2¼	9¼
	do	6.00	56	4 ounces sections (no membrane)	13.44	2	7½
Small No. 250	Pound	1.00		1 whole	3.00	8½	33½
	Dozen	4.00	50	4 fluid ounces juice	7.34	3½	13¾
	do	4.00	56	4 ounces sections (no membrane)	8.96	3	11¼
Orange segments	½-gallon jar	4.28	100	4 ounces	17.12	1½	6
Peaches	Pound	1.00		1 medium	4.00	6¼	25
	do	1.00	76	3 ounces sliced or diced	4.05	6¼	24¾
	Bushel	48.00	76	do	194.56	(2)	(2)
	Pound	1.00		⅙ 9-inch pie (1.88 pound per pie)	3.19	8	31½
	do	1.00		⅛ 9-inch pie	4.26	6	23½
Pears	do	1.00		1 medium	3.00	8½	33½
	do	1.00	78	3 ounces sliced or diced	4.16	6¼	24¼
	Bushel	46.00	78	do	191.36	(2)	(2)

Pineapples	Pound	1.00	52	3 ounces cubed	2.77	9¼	36¼
	½ crate	35.00	52	do	97.07	[2]	1¼
Pineapple chunks	½-gallon jar	4.36	100	4 ounces	17.44	1½	5¾
Plums	Pound	1.00		3 medium	2.67	9½	37½
	do	1.00	94	3 ounces halves pitted	5.01	5	20
	4-basket crate	28.00	94	do	140.37	[2]	[2]
Raspberries	Quart	1.47	97	1 ounce salad garnish	22.87	1¼	4½
	do	1.47	97	3 ounces	7.62	3½	13¼
	Crate (24 quarts)	35.00	97	do	181.07	[2]	[2]
	Quart	1.46		⅙ 9-inch pie (0.68 quart per pie)	8.85	3	11½
	do	1.46		⅛ 9-inch pie	11.76	2¼	8¾
Rhubarb, trimmed	Pound	1.00	103	3 ounces cooked	5.49	4¾	18¼
	do	1.00		⅙ 9-inch pie (1.44 pounds per pie)	4.17	6	24
	do	1.00		⅛ 9-inch pie	5.56	4½	18
Strawberries	Quart	1.48	87	1 ounce salad garnish	20.53	1¼	5
	do	1.48	87	3 ounces	6.84	3¾	14¾
	Crate (24 quarts)	35.00	87	do	162.40	[2]	[2]
	Quart	1.46		⅙ 9-inch pie (1 quart per pie)	6.00	4¼	16¾
	do	1.46		⅛ 9-inch pie	8.00	3¼	12½
Tangerines	Pound	1.00		1 medium	4.00	6¼	25
	Box	45.00		do	180.00	[2]	[2]
	Pound	1.00	74	3 ounces sections	3.95	6½	25½
Watermelon	do	1.00	46	3 ounces	2.45	10¼	41
	1 melon	18 to 30		⅟₁₆ melon	16.00	1¾	6¼

[1] Legal weights for contents of bushels, lugs, crates, and boxes vary among States.

[2] Number of purchase units needed is less than one.

TABLE 14.—FRUITS—CANNED

Canned fruits as purchased	Unit of purchase	Weight per unit	Yield, as served	Portion as served	Portions per purchase unit	Approximate purchase units for— 25 portions	100 portions
		Pounds	*Percent*		*Number*	*Number*	*Number*
Apples, solid pack	No. 2 can	1.12	100	4 ounces	4.48	5¾	22½
	No. 2½ can	1.62	100	do	6.48	4	15½
	No. 10 can	6.00	100	4 ounces	24.00	1¼	4¼
				⅙ 9-inch pie	24.00	1¼	4¼
Apple juice	23-fluid-ounce can	1.57	100	4 fluid ounces	5.75	4⅓	17½
	46-fluid-ounce can	3.14	100	do	11.50	2¼	8¾
	96-fluid-ounce can	6.56	100	do	24.00	1¼	4¼
Applesauce	No. 303 can	1.00	100	4 ounces	4.00	6¼	25
	No. 2½ can	1.81	100	do	7.24	3½	14
	No. 10 can	6.75	100	do	27.00	1	3¾
Apricots, halves	No. 303 can	1.00		3–5 medium	4.00	6¼	25
	No. 2½ can	1.88		do	7.00	3¾	14½
	No. 10 can	6.62		do	25.00	1	4
Blackberries	No. 303 can	1.00	100	4 ounces	4.00	6¼	25
	No. 10 can	6.62	100	do	26.48	1	4
Blueberries	No. 300 can	.91	100	do	3.64	7	27½
	No. 10 can	6.56	100	do	26.24	1	4
Boysenberries	No. 303 can	.94	100	do	3.76	6¾	26¾
	No. 10 can	6.62	100	do	26.48	1	4
Cherries:							
Red, sour, pitted	No. 303 can	1.00	100	do	4.00	6¼	25
	No. 10 can	6.56	100	4 ounces	26.24	1	4
				⅙ 9-inch pie	24.00	1¼	4¼
Sweet	No. 303 can	1.00	100	4 ounces	4.00	6¼	25
	No. 2½ can	1.81	100	do	7.24	3½	14
	No. 10 can	6.75	100	do	27.00	1	3¾
Cranberries, strained or whole	No. 300 can	1.00	100	2 ounces	8.00	3¼	12½
	No. 10 can	7.31	100	do	58.50	(1)	1¾
Cranberry juice	1 pint	1.11	100	4 fluid ounces	4.00	6¼	25
	1 quart	2.23	100	do	8.00	3¼	12½
	1 gallon	8.92	100	do	32.00	(1)	3¼
Figs	No. 303 can	1.06		3–4 figs	4.00	6¼	25
	No. 2½ can	1.88		do	7.00	3¾	14½
	No. 10 can	7.00		do	25.00	1	4

34

FOOD PURCHASING GUIDE

Food	Purchase unit	Weight (pounds) per purchase unit	Percent yield	Serving size	Servings per purchase unit	Purchase units for 25 servings	Purchase units for 100 servings[1]
Fruit cocktail or salad	No. 303 can	1.06	100	4 ounces	4.24	6	23¾
	No. 2½ can	1.88	100	do	7.52	3½	13¼
	No. 10 can	6.75	100	do	27.00	1	3¾
Grapefruit juice	18-fluid-ounce can	1.24	100	4 fluid ounces	4.50	5¾	22¼
	46-fluid-ounce can	3.14	100	do	11.50	2¼	8¾
	96-fluid-ounce can	6.57	100	do	24.00	1¼	4¼
Grapefruit sections	No. 303 can	1.00	100	4 ounces	4.00	6¼	25
	No. 3 cylinder	3.12	100	do	12.48	2¼	8¼
Lemon juice	32 fluid-ounce bottle	2.16	100	2 fluid ounces	16.00	1¾	6¼
Lime juice	do	2.17	100	do	16.00	1¾	6¼
Orange juice	18-fluid-ounce can	1.24	100	4 fluid ounces	4.50	5¾	22¼
	46-fluid-ounce can	3.16	100	do	11.50	2¼	8¾
	96-fluid-ounce can	6.59	100	do	24.00	1¼	4¼
Oranges, mandarin	No. 10 can	6.38	100	4 ounces	25.50	1	4
Peaches:							
Halves or slices	No. 303 can	1.00	—	2 medium	3.00	8½	33½
	No. 2½ can	1.81	—	do	7.00	3¾	14½
	No. 10 can	6.75	—	{2 medium / ⅙ 9-inch pie}	25.00 / 24.00	1 / 1¼	4 / 4¼
Whole, spiced	do	6.88	—	1 each	25.00	1	4
Pears, halves	No. 303 can	1.00	—	2 medium	3.00	8½	33½
	No. 2½ can	1.81	—	do	7.00	3¾	14½
	No. 10 can	6.62	—	do	25.00	1	4
Pineapple:							
Chunks and cubes	No. 2½ can	1.88	100	4 ounces	7.52	3½	13½
	No. 10 can	6.75	100	do	27.00	1	3¾
Crushed	No. 2½ can	1.88	100	do	7.52	3½	13½
	No. 10 can	6.81	100	do	27.24	1	3¾
Sliced	No. 2½ can	1.88	100	1 large or 2 small	8.00	3¼	12½
	No. 10 can	6.81	100	1 large or 2 small	25.00	1	4
Pineapple juice	18-fluid-ounce can	1.24	100	4 fluid ounces	4.50	5¾	22¼
	46-fluid-ounce can	3.17	100	do	11.50	2¼	8¾
	96-fluid-ounce can	6.62	100	do	24.00	1¼	4¼
Plums	No. 2½ can	1.88	—	2-3 plums	7.00	3¾	14½
	No. 10 can	6.75	—	do	25.00	1	4
Prunes	No. 2½ can	1.88	100	4 ounces	7.52	3½	13¾
	No. 10 can	6.88	100	do	27.52	1	3¾
Raspberries	No. 303 can	1.00	100	do	4.00	6¼	25
	No. 10 can	6.75	100	do	27.00	1	3¾
Strawberries	No. 303 can	1.00	100	do	4.00	6¼	25
	No. 10 can	6.75	100	do	27.00	1	3¾

[1] Number of purchase units needed is less than one.

TABLE 15.—FRUITS—FROZEN

Frozen fruits as purchased	Unit of purchase	Weight per unit	Yield, as served	Portion as served	Portions per purchase unit	Approximate purchase units for— 25 portions	Approximate purchase units for— 100 portions
		Pounds	*Percent*		*Number*	*Number*	*Number*
Apples, sliced	Pound	1.00	106	4 ounces	4.24	6	23¾
				⅙ 9-inch pie (1.50 pounds per pie).	4.00	6¼	25
	Package	2.50	106	4 ounces	10.60	2½	9½
	do	5.00	106	do	21.20	1¼	4¾
	Can	30.00	106	do	127.20	(1)	(1)
Apricots	Pound	1.00	95	do	3.80	6¾	26½
	Can	25.00	95	do	95.00	(1)	1¼
	do	30.00	95	do	114.00	(1)	(1)
Blackberries	Pound	1.00	103	do	4.12	6¼	24½
	Can	30.00	103	do	123.60	(1)	(1)
Blueberries	Pound	1.00	108	do	4.32	6	23¼
	Package	2.50	108	do	10.80	2½	9½
	Can	25.00	108	do	108.00	(1)	1
	do	30.00	108	do	129.60	(1)	(1)
Cherries, red, sour, pitted	Pound	1.00	100	4 ounces	4.00	6¼	25
				⅙ 9-inch pie (1.50 pounds per pie).	4.00	6¼	25
	Can	30.00	100	4 ounces	120.00	(1)	(1)
Grapefruit sections	Pound	1.00	100	do	4.00	6¼	25
	Package	3.00	100	do	12.00	2¼	8½
Grapefruit juice, concentrate	6-fluid-ounce can	.46	400	4 fluid ounces	6.00	4¼	16¾
	32-fluid-ounce can	2.46	400	do	32.00	(1)	3¼
Grape juice, concentrate	6-fluid-ounce can	.48	400	do	6.00	4¼	16¾
	32-fluid-ounce can	2.54	400	do	32.00	(1)	3¼
Lemon juice, concentrate	4-fluid-ounce can	.31	500	2 fluid ounces	10.00	2½	10
	6-fluid-ounce can	.47	500	do	15.00	1¾	6¾
Lemonade, concentrate	6-fluid-ounce can	.49	700	do	21.00	1¼	5
	18-fluid-ounce can	1.46	700	do	63.00	(1)	1¾
Melon scoops	Pound	1.00	100	3 ounces	5.33	4¾	19
	Package	6.50	100	do	34.67	(1)	3

Orange juice, concentrate	6-fluid-ounce can	.46	400	4 fluid ounces	6.00	4¼	16¾
	12-fluid-ounce can	.93	400	do	12.00	2¼	8½
	32-fluid-ounce can	2.48	400	do	32.00	(1)	3¼
Peaches, sliced	Pound	1.00	95	4 ounces	3.80	6¾	26½
				⅙ 9-inch pie (1.33 pounds per pie).	4.50	5¾	22¼
	Can	6.50	95	4 ounces	24.70	1¼	4¼
	do	10.00	95	do	38.00	(1)	2¾
	do	30.00	95	do	114.00	(1)	(1)
Pineapple:							
Chunks	Pound	1.00	100	do	4.00	6¼	25
	Can	10.00	100	do	40.00	(1)	2½
Crushed	do	30.00	100	do	120.00	(1)	(1)
Pineapple juice, concentrate	6-fluid-ounce can	.47	400	4 fluid ounces	6.00	4¼	16¾
	32-fluid-ounce can	2.53	400	do	32.00	(1)	3¼
Raspberries	Pound	1.00	100	4 ounces	4.00	6¼	25
	Can	6.50	100	do	26.00	1	4
	do	10.00	100	do	40.00	(1)	2½
	do	30.00	100	do	120.00	(1)	(1)
Rhubarb	Pound	1.00	106	4 ounces	4.24	6	23¾
				⅙ 9-inch pie (1.50 pounds per pie).	4.00	6¼	25
	Package	2.50	106	4 ounces	10.60	2½	9½
	Can	10.00	106	do	42.40	(1)	2½
	do	25.00	106	do	106.00	(1)	1
	do	30.00	106	do	127.20	(1)	(1)
Strawberries	Pound	1.00	100	do	4.00	6¼	25
	Can	6.50	100	do	26.00	1	4
	do	10.00	100	do	40.00	(1)	2½
	do	30.00	100	do	120.00	(1)	(1)
Tangerine juice, concentrate	6-fluid-ounce can	.47	400	4 fluid ounces	6.00	4¼	16¾
	32-fluid-ounce can	2.48	400	do	32.00	(1)	3¼

[1] Number of purchase units needed is less than one.

TABLE 16.—FRUITS—DRIED

Fruits, dried, regular and low-moisture, as purchased	Unit of purchase	Weight per unit	Yield, as served	Portion as served	Portions per purchase unit	Approximate purchase units for— 25 portions	100 portions
		Pounds	*Percent*		*Number*	*Number*	*Number*
REGULAR							
Apple slices	Pound	1.00	412	4 ounces	16.48	1¾	6¼
				⅙ 9-inch pie (⅓ pound per pie)	18.00	1½	5¾
	Carton	5.00	412	4 ounces	82.40	([1])	1¼
Apricots	11-ounce package	.69	344	do	9.46	2¾	10¾
	Pound	1.00	344	do	13.76	2	7½
	Carton	30.00	344	do	412.80	([1])	([1])
Dates	12-ounce package	.75	100	3 ounces	4.00	6¼	25
	Pound	1.00	100	do	5.33	4¾	19
	Carton	15.00	100	do	80.00	([1])	1¼
Peaches	11-ounce package	.69	422	4 ounces	11.60	2¼	8¾
	Pound	1.00	422	4 ounces	16.88	1½	6
				⅙ 9-inch pie (⅓ pound per pie)	18.00	1½	5¾
	Carton	30.00	422	4 ounces	506.40	([1])	([1])
Prunes	Pound	1.00	253	do	10.12	2½	10
	2-pound package	2.00	253	do	20.24	1¼	5
	Carton	30.00	253	do	303.60	([1])	([1])
Raisins	Pound	1.00	100	½ cup	6.00	4¼	16¾
LOW-MOISTURE							
Apples	Pound	1.00	584	4 ounces	23.36	1¼	4½
				⅙ 9-inch pie (¼ pound per pie).	24.00	1¼	4¼
	No. 10 can	1.50	584	4 ounces	35.04	([1])	3
Applesauce	Pound	1.00	911	do	36.44	([1])	2¾
	No. 10 can	2.50	911	do	91.10	([1])	1¼
Apricots	Pound	1.00	505	do	20.20	1¼	5
	No. 10 can	3.50	505	do	70.70	([1])	1½
Fruit cocktail	Pound	1.00	558	do	22.32	1¼	4½
	No. 10 can	2.75	558	do	61.38	([1])	1¾
Peaches	Pound	1.00	534	4 ounces	21.36	1¼	4¾
				⅙ 9-inch pie (¼ pound per pie).	24.00	1¼	4¼
	No. 10 can	3.00	534	4 ounces	64.08	([1])	1¾
Prunes, whole, pitted	Pound	1.00	462	do	18.48	1½	5½
	No. 10 can	3.00	462	do	55.44	([1])	2

[1] Number of purchase units needed is less than one.

TABLE 17.—FLOUR, CEREALS, AND MIXES

Flour, cereals, and mixes as purchased	Unit of purchase	Weight per unit	Yield, as served	Portion as served or used	Portions per purchase unit	Approximate purchase units for—	
						25 portions	100 portions
		Pounds	*Percent*		*Number*	*Number*	*Number*
Flour	5-pound bag	5.00		1 cup	20.00	(1)	(1)
	25-pound bag	25.00		do	100.00	(1)	(1)
	100-pound sack	100.00		do	400.00	(1)	(1)
Cereals, uncooked:							
Bulgur, cracked wheat (USDA)	Pound	1.00	401	¾ cup cooked	10.67	2½	9½
				1 cup uncooked	2.67	(1)	(1)
Cornmeal	1-pound box	1.00	628	¾ cup cooked	15.33	1¾	6¾
	5-pound bag	5.00	628	do	76.65	(2)	1½
	10-pound bag	10.00	628	do	153.30	(2)	(2)
	1-pound box	1.00	100	1 cup uncooked	3.00	(1)	(1)
Corn grits	do	1.00	628	¾ cup cooked	16.43	1¾	6¼
	do	1.00	100	1 cup uncooked	2.75	(1)	(1)
Farina	do	1.00	855	¾ cup cooked	21.92	1¼	4¾
	5-pound bag	5.00	855	do	109.60	(2)	1
Macaroni	1-pound box	1.00	311	do	12.00	2¼	8½
	20-pound box	20.00	311	do	240.00	(2)	(2)
	1-pound box	1.00	100	1 cup uncooked	3.75	(1)	(1)
Noodles	do	1.00	329	¾ cup cooked	10.67	2½	9½
	20-pound box	20.00	329	do	213.40	(2)	(2)
	1-pound box	1.00	100	1 cup uncooked	7.25	(1)	(1)
Rice	do	1.00	320	¾ cup cooked	11.27	2¼	9
	10-pound box	10.00	320	do	112.70	(2)	(2)
	100-pound sack	100.00	320	do	1,127.00	(2)	(2)
	1-pound box	1.00	100	1 cup uncooked	2.75	(1)	(1)
Rolled oats	do	1.00	610	¾ cup cooked	15.33	1¾	6¾
	3-pound box	3.00	610	do	46.00	(2)	2¼
	50-pound sack	50.00	610	do	766.50	(2)	(2)
	1-pound box	1.00	100	1 cup uncooked	4.50	(1)	(1)
Rolled wheat (USDA)	do	1.00	375	¾ cup cooked	8.89	3	11¼
	3-pound box	3.00	375	do	26.67	(2)	3¾
Spaghetti	1-pound box	1.00	359	do	12.12	2¼	8¼
	20-pound box	20.00	359	do	242.40	(2)	(2)
	1-pound box	1.00	100	1 cup uncooked	6.06	(1)	(1)
Whole wheat	do	1.00	608	¾ cup cooked	15.20	1¾	6¾
	4½-pound box	4.50	608	do	68.40	(2)	1½
	50-pound sack	50.00	608	do	760.00	(2)	(2)

See footnotes at end of table.

TABLE 17.—FLOUR, CEREALS, AND MIXES—Continued

Flour, cereals, and mixes as purchased	Unit of purchase	Weight per unit	Yield, as served	Portion as served or used	Portions per purchase unit	Approximate purchase units for— 25 portions	100 portions
		Pounds	*Percent*		*Number*	*Number*	*Number*
Cereals, ready-to-eat:							
Bran flakes (25–40%)	Pound	1.00	100	1 ounce	16.00	1¾	6¼
	14½-ounce package	.91	100	do	14.50	1¾	7
	10-pound package	10.00	100	do	160.00	[2]	[2]
Bran flakes with raisins	Pound	1.00	100	1¼ ounces	12.80	2	8
	14-ounce package	.88	100	do	11.20	2¼	9
	200 individuals	15.62	100	do	200.00	[2]	[2]
Corn flakes	Pound	1.00	100	1 ounce	16.00	1¾	6¼
	12-ounce package	.75	100	do	12.00	2¼	8½
	10-pound package	10.00	100	do	160.00	[2]	[2]
Puffed rice	Pound	1.00	100	⅝ ounce	25.60	1	4
	8-ounce package	.50	100	do	12.80	2	8
	10-pound package	10.00	100	do	256.00	[2]	[2]
Puffed wheat	Pound	1.00	100	½ ounce	32.00	[2]	3¼
	8-ounce package	.50	100	do	16.00	1¾	6¼
	10-pound package	10.00	100	do	320.00	[2]	[2]
Puffed wheat, presweetened	Pound	1.00	100	⅞ ounce	18.29	1½	5½
	9-ounce package	.56	100	do	10.29	2½	9¾
	200 individuals	10.94	100	do	200.00	[2]	[2]
Rice flakes	Pound	1.00	100	do	18.29	1½	5½
	9½-ounce package	.59	100	do	10.86	2½	9¼
	10-pound package	10.00	100	do	182.86	[2]	[2]
Shredded wheat	Pound	1.00	100	1⅗ ounces	10.00	2½	10
	12-ounce package	.75	100	1⅗ ounces (2 small)	7.50	3½	13½
	200 individuals	20.00	100	1⅗ ounces	200.00	[2]	[2]
Wheat flakes	Pound	1.00	100	1 ounce	16.00	1¾	6¼
	10-ounce package	.62	100	do	10.00	2½	10
	10-pound package	10.00	100	do	160.00	[2]	[2]
Mixes: [3]							
Cake:							
Angel food	Pound	1.00		1/12 10-in. cake	12.00	2¼	8½
	12-cake case	12.00		do	144.00	[2]	[2]
Other	Pound	1.00		2 in. x 3 in. cut	15–20	1¾	6¾
				Cupcake	20.00	1¼	5
	5-pound box	5.00		2 in. x 3 in. cut	75–100	[2]	1½
				Cupcake	100.00	[2]	1
Frosting	Pound	1.00		2 in. x 2 in.	38–39	[2]	2¾
				Cupcake	36–37	[2]	3
	5-pound box	5.00		2 in. x 2 in.	190–195	[2]	[2]
				Cupcake	180–185	[2]	[2]

Cookie:							
Basic sugar	Pound	1.00		2 ½-ounce cookies	17–20	1½	6
	5-pound box	5.00		do	85–100	(²)	1¼
Brownie	Pound	1.00		2 in. x 2 in.	20–30	1¼	5
	5-pound box	5.00		do	100–150	(²)	1
Hot bread:[3]							
Biscuit	Pound	1.00		2-inch biscuit	20.00	1¼	5
	5-pound box	5.00		do	100.00	(²)	1
Muffins	Pound	1.00		1½-ounce muffin	14–16	2	7¼
	5-pound box	5.00		do	70–80	(²)	1½
Rolls:							
Sweet	Pound	1.00		1¼-ounce roll	18–19	1½	5¾
	5-pound box	5.00		do	90–95	(²)	1¼
Yeast	Pound	1.00		1-ounce roll	23–25	1¼	4½
	5-pound box	5.00		do	115–120	(²)	(²)
Piecrust	Pound	1.00		9-inch shell	3.00	8½	33½
	5-pound box	5.00		do	16.00	1¾	6¼

[1] Number of purchase units needed is determined by use.
[2] Number of purchase units needed is less than one.
[3] Yields of mixes vary widely, depending on manufacturer, size of pan, and baking time and temperature. See instructions on package or box.

TABLE 18.—BAKERY FOODS

Bakery foods as purchased	Unit of purchase	Weight per unit	Portion as served	Portions per purchase unit	Approximate purchase units for— 25 portions	Approximate purchase units for— 100 portions
		Pounds		*Number*	*Number*	*Number*
Bread: [1]						
Raisin	1-pound loaf	1.00	1 slice	18.00	1½	5¾
	2-pound loaf	2.00	do	36.00	(2)	3
Rye	1-pound loaf	1.00	do	23.00	1¼	4½
	1½-pound loaf	1.50	do	28.00	1	3¾
	2-pound loaf	2.00	do	33.00	(2)	3¼
White and whole wheat	1-pound loaf	1.00	⅝-inch slice	16.00	1¾	6¼
	1¼-pound loaf	1.25	do	19.00	1½	5½
	1½-pound loaf	1.50	do	24.00	1¼	4¼
	2-pound loaf	2.00	½-inch slice	28.00	1	4
			⅜-inch slice	36.00	(2)	3
	3-pound loaf	3.00	½-inch slice	44.00	(2)	2½
			⅜-inch slice	56.00	(2)	2
Cake:						
Layer	8-inch		1/12 cake	12.00	2¼	8½
	9-inch		1/16 cake	16.00	1¾	6¼
	12-inch		1/30 cake	30.00	(2)	3½
	14-inch		1/40 cake	40.00	(2)	2½
Loaf	Pound	1.00	⅛ cake	8.00	3¼	12½
			1 cup soft cubes or crumbs	18.00	1½	5¾
			1 cup toasted cubes	13.50	2	7½
			1 cup dry crumbs	6.00	4¼	16¾
Sheet	8-inch square		2 in. x 2 in. (small)	16.00	1¾	6¼
	9 in. x 13 in		3 in. x 3 in. (regular)	12.00	2¼	8½
	12 in. x 10 in		2 in. x 2 in	54.00	(2)	2
			3 in. x 3 in	24.00	1¼	4¼
	16 in. x 24 in		2 in. x 2 in	96.00	(2)	1¼
			3 in. x 3 in	40.00	(2)	2½
Cookies:						
Brownies	Pound	1.00	2 cookies	18.00	1½	5¾
Butter	do	1.00	do	46.50	(2)	2¼
Chocolate chip	do	1.00	do	21.50	1¼	4¾
Cream filled	do	1.00	do	19.50	1½	5¼
Fig bars	do	1.00	do	15.50	1¾	6½
Ginger snaps	do	1.00	do	30.00	(2)	3½
Shortbread	do	1.00	do	29.00	(2)	3½
Sugar	do	1.00	do	10.50	2½	9¾
Vanilla	do	1.00	do	46.50	(2)	2¼
Crackers:						
Graham	do	1.00	2 crackers	32.50	(2)	3¼
Saltines	do	1.00	do	65–70	(2)	1¾
Soda	do	1.00	do	30–35	(2)	3½

Rolls:						
Frankfurter	do	1.00	1 roll (1⅓ ounces)	12.03	2¼	8½
Hamburger	do	1.00	1 roll (1¾ ounces)	9.14	2¾	11
Hard, round	do	1.00	1 roll (1⅚ ounces)	8.74	3	11½
Plain, pan	do	1.00	1 roll (1⅓ ounces)	12.03	2¼	8½
Sweet, pan	do	1.00	1 roll (1½ ounces)	10.67	2½	9½
Pie	8-inch		⅙ pie	6.00	4¼	16¾
	9-inch		⅐ pie	7.00	3¾	14½
	10-inch		⅛ pie	8.00	3¼	12½

[1] End crusts of bread were excluded in determining portions per purchase unit.

[2] Number of purchase units needed is less than one.

Table 19.—FATS AND OILS

Fats and oils as purchased	Unit of purchase	Weight per unit	Portion as served or used	Portions per purchase unit	Approximate purchase units for— 25 portions	Approximate purchase units for— 100 portions
		Pounds		*Number*	*Number*	*Number*
Butter or margarine:						
Pound print	Carton	1.00	1 cup	2.00	(1)	(1)
			1 pat	72.00	(2)	1½
¼-pound print	do	1.00	1 pat	72.00	(2)	1½
Chips	Case	5.00	do	360.00	(2)	(2)
Lard	Carton	1.00	1 cup	2.00	(1)	(1)
	Can	50.00	do	100.00	(1)	(1)
Salad dressing (oil or mayonnaise type)	Pint	1.00	1 tablespoon	32.00	(2)	3¼
	Quart	2.00	do	64.00	(2)	1¾
	Gallon	8.00	do	256.00	(2)	(2)
Salad oil	Pint	.97	1 cup	2.00	(1)	(1)
	Quart	1.94	do	4.00	(1)	(1)
	Gallon	7.76	do	16.00	(1)	(1)
Shortening (Hydrogenated)	Can	1.00	do	2.50	(1)	(1)
	do	3.00	do	7.50	(1)	(1)
	do	50.00	do	125.00	(1)	(1)

[1] Number of purchase units needed is determined by use.

[2] Number of purchase units needed is less than one.

Table 20.—SUGAR AND SWEETS

Sugar and sweets as purchased	Unit of purchase	Weight per unit	Portion as served or used	Portions per purchase unit	Approximate purchase units for—	
					25 portions	100 portions
		Pounds		*Number*	*Number*	*Number*
Sugar:						
Brown, dark or light	Carton	1. 00	1 cup	2. 00	[1]	[1]
		25. 00	do	50. 00	[1]	[1]
Cubes	do	1. 00	2 cubes	40. 00	[2]	2½
	Bulk	25. 00	do	1, 000. 00	[2]	[2]
Granulated:						
Bulk	Carton	1. 00	2 level or 1 rounded teaspoon	54. 00	[2]	2
			1 cup	2. 25	[1]	[1]
	Bag	5. 00	1 cup	11. 25	[1]	[1]
	do	25. 00	do	56. 25	[1]	[1]
	Sack	100. 00	do	225. 00	[1]	[1]
Individuals	Package	1. 50	1 packet	100. 00	[2]	1
	Carton	45. 00	do	3, 000. 00	[2]	[2]
Powdered (confectioners)	do	1. 00	1 cup	3. 50	[1]	[1]
	Sack	25. 00	do	87. 50	[1]	[1]
Sirup:						
Blends	12-fluid-ounce bottle	1. 03	2 tablespoons	12. 00	2¼	8½
	Quart	2. 83	do	32. 00	[2]	3¼
	No. 10 can	8. 50	do	96. 00	[2]	1¼
	Gallon	11. 00	do	128. 00	[2]	[2]
Corn	Pint	1. 50	do	16. 00	1¾	6¼
	5-pound can	5. 00	do	53. 33	[2]	2
	No. 10 can	8. 79	2 tablespoons	93. 76	[2]	1¼
			1 cup	11. 72	[1]	[1]
Maple	Pint	1. 38	2 tablespoons	16. 00	1¾	6¼
	Gallon	11. 00	do	128 00	[2]	[2]
Molasses	Pint	1. 50	do	16. 00	1¾	6¼
	Jar	2. 00	do	21. 00	1¼	5
	No. 10 can	9. 31	do	99. 00	[2]	1
Jam, jelly, marmalade:						
Bulk	Jar	1. 00	1 tablespoon	23. 00	1¼	4½
	No. 10 can	8. 38	do	192. 00	[2]	[2]
Individuals	Carton		1 packet	200. 00	[2]	[2]
Other sweets:						
Apple butter	Jar	1. 00	do	11. 00	2½	9¼
	No. 10 can	7. 50	do	81. 00	[2]	1¼
Honey	Jar	1. 00	do	11. 00	2½	9¼
	2-pound can	2. 00	do	22. 00	1¼	4¾
	5-pound can	5. 00	do	54. 00	[2]	2
Desserts, dry:						
Gelatin, flavored	3-ounce package	. 19	½ cup	4. 00	6¼	25
	6-ounce package	. 38	do	8. 00	3¼	12½
	Pound	1. 00	do	21. 33	1¼	4¾

Pudding, pie filling:						
Chocolate	4-ounce package	.25	do	4.00	6¼	25
	Pound	1.00	4 ounces	20.00	1¼	5
			Fill for ⅛ 9-inch pie	18.67	1⅓	5⅓
Lemon chiffon	do	1.00	Fill for ⅛ 9-inch pie	32.00	(²)	3¼
Vanilla	3-ounce package	.19	½ cup	4.00	6¼	25
	Pound	1.00	4 ounces	25.60	1	4
			Fill for ⅛ 9-inch pie	24.00	1¼	4¼
Pudding, instant:						
Chocolate	4½-ounce package	.28	½ cup	4.00	6¼	25
	Pound	1.00	do	14.29	1¾	7
Vanilla	3¾-ounce package	.23	do	4.00	6¼	25
	Pound	1.00	do	17.39	1½	5¾

[1] Number of purchase units needed is determined by use.

[2] Number of purchase units needed is less than one.

Table 21.—BEVERAGES

Beverages as purchased	Unit of purchase	Weight per unit	Portion as served	Portions per purchase unit	Approximate purchase units [1] for— 25 portions	Approximate purchase units [1] for— 100 portions
		Pounds		*Number*	*Number*	*Number*
Carbonated drinks:						
6-ounce bottles	Case (24)		6 fluid ounces	24.00		
12-ounce bottles	do		do	48.00		
16-ounce bottles	do		do	64.00		
Cocoa:						
Regular, unsweetened	Pound	1.00	1 measuring cup, prepared	50.00	½	2
Instant, sweetened:						
Bulk	8-ounce carton	.50	1 cup	28.00	(1½ c.)	(6 c.).
	38-ounce carton	2.38	do	133.00	(1½ c.)	(6 c.).
Individuals	Carton (50)		1 packet	50.00	½	2
Sirup, sweetened	16-ounce can	1.00	1 cup	29.00	1	3½.
Coffee:						
Ground	Pound	1.00	1 measuring cup, prepared	[2] 37.00		
Instant:						
Bulk	6-ounce jar	.38	1 level teaspoon	180.00	(½ c.+1 t.)	(2 c.+4 t.).
			1 rounded teaspoon	90.00	(½ c.+1 t.)	(2 c.+4 t.).
	10-ounce jar	.62	1 level teaspoon	300.00	(½ c.+1 t.)	(2 c.+4 t.).
Individuals	Carton (72)		1 packet	72.00		
Tea:						
Bulk	Pound	1.00	1 measuring cup, prepared	256.00		(6¼ oz.).
Bags	Package (48)	.24	1 measuring cup or more	48.00		
	Carton (100)	.50	do	100.00	¼	1
Instant	1½-ounce jar	.09	1 cup hot tea	96.00	(½ c.+1 t.)	(2 c.+4 t.).
			1 cup iced tea	64.00	(¾ c.)	(3 c.).

[1] Numbers in parentheses refer to approximate measure to serve 25 and 100 portions: c., cup; t., teaspoon; oz., ounces.

[2] Varies depending on brand of coffee used and method of preparation.

OTHER USEFUL INFORMATION FOR ESTIMATING FOOD QUANTITIES

TABLE 22.—*Conversion factors for computing the number of purchase units needed for portions of various sizes*

Portion size given in purchase tables (ounces)	Conversion factors for specified portion size, ounces									
	1	2	3	4	5	6	7	8	9	10
1	1.00	2.00	3.00	4.00	5.00	6.00	7.00	8.00	9.00	10.00
2	.50	1.00	1.50	2.00	2.50	3.00	3.50	4.00	4.50	5.00
3	.33	.67	1.00	1.33	1.67	2.00	2.33	2.67	3.00	3.33
4	.25	.50	.75	1.00	1.25	1.50	1.75	2.00	2.25	2.50
5	.20	.40	.60	.80	1.00	1.20	1.40	1.60	1.80	2.00
6	.17	.33	.50	.67	.83	1.00	1.17	1.33	1.50	1.67
7	.14	.29	.43	.57	.71	.86	1.00	1.14	1.29	1.43
8	.12	.25	.38	.50	.62	.75	.88	1.00	1.12	1.25

How To Use Table 22:

This table is to be used to help determine the number of purchase units if the size of portion is different from that specified in tables 1 to 21. For example, for 3-ounce portions of snap beans, five No. 10 cans are required (table 10); for other size portions, conversion factors in this table can be used to determine the number of No. 10 cans required.

The figures in the left-hand column of the conversion table represent the portion sizes given in tables 1 to 21. The figures across the top represent portion sizes that may be desired. If a 4-ounce instead of a 3-ounce portion of canned snap beans is to be used, for example, find the 3-ounce line in the left-hand column of the conversion table. Follow this line across to the factor in the 4-ounce column. Multiply this factor (1.33) by the number of purchase units (five No. 10 cans) given in table 10 for 100. Thus: 5 (No. 10 cans) × 1.33=6.65 No. 10 cans (round to 6¾ No. 10 cans) to serve 100 people each a 4-ounce portion.

Portion sizes in the purchase tables are sometimes given in terms of tablespoons, cups, slices, etc. Any of these measures can be substituted for ounces in this conversion table and the same computations performed.

TABLE 23.—*Cost per portion for food priced from 10 cents to $2 per purchase unit*

Price per purchase unit (cents)	Cost per portion for indicated portions per purchase unit							
	4	6	8	10	12	16	20	24
	Cents	*Cents*	*Cents*	*Cents*	*Cents*	*Cents*	*Cents*	*Cents*
10	2.5	1.7	1.2	1.0	0.8	0.6	0.5	0.4
15	3.8	2.5	1.9	1.5	1.2	.9	.8	.6
20	5.0	3.3	2.5	2.0	1.7	1.2	1.0	.8
25	6.2	4.2	3.1	2.5	2.1	1.6	1.2	1.0
30	7.5	5.0	3.8	3.0	2.5	1.9	1.5	1.2
35	8.8	5.8	4.4	3.5	2.9	2.2	1.8	1.5
40	10.0	6.7	5.0	4.0	3.3	2.5	2.0	1.7
45	11.2	7.5	5.6	4.5	3.7	2.8	2.2	1.9
50	12.5	8.3	6.2	5.0	4.2	3.1	2.5	2.1
60	15.0	10.0	7.5	6.0	5.0	3.8	3.0	2.5
70	17.5	11.7	8.8	7.0	5.8	4.4	3.5	2.9
80	20.0	13.3	10.0	8.0	6.7	5.0	4.0	3.3
90	22.5	15.0	11.2	9.0	7.5	5.6	4.5	3.7
100	25.0	16.7	12.5	10.0	8.3	6.2	5.0	4.2
110	27.5	18.3	13.8	11.0	9.2	6.9	5.5	4.6
120	30.0	20.0	15.0	12.0	10.0	7.5	6.0	5.0
130	32.5	21.7	16.2	13.0	10.8	8.1	6.5	5.4
140	35.0	23.3	17.5	14.0	11.7	8.8	7.0	5.8
150	37.5	25.0	18.8	15.0	12.5	9.4	7.5	6.2
160	40.0	26.7	20.0	16.0	13.3	10.0	8.0	6.7
170	42.5	28.3	21.2	17.0	14.2	10.6	8.5	7.1
180	45.0	30.0	22.5	18.0	15.0	11.2	9.0	7.5
190	47.5	31.7	23.8	19.0	15.8	11.9	9.5	7.9
200	50.0	33.3	25.0	20.0	16.7	12.5	10.0	8.3

How To Use Table 23:

Determine the number of portions per unit of purchase through use of the food item or from the column, "Portions per purchase unit," in appropriate table. Locate the column in the table above that is nearest to that number. Then locate in that column the number horizontal to the price paid for the purchase unit in the left-hand column. This number represents the approximate cost of a portion.

FOOD PURCHASING GUIDE

TABLE 24.—BEEF: *Approximate percentage of edible meat [1] from the carcass and wholesale cuts of Choice, Good, and Standard grades of beef*

[Steers ranging from 11 to 21 months in age]

Beef	Grade of carcass		
	Choice	Good	Standard
	Percent	*Percent*	*Percent*
Carcass	85	84	82
Wholesale cuts:			
Brisket	88	87	85
Chuck	86	85	83
Flank	100	100	100
Foreshank	58	58	56
Loin end	89	88	86
Round, with hindshank	85	84	82
Rump, knuckle out	87	86	84
Short loin	90	89	87
Standing rib	85	83	80
Short plate	90	89	86

[1] The remaining percentage of beef consists of bone, ligament, and tendon.

TABLE 25.—LAMB: *Approximate percentage of edible meat [1] from the carcass and wholesale cuts of Prime, Choice, and Good grades of lamb*

Lamb	Grade of carcass		
	Prime	Choice	Good
	Percent	*Percent*	*Percent*
Carcass	86	83	82
Wholesale cuts:			
Breast and flank	89	86	86
Leg	87	85	84
Loin	90	87	86
Neck	79	75	75
Rib cut (9 ribs)	86	82	80
Shoulder (3 ribs)	87	85	84

[1] The remaining percentage of lamb consists of bone and ligament.

TABLE 26.—PORK: *Approximate percentage of edible meat [1] from the carcass and wholesale trimmed cuts from hogs of 3 weight groups*

Pork	Weight of carcass [2]		
	200 pounds live, 158 pounds dressed	225 pounds live, 178 pounds dressed	250 pounds live, 197 pounds dressed
	Percent	*Percent*	*Percent*
Carcass	79	80	82
Wholesale cuts:			
Bacon	92	93	94
Ham	85	85	86
Head, full cut	47	50	53
Loin	78	79	79
Shoulder, full cut	84	85	86
Shoulder, ribs	40	42	45
Spareribs	58	61	63

[1] The remaining percentage consists of bone and skin.
[2] The average yield of lard per hog slaughtered is 14 percent per 100 pounds live weight. This percentage includes lard and rendered pork fat, and excludes bacon and salt pork.

TABLE 27.—VEGETABLES OR FRUITS: *Approximate amount of canned and frozen product obtained from specified quantities of fresh vegetables and fruits*

Vegetables or fruits	Home canning methods		Commercial canning methods		Frozen		
	Fresh	Yield, canned	Fresh	Yield of #10 cans, canned	Fresh	Yield, frozen	Fruit-to-sugar ratio
		Quarts		Number		Pounds	
Vegetables:							
Asparagus	2½ to 4½ pounds		8 to 9 pounds	1	1 crate	15	
	1 crate	7-12	1 crate	3-4			
Beans, lima	3 to 5 pounds [1]	1	5 pounds [2]	1	1 bushel [2]	29	
	1 bushel [1]	6-11	1 bushel [2]	6			
Beans, snap	1½ to 2½ pounds	1	4 to 5 pounds	1	1 bushel	24	
	1 bushel	12-20	1 bushel	6-8			
Beets, without tops	2 to 3½ pounds	1	8 pounds	1			
	1 bushel	15-26	1 bushel	6-7			
Broccoli					1 crate	23	
Carrots, without tops	2 to 3 pounds	1	8 pounds	1	1 bushel	25	
	1 bushel	17-25	1 bushel	6-7			
Corn, sweet, in husks	3 to 6 pounds	1	17 to 18 pounds	3 [1]			
Okra	1 bushel	6-12	1 bushel	2 [2]	1 bushel	8 [3]	
	1½ pounds	1	7 pounds	1			
Peas, green	3 to 6 pounds [1]	1	4 to 5 pounds [2]	1	1 bushel [2]	27	
	1 bushel [1]	5-10	1 bushel [2]	6-8			
Pumpkin and winter squash	1½ to 3 pounds	1	17 to 18 pounds	3	1 bushel	32	
	1 bushel	17-33	1 bushel	3			
Spinach, other greens	2 to 6 pounds	1	8 pounds	1	1 bushel	10-11	
	1 bushel	3-10	1 bushel	2-3			
Sweetpotatoes	2 to 3 pounds	1	7 pounds	1			
	1 bushel	17-25	1 bushel	7			
Tomatoes	2½ to 3½ pounds	1	12 pounds	1			
	1 bushel	15-21	1 bushel	4-5			
Tomato catsup			19 pounds	1			
			1 bushel	2-3			
Tomato paste			40 to 41 pounds	1			
			1 bushel	1-2			
Tomato sauce			21 pounds	1			
			1 bushel	3-4			

FOOD PURCHASING GUIDE

Fruits:						
Apples	2½ to 3 pounds	15-20	10 pounds	4-5	1 bushel	20-31	5 to 1
Berries, except strawberries	1½ to 3 pounds		1 bushel	1	1 crate	34	4 to 1
Cherries, sour	1 crate	12-24	5 pounds	7			
	2 to 2½ pounds	22-28	7 pounds	1	1 bushel	53	4 to 1
Peaches	2 to 3 pounds		1 bushel	8			
	1 bushel	15-25	1 bushel	1	1 bushel	41-44	3 to 1
Pears	2 to 3 pounds		8 pounds	6-7			
	1 bushel	15-24	1 bushel	1			
Plums	1½ to 2½ pounds		5 pounds	5-6			
	1 bushel	10-32	1 bushel	1			
Strawberries	1½ to 3 pounds		6 pounds	9-10			
	1 crate	12-24	1 crate	6	1 crate	42	3 to 1

[1] In pods. [2] Shelled basis. [3] Whole kernel.

TABLE 28.—*Common can and jar sizes*

Can size (Industry term)	Container — Consumer description — Average net weight or fluid measure per can [1] (check label)	Average cups per can	Cans per case	Principal products
		Number	*Number*	
8 ounces	8 ounces	1	48 and 72	Small cans—ready-to-serve soups, fruits, and vegetables.
No. 1 picnic	10½ to 12 ounces	1¼	48	Small cans—condensed soups, some fruits, vegetables, meat, and fish.
No. 300	14 to 16 ounces	1¾	24	Small cans—fruits, vegetables, some meat and poultry products, and ready-to-serve soups.
No. 303	16 to 17 ounces	2	24	Do.
No. 2	1 pound, 4 ounces (20 ounces) or 1 pint, 2 fluid ounces (18 fluid ounces).	2½	24	Family size—juices, ready-to-serve soups, and some fruits.
No. 2½	1 pound, 13 ounces (29 ounces)	3½	24	Family size—fruits and some vegetables.
No. 3 cylinder	3 pounds, 3 ounces (51 ounces) or 1 quart, 14 fluid ounces (46 fluid ounces).	5¾	12	"Economy family size"—fruit and vegetable juices. Institutional size—condensed soups, some vegetables, and meat and poultry products.
No. 10	6 pounds, 8 ounces (104 ounces) to 7 pounds, 5 ounces (117 ounces).	12 to 13	6	Institutional size—fruits, vegetables, and some other foods.

[1] The label on one product may show net weight that differs slightly from the label on another product in cans or jars of identical size. (An example would be lima beans (1 pound) and blueberries (14 ounces) in the same size can.)

Source: National Canners Association.

Ounce equivalents in decimal parts of pound

Ounces	Pound	Ounces	Pound
1	0.06	9	.56
2	.12	10	.62
3	.19	11	.69
4	.25	12	.75
5	.31	13	.81
6	.38	14	.88
7	.44	15	.94
8	.50	16	1.00

Approximate scoop equivalents

Scoop No.[1]	Level measure	Scoop No.[1]	Level measure
6	⅔ cup	20	3⅓ tablespoons
8	½ cup	24	2⅔ tablespoons
10	⅜ cup	30	2⅕ tablespoons
12	⅓ cup	40	1⅗ tablespoons
16	¼ cup		

[1] A serving spoon may be used to replace a scoop. Since serving spoons are not identified by number, it is necessary to measure or weigh the quantity of food from sizes of spoons used to obtain the approximate serving size desired.

Common food-measure equivalents

3 teaspoons	1 tablespoon	16 tablespoons	1 cup
2 tablespoons	1 fluid ounce	1 cup	8 fluid ounces
4 tablespoons	¼ cup	2 cups	1 pint
6 tablespoons	⅜ cup	2 pints	1 quart
8 tablespoons	½ cup		

INDEX OF FOODS IN TABLES 1 THROUGH 21

Food	Page
Almonds	17
Apple butter, canned	42
Apple juice, canned	32
Apples:	
canned	32
dried	36
fresh	29
frozen	34
Applesauce:	
canned	32
dried	36
Apricots:	
canned	32
dried	36
fresh	29
frozen	34
Asparagus:	
canned	23
fresh	20
frozen	26
Avocados, fresh	29
Bacon	5
Bananas, fresh	29
Beans, butter (lima) frozen	26
Beans, dried:	
canned	23
raw	28
Beans, lima, green:	
canned	23
fresh	20
frozen	26
Beans, snap, green or wax:	
canned	23
fresh	20
frozen	26
Bean sprouts, canned	23
Beans with frankfurters in sauce, canned	8
Beans with ham in sauce, canned	8
Beans with meat in chili sauce, canned	8
Beef:	
canned	5
dried	5
fresh or frozen	3
Beef goulash:	
canned	8
frozen	8
Beef stew, canned	8
Beef with barbecue sauce, canned	8
Beef with gravy, canned	8
Beet greens, fresh	20
Beets:	
canned	23
fresh	20
Biscuit mix	39
Blackberries:	
canned	32
fresh	29
frozen	34
Blackeye peas:	
fresh	20
frozen	26
Blueberries:	
canned	32
fresh	29
frozen	34
Boysenberries, canned	32

Food	Page
Bran flakes	38
Bran flakes with raisins	38
Brazil nuts	17
Bread	40
Broccoli:	
fresh	20
frozen	26
Brunswick stew, canned	8
Brussel sprouts:	
fresh	20
frozen	26
Bulgar, cracked wheat	37
Butter	41
Cabbage, Chinese, fresh	20
Cabbage, fresh	20
Cake:	
mixes	38
ready-to-eat	40
Canadian bacon	5
Cantaloup, fresh	29
Carbonated drinks	43
Carrots:	
canned	23
fresh	20
frozen	26
Cashew nuts	17
Cauliflower:	
fresh	20
frozen	26
Celery, fresh	20
Cereals:	
ready-to-eat	38
uncooked	37
Chard, fresh	20
Cheese:	
cheddar	18
cottage	18
cream	18
processed	18
Cherries:	
canned	32
fresh	29
frozen	34
Chestnuts	17
Chicken:	
canned	10
fresh or frozen	10
Chicken combinations, canned or frozen:	
a la king	12
burgers	12
cacciatore	12
chop suey	12
chow mein	12
creamed	12
fricassee	12
minced, barbecue	12
noodles or dumplings	12
potpie	12
sliced with gravy	12
stew	12
tamales	12
Chicken parts, fresh or frozen	10
Chicory	21
Chili con carne, canned	8
Chili con carne with beans, canned	8
Chili mac, canned	8

INDEX

Entry	Page
Chop suey or chow mein vegetables with meat:	
canned	9
frozen	9
Chop suey vegetables, canned	23
Clam chowder	14
Clam juice	14
Clams:	
fresh (live in shell)	14
fresh or frozen, shucked	15
frozen, breaded	15
minced	14
Cocoa	43
Coconut	17
Cod, dried	13
Coffee	43
Collards:	
canned	23
fresh	20
frozen	26
Cookies:	
mixes	39
ready-to-eat	40
Corn:	
canned	23
fresh	20
frozen	26
Corn flakes	38
Corn grits	37
Cornmeal	37
Crabcakes, frozen	15
Crabmeat:	
canned	14
fresh or frozen	15
Crabs:	
fresh (live in shell)	14
fresh or frozen (cooked in shell)	15
Crackers	40
Cranberries:	
canned	32
fresh	29
Cranberry juice	32
Cream	18
Cucumbers, fresh	21
Dates, dried	36
Desserts, dry	42
Duck, fresh or frozen	11
Eggplant	21
Eggs	16
Endive	21
Escarole	21
Farina	37
Figs:	
canned	32
fresh	29
Filberts	17
Fish:	
canned	13
dried	13
fresh or frozen:	
drawn	13
dressed	13
fillets	13
steaks	13
whole or round	13
Fish (portions), frozen:	
breaded	14
unbreaded	14
Fish sticks, breaded	14
Flour	37
Frankfurters	7
Frosting mixes	38
Fruit cocktail or salad:	
canned	33
dried	36
Fruit juices. (*See* specific kind.)	
Gefiltefish, canned	13
Gelatin, flavored	42
Goose, fresh or frozen	11
Grapefruit:	
canned sections	33
fresh	30
fresh segments	30
frozen sections	34
Grapefruit juice:	
canned	33
frozen concentrate	34
Grape juice, frozen concentrate	34
Grapes, fresh	30
Hash, beef, canned	9
Honey	42
Honeydew melon	30
Hot bread mixes	39
Ice cream	18
Jam	42
Jelly	42
Kale:	
canned	23
fresh	21
frozen	26
Kohlrabi, fresh	21
Lamb, fresh or frozen	5
Lamb stew, canned	9
Lard	41
Lemonade, frozen concentrate	34
Lemon juice:	
canned	33
frozen concentrate	34
Lemons, fresh	30
Lentils	28
Lettuce	21
Lime juice, canned	33
Limes, fresh	30
Lobster, fresh or frozen (cooked in shell)	15
Lobster meat, fresh or frozen	15
Lobster, spiny tails, frozen	15
Luncheon meats (all meat varieties)	7
Macaroni	37
Macaroni and beef in tomato sauce, canned	9
Mackerel, canned	13
Mangoes	30
Margarine	41
Marmalade	42
Meatballs with gravy:	
canned	9
frozen	9
Melon, honeydew	30
Melon scoops, frozen	34
Milk	19
Mixes:	
cake	38
cookie	39
frosting	38
hot bread	39
piecrust	39
Molasses	42
Muffin mix	39
Mushrooms:	
canned	23
fresh	21
Mustard greens:	
canned	23
fresh	21
frozen	27
Noodles	37
Noodles with chicken, canned	12
Nuts	17
Oats, rolled	37
Okra:	
canned	23
fresh	21
frozen	27

INDEX

Item	Page
Okra and tomatoes, canned	23
Olives, canned	24
Onions:	
canned	24
dried	28
fresh:	
green	21
mature	21
Orange juice:	
canned	33
frozen concentrate	35
Oranges:	
fresh	30
fresh segments	30
mandarin, canned	33
Oysters:	
canned	14
fresh (live in shell)	15
fresh or frozen, shucked	15
frozen, breaded	15
Oyster stew	14
Parsley	21
Parsnips	21
Peaches:	
canned	33
dried	36
fresh	30
frozen	35
spiced	33
Peanut butter	17
Peanuts	17
Pears:	
canned	33
fresh	30
Peas, dried	28
Peas, green:	
canned	24
fresh	21
frozen	27
Peas and carrots:	
canned	24
frozen	27
Pecans	17
Peppers, green:	
fresh	21
frozen	27
Pickle relish	24
Pickles	24
Pie, ready-to-eat	41
Piecrust mix	39
Pie filling, fruit. (*See* appropriate fruit.)	
Pie filling, mix	43
Pimientos, canned	24
Pineapple:	
canned	33
fresh	31
frozen	35
Pineapple juice:	
canned	33
frozen concentrate	35
Plums:	
canned	33
fresh	31
Pork:	
canned	6
cured	5
fresh	6
Pork with barbecue sauce:	
canned	9
in waxed tub	9
Pork with gravy, canned	9
Potatoes:	
canned	24
dried	28

Item	Page
Potatoes—Continued	
fresh	21
frozen	27
Prunes:	
canned	33
dried	36
Pudding, instant mix	43
Pudding mix	43
Pumpkin:	
canned	24
fresh	22
Radishes	22
Raisins	36
Raspberries:	
canned	33
fresh	31
frozen	35
Ravioli with meat in sauce, canned	9
Rhubarb:	
fresh	31
frozen	35
Rice	37
Rice, puffed	38
Rice flakes	38
Rolls:	
mix	39
ready-to-eat	41
Rutabagas, fresh	22
Salad dressing	41
Salad oil	41
Salmon, canned	13
Sardines, canned:	
Maine	13
Pacific	13
Sauerkraut, canned	24
Sausage	6
Scallops:	
fresh or frozen, shucked	15
frozen, breaded	15
Sherbet	19
Shortening	41
Shrimp:	
canned	14
fresh or frozen (cooked and raw)	15
frozen, breaded	15
Sirup:	
blends	42
corn	42
maple	42
Soups:	
canned	25
condensed	25
ready-to-serve	25
Spaghetti	37
Spaghetti with meatballs and sauce, canned	9
Spinach:	
canned	25
fresh	22
frozen	27
Split peas	28
Squash, summer:	
canned	25
fresh	22
frozen	27
Squash, winter:	
canned	25
fresh	22
frozen	27
Strawberries:	
canned	33
fresh	31
frozen	35
Succotash:	
canned	25
frozen	27
Sugar	42

INDEX

Sweetpotatoes:	Page
canned	25
dried	28
fresh	22
frozen	27
Tamales, frozen	9
Tamales with gravy or sauce, canned	9
Tangerine juice, frozen concentrate	35
Tangerines, fresh	31
Tea	43
Tomatoes:	
canned	25
fresh	22
Tomato products:	
catsup	25
chili sauce	25
juice, concentrate	25
Tuna, canned	13
Turkey:	
canned	11
fresh or frozen	11
stuffed, whole, frozen	11
Turkey combinations, canned or frozen:	
a la king	12
creamed	12
fricassee	12

Turkey etc.—Continued	Page
potpie	12
sliced with gravy	12
Turkey parts, fresh or frozen	11
Turkey rolls, frozen	11
Turnip greens:	
canned	25
fresh	22
frozen	27
Turnip greens with turnips, frozen	27
Turnips, fresh	22
Veal, fresh or frozen	7
Vegetable juices, canned	25
Vegetables, mixed:	
canned	25
frozen	27
Vienna sausage	7
Walnuts	17
Watercress, fresh	22
Watermelon, fresh	31
Wheat:	
flakes	38
puffed	38
puffed, presweetened	38
rolled	37
shredded	38
whole	37

FOOD SERVICE GLOSSARY

TABLE OF CONTENTS

	Page
Absorption Capability … Antioxidant	1
Antipasti or Antipasto … Bavarian	2
Beat … Brown	3
Brunswick Stew … Chili con Carne	4
Chill … Croutons	5
Crullers … Disinfectant	6
Disposables … Éclair	7
Edible … Fold	8
Fold In … Fricassee	9
Fritters … Goulash	10
Gourmet … Horseshoes	11
Host … Kebab	12
Knead … Marinade	13
Marinate … Mulligatawny	14
Myocide … Pare	15
Parkerhouse Rolls … Potable	16
Potentially Hazardous pH … Reconstitute	17
Rehydrate … Saponify	18
Saturation … Skim	19
Slack Dough … Steep	20
Sterilize … Tartar	21
Tarts … Truss	22
Vacuum Drying … Zwieback	23

FOOD SERVICE GLOSSARY

A

ABSORPTION CAPABILITY
The property of flour to absorb and hold liquid.

ACIDITY
Sourness or tartness in a food product; in yeast doughs, a condition indicating excess fermentation; a factor in generating carbon dioxide for cake leavening.

AERATION
See LEAVENING.

AEROBIC BACTERIA
Those that require the presence of free oxygen as found in the air for growth.

A LA CARTE
On the menu alone, not in combination with a total meal.

A LA KING
A dish served with a cream sauce, usually containing green peppers and pimentos, and sometimes mushrooms and onions.

A LA MODE
In a fashion or the style of; for example, desserts served with ice cream or pot roast of beef cooked with vegetables.

ALBUMEN
Egg white.

AMBROSIA
A favorite southern dessert made of oranges, bananas, pineapple, and shredded coconut.

AMEBA
A simple animal-like organism that grows in water.

ANAEROBIC BACTERIA
Those that grow in oxygen-free atmosphere, deriving oxygen from solid or liquid materials and producing toxic substances.

ANTIBIOTICS
Substances produced by microorganisms and capable of inhibiting or killing other microorganisms.

ANTIOXIDANT
A chemical solution in which fruits and vegetables are dipped to prevent darkening.

ANTIPASTI or ANTIPASTO
An appetizer, or a spicy first course, consisting of relishes, cold sliced meats rolled with or without stuffings, fish, or other hors d'oeuvres eaten with a fork.

ANTISEPTIC
An agent that may or may not kill microorganisms, but does inhibit their growth. Peroxide is an example.

APPETIZER
A small portion of food or drink before or as the first course of a meal. These include a wide assortment of items ranging from cocktails, canapes, and hors d'oeuvres to plain fruit juices. The function of an appetizer is to pep up the appetite.

AU GRATIN
A thin surface crust formed by either bread or cheese, or both. Sometimes used with a cream sauce.

AU JUS
With natural juice. Roast rib au jus, for example, is beef served with unthickened gravy.

B

BACILLI
Cylindrical or rod-shaped bacteria responsible for such diseases as botulism, typhoid fever, and tuberculosis.

BACTERIA
Microscopic, one-cell microbes found in soil, water, and most material throughout nature. Some are responsible for disease and food spoilage, others are useful in industrial fermentation.

BACTERICIDE
Any substance that kills bacteria and related forms of life.

BAKE
To cook by dry heat in an oven. When applied to meats, it is called roasting.

BARBECUE
To roast or broil in a highly seasoned sauce.

BASTE
To moisten foods while cooking, especially while roasting meat. Melted fat, meat drippings, stock, water, or water and fat may be used.

BATTER
A homogeneous mixture of ingredients with liquid to make a mass that is of a soft plastic character.

BAVARIAN
A style of cooking that originated in the Bavarian section of Germany.

BEAT
  To make a mixture smooth or to introduce air by using a lifting motion with spoon or whip.

BENCH TOLERANCE
  The property of dough to ferment at a rate slow enough to prevent overfermentation while dough is being made up into units on the bench.

BLANCH
  To rinse with boiling water, drain, and rinse in cold water. Used for rice, macaroni, and other pastas to prevent sticking. For potatoes, to cook in hot, deep fat for a short time until clear but not brown.

BLAND
  Mild flavored, not stimulating to the taste.

BLEACHED FLOUR
  Flour that has been treated by a chemical to remove its natural color and make it white.

BLEEDING
  Dough that has been cut and left unsealed at the cut, thus permitting the escape of leavening gas. This term also applies to icing that bleeds.

BLEND
  To mix thoroughly two or more ingredients.

BOIL
  To cook in a liquid that bubbles actively during the time of cooking. The boiling temperature of water at sea level is 212° F.

BOTULISM
  Acute food poisoning caused by botulin (toxin) in food.

BOUILLON
  A clear soup made from beef or chicken stock or soup and gravy base.

BRAISE
  To brown meat or vegetables in a small amount of fat, then to cook slowly, covered, at simmering temperature in a small amount of liquid. The liquid may be juices rendered from meat, or added water, milk, or meat stock.

BREAD
  To coat with crumbs of bread or other food; or to dredge in seasoned flour, dip in a mixture of milk and slightly beaten eggs, and then dredge again in crumbs.

BROIL
  To cook under or over direct heat.

BROWN
  To cook, usually at medium or high heat, until the item of food darkens.

BRUNSWICK STEW
A main dish composed of a combination of poultry, meats, and vegetables.

BUTTERFLY
A method of cutting double chops (usually pork) from boneless loin strips. One side of each double chop is hinged together with a thin layer of meat.

BUTTERHORNS
Basic sweet dough cut and shaped like horns.

C

CACCIATORE
Chicken cooked "hunter" style. Browned chicken is braised in a sauce made with tomatoes, other vegetables, stock, and herbs.

CANAPE
Any of many varieties of appetizers, usually spread on bread, toast, or crackers and eaten with the fingers.

CANDY
To cook in sugar or syrup.

CARAMELIZED SUGAR
Dry sugar heated with constant stirring until melted and dark in color, used for flavoring and coloring.

CARBOHYDRATES
Sugars and starches derived chiefly from fruits and vegetable sources and containing set amounts of carbon, hydrogen, and oxygen.

CARBON DIOXIDE
A colorless, tasteless edible gas obtained during fermentation or from a combination of soda and acid.

CARRIERS
Persons who harbor and disseminate germs without having symptoms of a disease. The individual has either had the disease at one time and temporarily continues to excrete the organism, or has never manifested symptoms because of good resistance to the disease.

CHIFFONADE DRESSING
A salad dressing containing chopped hard-cooked eggs and beets.

CHIFFON CAKE
A sponge cake containing liquid shortening.

CHILI
A special pepper or its fruits. Dried, ground chili peppers are used in chili powder.

CHILI CON CARNE
Ground beef and beans seasoned with chili powder.

CHILL
 To place in a refrigerator or cool place until cold.

CHOP
 To cut into pieces with a knife or chopper.

CHOP SUEY
 A thick Chinese stew of thin slices of pork and various vegetables, such as bean sprouts, celery, and onions.

CLEAR FLOUR
 Lower grade and higher ash content flour remaining after the patent flour has been separated. (Used in rye bread.)

COAGULATE
 To thicken or form into a consistent mass.

COAT
 To cover the entire surface of food with a selected mixture.

CONDIMENTS
 Seasonings that in themselves furnish little nourishment, but which improve the flavor of food.

CONGEALING POINT
 Temperature or time at which a liquid changes to a firm or plastic condition.

COOKING LOSSES
 Loss of weight, liquid, or nutrients, and possibly a lowered palatability of a cooked food.

COOL
 To let stand, usually at room temperature, until no longer warm to touch.

CREAM
 To mix until smooth, sugar, shortening, and other ingredients; to incorporate air so that resultant mixture increases appreciably in volume and is thoroughly blended.

CREAM PUFFS
 Baked puffs of cream-puff dough, which are hollow; usually filled with cream pudding, whipped topping, or ice cream.

CREOLE
 A cooked sauce for poultry or shrimp. Usually served with rice.

CRISP
 To make somewhat firm and brittle.

CROUTONS
 Bread cut into small cubes and either fried or browned in the oven, according to the intended use. Used as a garnish, croutons are fried; as soup accompaniments, baked.

CRULLERS
  Long, twisted doughnuts.

CRUMB
  The soft part of bread or cake; a fragment of bread (see also BREAD).

CRUST
  Hardened exterior of bread; pastry portion of pie.

CRUSTING
  Formation of dry crust on the surface of doughs.

CUBE
  To cut into approximately 1/4 to 1/2 inch squares.

CURDLE
  To change into curd; to coagulate or thicken.

CURING
  A form of processing meat, which improves its flavor and texture.

CURRY
  A powder made from many spice ingredients and used as a seasoning for Indian and Oriental-type dishes, such as shrimp and chicken curry.

CUSTOM FOODS (RATION-DENSE)
  Various types of labor- and space-saving foods, including canned, concentrated, dehydrated, frozen, and prefabricated items.

CUT IN (as for shortening)
  To combine firm shortening and flour with pastry blender or knife.

D

DANISH PASTRY
  A flaky yeast dough having butter or shortening rolled into it.

DASH
  A scant 1/8 teaspoon.

DEVILED
  A highly seasoned, chopped, ground, or whole mixture served hot or cold.

DICE
  To cut into 1/4 inch or smaller cubes.

DISINFECTANT
  A chemical agent that destroys bacteria and other harmful organisms.

DISPOSABLES
Disposable articles used for food preparation, eating, or drinking utensils, constructed wholly or in part from paper or synthetic materials and intended for one single service.

DISSOLVE
To mix a solid, dry substance with a liquid until the solid is in solution.

DIVIDER
A machine used to cut dough into a desired size or weight.

DOCKING
Punching a number of vertical impressions in a dough with a smooth round stick about the size of a pencil. Docking makes doughs expand uniformly without bursting during baking.

DOT
To place small pieces (usually butter) on the surface of food.

DOUGH
The thickened, uncooked mass of combined ingredients for bread, rolls, cookies, and pies, but usually applicable to bread.

DOUGH CONDITIONER
A chemical product added to flour to alter its properties to hold gas.

DOUGH TEMPERATURES
Temperature of dough at different stages of processing.

DRAIN
To remove liquid.

DREDGE
To sprinkle or coat with flour, sugar, or cornmeal.

DRIPPINGS
Fat and juice dripped from roasted meat.

DRY YEAST
A dehydrated form of yeast.

DU JOUR
Today's or of the day; for example, Specialite du jour — food specialty of the day.

DUSTING
Distributing a film of flour or starch on pans or work surfaces.

E

ECLAIR
A long, thin pastry made from cream puff batter, usually filled with cream pudding, whipped topping, or ice cream. The baked, filled shell is dusted with confectioner's sugar or covered with a thin layer of chocolate.

EDIBLE
Fit to eat, wholesome.

EMULSIFICATION
The process of blending together fat and water solutions of ingredients to produce a stable mixture that will not separate while standing.

ENCHILADAS
A dish consisting of tortillas, a sauce, a filling (cheese, meat, or beans) and garnished with a topping such as cheese, then rolled, stacked, or folded and baked.

ENRICHED BREAD
Bread made from enriched flour and containing federally prescribed amounts of thiamin, riboflavin, iron, and niacin.

ENTREE
An intermediary course of a meal, which in the United States is usually the "main" dish.

ENZYME
A substance, produced by living organisms, that has the power to bring about changes in organic materials.

EXTRACT
Essence of fruits or spices used for flavoring.

F

FAT ABSORPTION
Fat that is absorbed in food products as they are fried in deep fat.

FERMENTATION
The chemical changes of an organic compound caused by action of living organisms (yeast or bacteria), usually producing a leavening gas.

FILET
The English term is "fillet," designating a French method of dressing fish, poultry, or meat to exclude bones and include whole muscle strips.

FLIPPER
A can of food that bulges at one end, indicating food spoilage. If pressed, the bulge may "flip" to the opposite end. Can and contents should be discarded.

FOAM
Mass of beaten egg and sugar, as in sponge cake before the flour is added.

FOLD
To lap yeast dough over onto itself. With cake batter, to lift and lap the batter onto itself to lightly incorporate ingredients.

FOLD IN
To combine ingredients gently with an up-and-over motion by lifting one up through the other.

FOOD-CONTACT SURFACES
Those parts and areas of equipment and utensils with which food normally comes in contact. Also those surfaces with which food may come in contact and drain back into surfaces normally in contact with food.

FOOD INFECTION
A food-borne illness from ingesting foods carrying bacteria that later multiply within the body and produce disease.

FOOD INTOXICATION
Another term used synonymously with food poisoning, or the ingestion of a food containing a poisonous substance.

FOOD POISONING
A food-borne illness contracted through ingesting food that contains some poisonous substance.

FOOD VALUE
The quantity of a nutrient contained in a food substance.

FOO YOUNG
A popular dish made with scrambled eggs or omelets with cut Chinese vegetables, onions, and meat. Usually, the dish is served with a sauce.

FORMULA
A recipe giving ingredients, amounts to be used, and the method of preparing the finished product.

FRANCONIA POTATOES
Potatoes are parboiled, then oven-browned in butter.

FREEZE DRYING
Drying method where the product is first frozen and then placed within a vacuum chamber (freeze dehydration). Aided by small controlled inputs of thermal or microwave energy, the moisture in the product passes directly from the ice-crystalline state to moisture vapor that is evacuated.

FRENCH BREAD
A crusty bread, baked in a narrow strip and containing little or no shortening.

FRENCH FRY
To cook in deep fat.

FRICASSEE
To cook by braising; usually applied to fowl or veal cut into pieces.

FRITTERS
Fruit, meat, poultry, or vegetables that are dipped in batter and fried.

FRIZZLE
To cook in a small amount of fat until food is crisp and curled at the edges.

FRY
To cook in hot fat. When a small amount of fat is used, the process is known as pan-frying or sauteing; when food is partially covered, shallow frying; and when food is completely covered, deep-fat frying.

FUMIGANT
A gaseous or colloidal substance used to destroy insects or pests.

FUNGICIDE
An agent that destroys fungi.

G

GARNISH
To ornament or decorate food before serving.

GELATINIZE
To convert into a gelatinous or jelly-like form.

GERM
A pathogenic, or disease-producing bacteria. A small mass of living substance capable of developing into an organism or one of its parts.

GERMICIDE
A germ-destroying agent.

GIBLETS
The heart, gizzard, and liver of poultry cooked with water for use in preparing chicken or turkey stock or gravy.

GLAZE
A thick or thin sugar syrup or sugar mixture used to coat certain types of pastry and cakes.

GLUTEN
The elastic protein mass formed when the protein material of the wheat flour is mixed with water.

GOULASH
A Hungarian stew variously made in the United States of beef, veal, or frankfurters with onions and potatoes. The sauce has tomato paste and paprika as ingredients, served with sour cream if desired.

GOURMET
A connoisseur, or a critical judge, of good food and drink.

GRATE
To separate food into small pieces by rubbing it on a grater.

GREASE
To rub lightly with butter, shortening, or oil.

GRIDDLE
A flat surface or pan on which food is cooked by dry heat. Grease is removed as it accumulates. No liquid is added.

GRILL
See BROIL.

GRIND
To force food materials through a food chopper.

GUMBO
A Creole dish resembling soup, thickened somewhat with okra, its characteristic ingredient.

H

HARD SAUCE
A dessert sauce made of butter and confectioner's sugar, thoroughly creamed. The mixture is thinned or tempered with boiling water.

HASH
A baked dish made of chopped or minced meat and/or vegetables mixture in brown stock.

HEARTH
The heated baking surface of the floor of an oven.

HERMITS
A rich short-flake cookie.

HOLLANDAISE
A sauce made with egg yolks and butter and usually served over vegetables.

HONEY
A sweet syrupy substance produced by bees from flower nectar.

HORS D'OEUVRES
Light, snack-type foods eaten hot or cold at the beginning of a meal.

HORSESHOES
Danish pastry, shaped like horseshoes.

HOST
   Any living animal or plant affording food for growth to a parasite.

HOT CROSS BUNS
   Sweet, spicy, fruity buns with cross-cut on top, which usually is covered with a plain frosting.

HOT AIR DRYING
   Products are cut in small pieces and spread on slat or wire bottom trays. Hot air is passed over and under trays to dry products.

HUMIDITY
   The percent of moisture in air related to the total moisture capacity of that air at a particular temperature. Usually expressed as relative humidity.

HUNTER STYLE
   Browned meat, usually chicken, braised in various combinations of tomatoes and other vegetables, stock, oil, garlic, and herbs.

HUSH PUPPIES
   Deep-fried cornbread batter seasoned with onions. Used mostly in the South, usually with fish.

I

INCUBATION PERIOD
   That time between entrance of disease-producing bacteria in a person and the first appearance of symptoms.

INSECTICIDE
   Any chemical substance used for the destruction of insects.

ITALIENNE
   Italian style of cooking.

J

JARDINIERE
   A meat dish or garnish, "garden" style, made of several kinds of vegetables.

JULIENNE
   A method of cutting meat, poultry, vegetables (especially potatoes), and fruits in long, thin strips.

K

KEBAB
   Various Turkish-style dishes whose principal feature is skewered meat, usually lamb.

KNEAD
To work and press dough with the palms of the hands, turning and folding the dough at rapid intervals.

KOLACHES
A bread bun made from a soft dough and topped with fruit.

L

LACTIC ACID
An organic acid sometimes known as the acid of milk because it is produced when milk sours. Bacteria cause the souring.

LARDING
To cover uncooked lean meat or fish with strips of fat, or to insert strips of fat with a skewer.

LASAGNA
An Italian baked dish with broad noodles, or lasagna noodles, which has been cooked, drained, and combined in alternate layers with Italian meat sauce and cheese of two or three types (cottage, parmesan, and mozzarella).

LEAVENING
The aeration of a product (raising or lightening by air, steam, or gas (carbon dioxide)) that occurs during mixing and baking. The agent for generating gas in a dough or batter is usually yeast or baking powder.

LUKEWARM
Moderately warm or tepid.

LYONNAISE
A seasoning with onions originating in Lyons, France. Sauteed potatoes, green beans, and other vegetables are seasoned this way.

M

MAKEUP
Manual or mechanical manipulation of dough to provide a desired size and shape.

MARBLE CAKE
A cake of two or three colored batters partially mixed.

MARBLING
The intermingling of fat with lean in meat. Meat cut across the grain will show the presence or absence of marbling and may indicate its quality and palatability.

MARINADE
A preparation containing spices, herbs, condiments, vegetables, and a liquid (usually acid) in which a food is placed for a period of time to enhance its flavor, or to increase its tenderness.

MARINATE
To cover with dressing and allow to stand for a short length of time.

MARMALADE
A type of jam or preserve made with sliced fruits. Crushed fruits or whole fruits are used more commonly in jam.

MEAT SUBSTITUTE
Any food used as an entree that does not contain beef, veal, pork, or lamb. Some substitutes are protein-rich dishes such as eggs, fish, dried beans, and cheese.

MEDIA
The plural of medium.

MEDIUM
A material or combination of materials used for cultivation of microorganisms.

MELTING POINT
The temperature at which a solid becomes a liquid.

MERINGUE
A white frothy mass of beaten egg whites and sugar.

MILK FAT
The fat in milk and milk products.

MILK LIQUID
Fresh fluid milk or evaporated or powdered milk reconstituted to the equivalent of fresh fluid milk.

MINCE
To cut or chop into very small pieces, using knife or chopper.

MINESTRONE
Thickened vegetable soup containing lentils or beans.

MIXING
To unite two or more ingredients.

MOCHA
A flavor combination of coffee and chocolate, but predominately that of coffee.

MOLD
Microscopic, multicellular, thread-like fungi growing on moist surfaces of organic material.

MOLDER
Machine that shapes dough pieces for various shapes.

MULLIGATAWNY
A soup with a chicken-stock base highly seasoned, chiefly by curry powder.

MYOCIDE
An agent that destroys molds.

N

NUTRIENT
A food substance that humans require to support life and health.

O

O'BRIEN
A style of preparing sauteed vegetables with diced green peppers and pimientos.

OLD DOUGHS
Overfermented yeast dough that produces a finished baked loaf, dark in crumb color, sour in flavor, low in volume, coarse in grain, and tough in texture.

OMELET
Eggs beaten to a froth, cooked with stirring until set, and served in a half-round form by folding one half over the other.

OVEN
A chamber used for baking, heating, or drying.

OYSTER MUSCLE
Tender, oval piece of dark poultry meat found in the recess on either side of the back.

P

PALATABLE
Agreeable to the palate or taste.

PAN BROIL
See BROIL.

PAN FRY
See FRY.

PARASITES
Organisms that live in or on a living host.

PARBOIL
To boil in water until partially cooked.

PARE
To trim and remove all superfluous matter from any article.

PARKERHOUSE ROLLS
Folded buns of fairly rich dough.

PARMESAN
A very hard, dry cheese with a sharp flavor.

PASTA (or PASTE)
Any macaroni product, including spaghetti, noodles, and the other pastas.

PATHOGENS
Disease-producing microorganisms.

PEEL
To remove skin, using a knife or peeling machine.

PEPPER POT
Any of a wide variety of styles of highly seasoned soup or stew.

PICKLE
A method of preserving food by a salt and water (or vinegar) solution.

PILAF
An oriental or Turkish dish made of rice cooked in beef or chicken stock and mildly flavored with onions.

PIQUANT
A tart, pleasantly sharp flavor. A piquant sauce or dressing contains lemon juice or vinegar.

PIT
To remove pits or seeds (as from dates or avocados).

PLASTICITY
The consistency or feel of shortening.

POACH
Method of cooking food in a hot liquid that is kept just below the boiling point.

POLONAISE
A garnish consisting of chopped egg and parsley served on cauliflower, asparagus, or other dishes. Bread crumbs are sometimes added.

PPM
Parts per million.

PORCUPINE
A preparation of ground beef and rice shaped into balls and cooked in tomato sauce.

POTABLE
Suitable for drinking.

POTENTIALLY HAZARDOUS pH
　　Any perishable food which consists in whole or in part of milk or milk products, eggs, meat, poultry, fish, shellfish, synthetic food, or other ingredient capable of supporting rapid and progressive growth of pathogens.

PREHEAT
　　To heat to the desired baking temperature before placing food in the oven.

PROOF BOX
　　A tightly closed box or cabinet equipped with shelves to permit the introduction of heat and steam; used for fermenting dough.

PROOFING PERIOD
　　The time between molding and baking during which dough rises.

PROTOZOA
　　Minute, one-celled animals.

PROVOLONE
　　A cured, hard cheese that has a smoky flavor.

PSYCHROPHILIC BACTERIA
　　Microorganisms that grow at temperatures near freezing.

PUREE
　　The pulp of a boiled food that has been rubbed through a sieve. Soup is called puree when it has been thickened with its sieved, pulpy ingredients.

Q

QUICK BREADS
　　Bread products baked from a lean, chemically leavened batter.

R

RABBIT OR RAREBIT
　　A melted-cheese dish.

RAGOUT
　　The French word for "stew."

RANCID
　　A disagreeable odor or flavor. Usually used to describe foods with high fat content, when oxidation occurs.

READY-TO-COOK POULTRY
　　Drawn or eviscerated poultry.

RECONSTITUTE
　　To restore the water taken from a food when it was dehydrated.

REHYDRATE
Combining a food with the same quantity of water that has been removed from it (see also RECONSTITUTE).

RELISH
A side dish, usually contrasting in color, shape, and texture to the meal. Usually designed to add flavor, zest, and interest to a meal.

RISSOLE
A French term meaning to obtain a crackling food by means of heat. Rissole potatoes are cooked to a golden brown crispness in fat.

ROAST
See BAKE.

ROPE
A spoiling bacterial growth in bread experienced when the dough becomes infected with bacterial spores. Poor sanitation can result in rope.

ROUNDING OR ROUNDING UP
Shaping of dough pieces into a ball to seal end and prevent bleeding and escape of gas.

ROUX
Preparation of flour and melted butter (or fat) used to thicken sauces, gravies, and soups.

ROYAL FROSTING
Decorative frosting of cooked sugar and egg whites.

S

SAFE HOLDING TEMPERATURE
A range of cold and hot temperatures considered safe for holding potentially hazardous foods, including those refrigeration temperatures 40° F, or below, or heating temperatures 140° F, or above.

SALISBURY STEAK
A ground meat dish cooked with onions and made to resemble steak in shape. Sometimes referred to as hamburg steak.

SALMONELLA INFECTION
A type of food poisoning transmitted through foods such as poultry and poultry products containing salmonella bacteria.

SANITIZE
Effective bactericidal treatment of clean surfaces of equipment and utensils by an established process that is effective in destroying microorganisms.

SAPONIFY
To convert to soap.

SATURATION
   Absorption to the limit of the capacity.

SAUERBRATEN
   A beef pot roast cooked in a sour sauce variously prepared with spices and vinegar, and sometimes served with sour cream.

SAUTE
   See FRY.

SCALD
   To heat a liquid over hot water or direct heat to a temperature just below the boiling point.

SCALE
   An instrument for weighing.

SCALING
   Apportioning batter or dough according to unit of weight.

SCALLOP
   To bake food, usually cut in pieces, with a sauce or other liquid.

SCORE
   To cut shallow slits or gashes in the surface of food with a knife.

SCORING
   Judging finished goods according to points of perfection; or to cut or slash the top surface of dough pieces.

SEASON
   To add, or sprinkle, with seasonings or condiments.

SHRED
   To cut or tear into thin strips or pieces using a knife or a shredder attachment.

SIFTING
   Passing through fine sieve for effective blending and to remove foreign or oversize particles.

SIMMER
   To cook in liquid at a temperature just below the boiling point.

SKEWER
   A sharp metal or wood pin used to hold parts of poultry meat or skin together while being roasted.

SKIM
   To remove floating matter from the surface of a liquid with a spoon, ladle, or skimmer.

SLACK DOUGH
This is a dough that is soft and extensible but has lost its resiliency.

SLIVER
To cut or split into long, thin pieces.

SMOKING
A treatment used on most cured meat to add color and flavor.

SMORGASBORD
A Scandinavian-type luncheon or supper, served buffet style. Many different dishes are served, including hot and cold hors d'oeuvres, pickled vegetables, fish, assorted cheeses, jellied salads, cold and hot fish, and meats.

SMOTHER
To cook in a covered container, as smothered onions.

SNAPS
Small cookies that run flat during baking and become crisp on cooking.

SNICKERDOODLE
A coffeecake with a crumb topping.

SOLIDIFYING POINT
Temperature at which a fluid changes to a solid.

SPORE
Any one of various small or minute primitive reproductive bodies, capable of maintaining and reproducing itself. These are unicellular, produced by plants, molds, and bacteria.

SPRAY DRYING
Used for liquids and thick materials such as soup. Hot air coming into a drier contacts the small globules of the product and causes the water to be evaporated.

SPRINGER
A marked bulging of a food can at one or both ends. Improper exhausting of air from the can before sealing, or bacterial or chemical growth may cause swelling and spoilage.

SPRINKLE
To scatter in drops or small particles, such as chopped parsley, over a finished product.

STAPHYLOCOCCI
A family of bacteria formed in grapelike clusters, living as parasites on the outer skin and mucous membrane.

STEAM
To cook in steam with or without pressure.

STEEP
To let stand in hot liquid below boiling temperature to extract flavor, color, or other qualities from a specific food.

STERILIZE
To destroy microorganisms by chemical or mechanical means.

STEW
To simmer in liquid.

STIR
To blend or mix ingredients by using a spoon or other implement.

STREPTOCOCCI
Single-celled, globular-shaped bacteria.

STROGANOFF
Beef prepared with sour cream.

STRONG FLOUR
One that is suitable for the production of bread of good volume and quality.

SUCCOTASH
A combination of corn and lima beans.

SUGAR
To sprinkle or mix with sugar; refers to granulated unless otherwise specified in recipe.

SUKIYAKI
A popular Japanese dish consisting of thin slices of meat fried with onions and other vegetables, including bean sprouts, and soy sauce containing seasoning, herbs, and spices.

SWELLER
A can of food having both ends bulging as a result of spoilage. Swellers should be discarded, except molasses, in which this condition is normal in a warm climate.

T

TABLEWARE
A general term referring to multi use eating and drinking utensils, including knives, forks, spoons, and dishes.

TACO
An open-face sandwich, Mexican style, made of fried tortillas shaped like a shell and filled with a hot meat-vegetable mixture.

TAMALE
A highly seasoned steamed dish made of cornmeal with ground beef or chicken rolled in the center.

TARTAR
A rich sauce made with salad dressing, onions, parsley, and sometimes pickle relish, olives, and cucumbers, served with fish and shellfish.

TARTS
Small pastries with heavy fruit or cream filling.

TEMPERING
Adjusting temperature of ingredients to a certain degree.

TETRAZINNI
An Italian dish with chicken, green peppers, and onions mixed in spaghetti and served with shredded cheese.

TEXTURE
The quality of the interior structure of a baked product. Usually sensed by the touch of the cut surface as well as by sight and taste.

THERMOSTAT
A device for maintaining constant temperature.

THICKEN
To transform a thin liquid into a thick one either by the gelatinization of flour starches or the coagulation of egg protein.

TOAST
To brown the surface of a food by the application of direct heat.

TORTILLA
A Mexican bread made with white corn flour and water. Special techniques are used in handling the dough to roll it thin as a pie crust. It is baked on an ungreased griddle or in the oven.

TOSS
To lightly mix one or more ingredients. Usually refers to salad ingredients.

TOXIN
A waste product, given off by an organism causing contamination of food and subsequent illness in human beings. It is the toxin of a disease-producing germ that causes the poisoning.

TRICHINOSIS
A food-borne disease transmitted through pork containing a parasite, Trichinella spirallis, or its larvae, which infects animals.

TROUGHS
Large containers, usually on wheels, used for holding large masses of raising dough.

TRUSS
To bind or fasten together the wings and legs of poultry with the aid of string or metal skewers.

V

VACUUM DRYING
Vacuum is applied to liquids and fills the liquid with bubbles, creating a puffing effect. The puffed product is then dried, leaving a solid fragile mass. This is then crushed to reduce bulk.

VERMICELLI
A pasta, slightly yellow in color, shaped like spaghetti and very thin.

VINAIGRETTE
A mixture of oil and vinegar seasoned with salt, pepper, and herbs, used in sauces and dressings.

VIRUS
A group of organisms of ultramicroscopic size that grow in living tissue and may produce disease in animals and plants. Viruses are smaller than bacteria and, hence, pass through membranes or filters.

W

WASH
A liquid brushed on the surface of an unbaked or baked product (may be water, milk, starch solution, thin syrup, or egg).

WATER ABSORPTION
Water required to produce a bread dough of desired consistency. Flours vary in ability to absorb water, depending on the age of the flour, moisture content, wheat from which it is milled, storage conditions, and milling process.

WHEY
Liquid remaining after the removal of fat, casein, and other substances from milk.

WHIP
To beat rapidly to increase volume by incorporating air.

Y

YEAST
A group of small, single-celled plants, oval in shape and several times larger than bacteria. Yeast helps to promote fermentation and is useful in producing bread, cheese, wine, and so on.

YOUNG DOUGHS
Underfermented yeast dough producing finished yeast goods that are light in color, tight in grain, and low in volume (heavy).

Z

ZWIEBACK
A toast made of bread or plain coffeecake dried in slow oven.

www.ingramcontent.com/pod-product-compliance
Lightning Source LLC
Chambersburg PA
CBHW081806300426
44116CB00014B/2255